Atlantic Loyalties

Americans in Spanish

West Florida, 1785–1810

ANDREW McMICHAEL

The University of Georgia Press · Athens and London

D0188389

Publication of this book was made possible in part by the Program for Cultural
Cooperation between Spain's Ministry of Culture and United States Universities.

Set in Minion by Bookcomp, Inc.
Printed and bound by Thomson-Shore
The paper in this book meets the guidelines for permanence
and durability of the Committee on Production Guidelines
for Book Longevity of the Council on Library Resources.
Printed in the United States of America

11   10   09   08   07   c   5   4   3   2   1

11   10   09   08   07   p   5   4   3   2   1

Library of Congress Cataloging-in-Publication Data

McMichael, F. Andrew (Francis Andrew), 1966–

Atlantic loyalties : Americans in Spanish West Florida,

1785–1810 / Andrew McMichael.

        p. cm.

Includes bibliographical references and index.

ISBN-13: 978-0-8203-3004-4 (hardcover : alk. paper)

ISBN-10: 0-8203-3004-3 (hardcover : alk. paper)

ISBN-13: 978-0-8203-3023-5 (softcover : alk. paper)

ISBN-10: 0-8203-3023-x (softcover : alk. paper)

1. West Florida—History.   2. Baton Rouge (La.)—History.

3. British Americans—West Florida—History.   4. British Americans—

West Florida—Ethnic identity.   5. Frontier and pioneer life—West Florida.

6. Allegiance—West Florida—History.   7. West Florida—Ethnic relations.

8. Florida—History—Spanish colony, 1784–1821.

9. Spain—Colonies—Administration—History—18th century.

10. Spain—Colonies—Administration—History—19th century.   I. Title.

F301.M15 2008

976.3'18030413—dc22   2007019059

British Library Cataloging-in-Publication Data available

 Atlantic Loyalties

To my wife, Lee, who puts up with a heck of a lot.

To my children, who hung the moon and the stars.

To my parents, who made it possible.

CONTENTS

MAPS, TABLES, AND FIGURES

ACKNOWLEDGMENTS

The cover of this book would have readers believe that this was the work of one person. Anyone who has written a monograph understands that such is never the case. This undertaking involved dozens of people, and it would be nearly impossible for me to acknowledge everyone who helped with the project.

I began this work in Jane Landers's borderlands graduate seminar at Vanderbilt University, trying to reconcile what I was reading in the Latin American primary sources with secondary sources written by U.S. historians. Anyone who has ever met Jane knows what a kind heart she has. As an advisor she gave her time more than generously, providing me with guidance, contacts among historians, and pointers for working in foreign archives. I owe her an intellectual and professional debt that I can never repay. I was proud to call myself her student—still prouder to call her a friend.

Don Doyle served as my primary advisor at Vanderbilt and helped me to understand the ways in which the development of the U.S. South might link to the southern borderlands. His conceptions of nationality, especially that of the Confederacy and in Italy, were insightful and contributed to my own intellectual framework for this book. Don was also willing to put down whatever he was doing to listen to crazy theories spilling out of the mouth of the graduate student who burst into his office.

The Southern Social History Group and numerous dissertation seminars at Vanderbilt University provided insightful and pointed readings as I was completing the first phase of this work. Tycho de Boer, Ed Harcourt, and Rob Lawson especially took the time for multiple critical readings that improved it dramatically. The members of the 1717 Society participated in many late-night seminars on this project. They deserve a great deal of thanks.

Barbara Oberg at the Papers of Thomas Jefferson at Princeton University taught me more about research, intellectual patience, and paleography in the two years I spent there than I had learned in my entire graduate career. Jim McClure and Elaine Pascu, also at the Papers, mentored me in more ways than they could know. My time there gave me professional training as well as access to a world-class library and a terrific intellectual community.

Research for this work took me to archives in Cuba, England, and Spain. In Cuba, Licenciada Coralia Alonso Valdéz, Licenciada Patria Cok Marquéz, Don Julio López Valdéz, and other folks at the Archivo Nacional de Cuba helped me navigate the archives there. Domestically the staff at the National Archives in

Washington, D.C., and College Park gave me stack access and left me alone to prowl millions of records. Dane Hartgrove at the National Historical Publications and Records Commission, especially, showed me where to find materials and how not to get lost in the maze of stacks.

Staff at the Hill Memorial Library at Louisiana State University helped me locate a great deal of material I would otherwise have missed. Research trips to Baton Rouge would not have been possible without Kurt Kemper, who provided a place to stay and hours of beer and college football. When I wanted to talk about research, he knew when to listen—and when to tell me to shut up. He is a good friend.

My current home of Western Kentucky University has provided assistance of every sort, and confining my thanks to these pages seems a disservice. Thousands of dollars in summer research grants helped send an Americanist to foreign language archives without so much as a furrowed brow. Colleagues here read drafts of the manuscript and helped me think of this work in different ways. Robert Dietle and Marion Lucas commented on drafts, Rick Keyser and Eric Reed helped correct my French and listened patiently to my ideas, and Patricia Minter provided guidance on legal theory. My department chair, Richard Weigel, gave me a great deal of latitude in my research endeavors. This institution is a great place to work.

I would like to thank several people who contributed more intangibly. Judy Schafer, Jim Roark, and Virginia Shadron taught me that genuine kindness to junior colleagues is easy. The late Mike Lanza; the history department at George Mason University, especially Roy Rosenzweig, Rosie Zagarri, Jane Censer, and Robert Hawkes; and Robert Townsend and Noralee Frankel at the American Historical Association all taught me how to be a student of history and a professional historian.

Derek Krissof and the editorial staff at the University of Georgia Press have been patient beyond belief.

Finally, I'd like to thank my family, and especially my wife, Lee. As a clinical social worker and therapist, she is the perfect mate for an archives rat. She is a wonderful wife, friend, and lover. My children inspire me.

Don Doyle once told me to keep track of anyone who ever lent me a paper clip, as I'd have to thank him or her in the acknowledgments. Historians are generous, and I hope that those I've forgotten will forgive me—they know that paper clips were the least of my needs. Many people read drafts of this work. They get credit for the improvements. The flaws are mine.

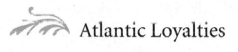 Atlantic Loyalties

INTRODUCTION

In August 1804, a gang of men led by three brothers named Kemper rode from the United States territory of Mississippi into Spanish-held West Florida. They carried a blue and white striped flag and a proclamation of independence demanding that the people of Spanish West Florida rise up against Spain and declare independence. No other West Floridians rallied to the Kemper-led gang, and many actively worked to track down and prosecute the invaders. Yet by November 1810—after Napoleon had kidnapped and deposed the Spanish king—a group of men in the territory of Spanish West Florida gathered to create a caretaker government, as occurred elsewhere in Spain's New World possessions. Similarly, West Floridians lamented the loss of their sovereign and vowed that their actions did not constitute a revolution—in fact, they argued in their declaration of independence that a number of events had necessitated their reluctant revolution. The convention repeatedly stressed its loyalty to the deposed king, insisting that it was merely taking control of the functions of government abdicated by its peninsular overseers.

West Floridians nonetheless constituted a unique element among Spain's New World revolutionaries in that they were overwhelmingly Anglo-American. Some had been in the territory for only a few years, while others had experienced the transitions from French to British to Spanish rule. If the residents and convention delegates were mostly Anglos, why, then, did they profess loyalty to Spain's deposed king? What was it about Spanish rule that engendered loyalty to the point that when presented with the opportunity to rise up under the Kempers, residents declined to rebel, only to do so within a few short years? Was it simply a matter of timing, or were there deeper issues of loyalty and economic self-interest? What engendered political fealty through 1804 and then caused its breakdown by 1810? These questions constitute the central theme of this book.

At its heart this book is about the immigration into, and the development of, the Baton Rouge district of Spanish West Florida from the 1780s to the revolution of 1810, focusing on the application of Spanish rule to the development of a frontier community, and the impact of Spanish institutions on whites and blacks living within the Spanish system. More importantly, though, it seeks to answer the question of how that development contributed to Spanish construction of national loyalty among Anglo-American borderland residents, how that loyalty held when tested, and then why it ultimately dissolved. This study also places the local into an international context by exploring the local effects of continental expansion by the United States and the Atlantic world context of West Florida's growth. In this respect it expands and revises the familiar narrative of West Florida by mixing local, national, and international sources, thereby drawing the narrative away from the local context and situating this area of the Latin American/U.S. borderlands within the larger Atlantic community.

American historians have long regarded the West Florida Revolution of 1810—which occurred only in the Baton Rouge district—as the inevitable by-product of what they have seen as long-standing Anglo-American dissatisfaction with Spain's government from 1785 through 1810.[1] (See map 1.) When Anglo-American resentment toward Spanish rule boiled over in 1810, the thinking goes, residents had finally triumphed in their struggle to rid the area of the hated Spaniards. What nationalist historians have passively accepted and described as a "foreign occupation" came to an end. Through this interpretation, histories of the period have portrayed United States expansion in West Florida—and by extension the rest of the southern borderlands from East Florida to California—as inevitable. These mostly diplomatic and political historians, and the very few social historians who have relied on their works, have regarded Anglo-American residents in West Florida as disaffected subjects of the Spanish Crown, who patiently waited until they could overthrow an alien system.

Southern borderlands history as applied to Louisiana and the South was in effect a muted version of the Turner thesis that implicitly accepted the notion of inevitable Anglo-American expansion into West Florida as a harbinger of the development of various cultures in the U.S. South. While Frederick Jackson Turner correctly argued that the peculiarity of the frontier molded the American character into something unique from the Old World whence it had originated, he at the same time romantically attached to that experience the origins of American democracy, pragmatism, and inventiveness. While historians have rejected those ideas in the context of U.S. history, they nonetheless continue to apply that model to West Florida.

American historians also seem to view the late colonial period of Louisiana before 1803, and West Florida before 1810, as a gray time when "some other" history took place. All too often studies using mostly local sources emphasize the French and American periods with little or no reference to the Spanish occupation. The assumption then follows that after the United States assumed control in both areas, "American" history began. As David Weber has explained, *la leyenda negra*, or the Black Legend, has informed much of Anglo scholarship since the late eighteenth century.[2] I would add that Black Legend historiography also served to justify the sense of inevitability with which American historians view the Spanish retreat from the New World, and that Americans' affinity for

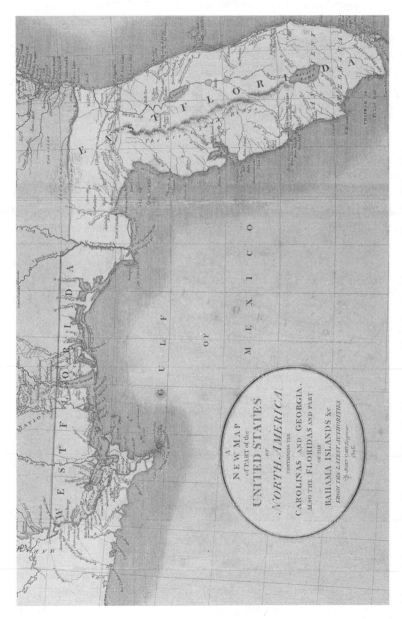

Map 1. Map showing East and West Florida, engraved by John Cary in 1806. Historical Map File, Georgia Surveyor General. RG 3-8-65, Georgia Archives.

the Black Legend grew alongside their perceptions of Spain as a barrier to western settlement.

However, a careful examination of this region during the late colonial period, using diaries, letters, court and shipping records, wills and probate documents, marriage documents, and especially records of slave and land sales, provides a more textured picture and reveals an abiding loyalty to Spain on the part of Anglo-American residents that lasted until after the revolution began.[3] The relationship between land and political loyalty in the British colonies has begun to receive more attention, especially from historians such as Woody Holton, studying frontier Virginia, and Leslie Hall, studying Revolutionary Georgia.[4] The pro-U.S. American nationalism that historians have assumed was so strong in West Floridians actually materialized after the beginning of the 1810 revolution and even then only in the absence of any other strong power that merited their loyalty or could provide protection. In that context this study examines the basis of Anglo-American loyalty in the Spanish borderlands and the social and cultural conflicts that came with living there, and provides an answer to why that loyalty shifted so suddenly in 1810 and brought about a revolution.

Although West Floridians' loyalty survived many tests, it evaporated rapidly in 1810, raising the question of whether genuine political and national loyalty to Spain had ever existed. What then motivated their political and national loyalty? It boiled down, perhaps ironically, to a political and economic version of Turner's frontier pragmatism. As long as the Spanish Crown could guarantee easy access to cheap land and a relatively stable regime, local residents willingly lived under Spanish rule and swore allegiance to the king. When those guarantees faded, so did local loyalty. In that sense West Floridians had little real political and national loyalty to Spain; what passed for allegiance to the Spanish Crown was instead only the exercise of individualistic pursuits that for most of the period from 1785 to 1810 occurred within the context of allegiance to the Spanish Crown. As long as the Spanish system suited them, West Floridians remained loyal to Spain and manifested that loyalty in various ways. In a move that demonstrated the flexibility of loyalty and national identity in the borderlands, residents got rid of the Spanish system when it no longer suited their needs. Beginning in 1810 the system of the United States appeared more convenient, so residents quickly shifted loyalties and, after a brief period of independence, brought the United States to West Florida.

Though Spanish West Florida at the time examined in this study extended to the Apalachicola River and included Pensacola and Mobile, I consider here only that area under rebellion in 1810: the Baton Rouge district from the Mississippi River east to the Pearl River. A clear treatment of the diplomatic, social, cultural, and political maneuvering that brought all of Florida from the Mississippi

River to the Atlantic Ocean under American rule is beyond the scope of this book. Works including James Cusick's *Other War of 1812: The Patriot War and the American Invasion of Spanish East Florida*, David Bice's *Original Lone Star Republic: Scoundrels, Statesmen and Schemers of the 1810 West Florida Rebellion*, and chapters in Paul E. Hoffman's *Florida's Frontiers* and Jane Landers' *Black Society in Spanish Florida* provide abundant details about the capture of West Florida, Mobile, and Pensacola and the transfer of the Floridas into U.S. hands.[5] Also, because this book is a study of the motivations for revolution, and not an analysis of the events that led to West Florida's incorporation into the United State, it substantially ends with West Florida's declaration of independence.

This book also seeks to address several historiographical oddities concerning West Florida and by extension the Mississippi Valley and Louisiana. The first issue involves the tendency of U.S. historians either to begin or to end their studies in 1803, and the inclination of Latin Americanists to treat post-1803 Louisiana and West Florida as the domain of U.S. historians. Instead, I demonstrate that the history of Americans in West Florida—and by extension Louisiana and the trans-Mississippi—is best understood as bridging the Louisiana Purchase. At the same time I would suggest that the year 1803—or even 1810 or 1819—does not mark the end of Latin American history in Louisiana, the Floridas, or even the South.

Yet the history of West Florida and Louisiana, and by extension the history of the U.S. South, requires a more nuanced approach, one that treats the first decade of the nineteenth century as a period when residents planted the South's American roots. Historians should not view the late colonial period around the time of the Louisiana Purchase—involving as it does French, Spanish, Irish, Scottish, British, Anglo American, African, and Indian residents and the resulting mix of planters, governments, settlers, and slaves—as simply the end of Spanish or French rule. Nor should historians view that time as an indicator of the beginning of American social and cultural history in that region. Instead, the period from 1785 to 1810 marks the social and cultural emergence of an American region within the context of Latin American, African, Caribbean, European, and American social, cultural, and political imperatives.

Finally, American scholars have generally downplayed the effectiveness of Spain in administering its New World territories. American historians have used Spain's loss of the colonies as ipso facto evidence of poor government in those colonies and then allowed that view to inform assumptions about life within the colonies. While a weak Spanish government led to the loss of their northern borderlands, that loss was by no means inevitable. After all, a weak American government in the West is frequently seen as contributing to progress in the late nineteenth century. In the case of Spain's territories, a reexamination of the end of Spanish rule in Louisiana cannot occur without careful attention to primary sources in Spanish and French as well as English. At the same time, much previous historiography must be disregarded if one is to synthesize the best of American, Latin American, *and* borderlands scholarship. Finally, the focus on the Louisiana Purchase and filibustering raids as a symbol of proto-Americanism has led historians to write about traditional political and military issues, focusing on "great men" and dramatic events. As a result, the time period lacks an integration of the events that created an American Louisiana in the American South, a shortcoming this book remedies.

To answer the questions outlined here, I examine the evolution and then the disruption of power in Spanish West Florida and the attendant effects on social, cultural, economic, and political relations in the area and provide an analytical framework through which we can understand both the early republic period of the United States and Spain's late colonial period. The broader goal of this project is to write the early history of Louisiana and the U.S. southern borderlands-frontier and reconcile it with the Spanish presence in West Florida. To accomplish this goal, I use the Baton Rouge district of Spanish West Florida as a case study.

The Baton Rouge area is significant for several reasons. First, along with Pensacola, Mobile, and Saint Augustine, it was the major settled region of Spanish Florida. Second, from the 1770s through 1810 it saw a huge influx of a wide variety of settlers with mixed motivations regarding political loyalty. Britons, for instance, came in large numbers, fleeing the American Revolution and seeking the stability of a monarchical government.[6] Third, the Louisiana Purchase created a surrounded borderland and with that a degree of instability for West Floridians that would serve as an indicator of the ability of the Spanish government to retain the residents' loyalty. Fourth, that area contained both frontier and nonfrontier areas: the town of Baton Rouge was relatively settled, while the Feliciana region to the north remained a borderland in many senses—it was in the process of settlement during 1783–1810, and it abutted American-held Mississippi at the thirty-first-degree longitude line. Finally, the Baton Rouge area is instructive because it declared independence while other areas of West Florida did not.

This book is constructed within a four-square model of history. It is first a history of the borderlands in a place that is unique among borderlands in North America, one whose ruling residents' cultural background did not originate from their ruling country. Within that context, I also address some problems common to borderlands everywhere: how do peoples on the peripheries of empire manifest (or not) their loyalty? By 1810 some 90 percent of the residents of Baton Rouge had immigrated either from the British North American colonies or from the United States. This made them not entirely unlike Texans in the 1830s and 1840s. Yet for most of the period from 1785 to 1810, their loyalty to Spain remained firm.

Second, this is an Atlantic history in the model of what David Armitage, borrowing a phrase from Thomas Jefferson, has called "cis-Atlantic" history, or the study of a unique place within its relation to the wider Atlantic world.[7] In Armitage's conception, cis-Atlantic history "seeks to define that uniqueness as a result of the interaction between local peculiarity and a wider web of connections."[8] The lives of West Floridians in many respects were subject to forces outside their control—forces that had a deep effect on the course of their lives and their relations to the Spanish Crown. Spain's land policy; its intercolonial rivalries with France, Great Britain, and the United States; Jefferson's 1807 embargo; France's invasion of Spain and Napoleon's subsequent jailing of Ferdinand VII; filibusters from outside Florida's borders; corrupt governors from Cuba; and trade within the Spanish Empire all helped determine the course of West Florida's history and deeply affected the sense of loyalty West Floridians held toward the Crown.

Third, as Ned Landesman has argued, "the need to re-think the historical meaning of national boundaries within the British state" should naturally lead historians to question how we view the European experience in the New World.[9] His argument should be extended to include the way we apply concepts of ethnicity to people living in borderland areas anywhere in the New World. More particularly the experiences of those living in that part of the borderland South that included West Florida require us to rethink what it meant to be southern, as well as American, during the period of the early republic.

Finally, this book follows a historiographical style sometimes referred to as contextualism. Whereas earlier historians have used their sources to extract social, political, cultural, or diplomatic histories, I have tried to let the sources dictate the type of history I have written. When the existing documents have suggested politics as the main frame of reference for the actors, I have written political history. When the context has suggested cultural, racial, or social history, I have written from those perspectives. Moreover, I have tried whenever possible to let the actors themselves tell the story. This provides a more integrated sense of the ways in which the people of the time saw their world— not as split into separate categories without influence on one another, but as a seamless whole, with all parts contributing to the fabric of their lives.

This book does not discuss Mississippi outside of its most immediate effect on West Florida. Three recent works, David Libby's *Slavery and Frontier Mississippi* (Jackson: University Press of Mississippi, 2004), Robert Haynes's "Territorial Mississippi, 1798–1817" (*Journal of Mississippi History* 64 [Winter 2002]:

283–305), and Christopher Morris's *Becoming Southern: The Evolution of a Way of Life, Warren County and Vicksburg, Mississippi, 1770–1860* already provide ample coverage of Mississippi during this period. Moreover, as noted, this study does not cover the events that led to the incorporation of Florida, West and East, into the United States. Given the cultural, military, and diplomatic wrangling that occurred in the context of that struggle, such a treatment requires a book in and of itself. Two recent works, Cusick's aforementioned *Other War of 1812* and Peter Kastor's *Nation's Crucible: The Louisiana Purchase and the Creation of America*, provide details for those events. Instead I focus on the making and breaking of national loyalty up to the West Florida Revolution of 1810.

This book is divided into three sections. The first section brings the reader from the wider world of settlement to West Florida and the lives of its residents. Chapter 1 traces the initial development of Louisiana and West Florida, from the initial French settlements to Spanish efforts to build political loyalty in West Florida through a liberal system of land grants. Chapter 2 demonstrates the ways in which the economy of the West Florida borderlands was built on slavery as well as the nature of slavery and race in the Spanish borderlands. Chapter 3 examines loyalty within the context of the Louisiana Purchase and its effect on Louisianans and West Floridians. In particular, this chapter explores the uncertainty with which the United States and French, Spanish, and even American residents managed the transfer of power and what that uncertainty meant for national loyalty.

The second section uses several case studies to focus on issues raised in the first section. Chapter 4 follows several filibustering raids in and around the borderland South, showing how residents reacted to instability by cementing their loyalty to the Spanish. Building on problems raised in the second chapter, chapter 5 examines, through a specific court case, the nature of Spanish slave law and how it was applied in the borderlands, especially in an area administered by a French-born governor and peopled by Anglo-Americans. For early eighteenth-century Americans in the U.S. South—the source of much immigration into West Florida—slavery was the main path to wealth. Spanish slave law operated on a different set of assumptions than that of the United States. Differences in such fundamental laws could have an impact on how Anglo-Americans related to the Spanish government.

The final section explores the local and international context of the demise of pro-Spanish loyalty in West Florida. Chapter 6 traces the internal breakdown, including the problem of increasing crime, the community's precarious position on the edge of the Mississippi territory, and a shift in Spanish land policy. Chapter 7 places several international and locally related administrative problems into perspective with regard to the revolution of 1810.

At its most basic level, this is one story of one portion of the geographical U.S. South. It is a U.S. South deserving closer scrutiny than most U.S. and Latin American historians have thus far given it. I hope that this work will prompt scholars to examine in greater detail borderland areas in general—not just the West Florida borderlands—in a greater Atlantic world context.

CHAPTER ONE

Settling the West Florida Frontier

Land, Wealth, and Loyalty

In September 1787 Carlos Benito Grangé and Margarita Angela Dubois entered into a marriage contract, uniting themselves and their posses-sions in the eyes of God and the Spanish Crown (the two also, after a fash-ion, married).[1] This was Margarita's second marriage—an occurrence with high probability for frontier women due to the high death rates among men. Official recognition of their union had been delayed for unknown reasons—perhaps in the confusion of the recent battles between Britain and Spain, perhaps because of the change in the administration of West Florida. Whatever the global con-text, they wished to formalize their marriage. Six days later in another part of the province, Spanish officials inventoried the estate of Ana Michel, who died intestate.[2] In October of that same year, Pedro Belly contracted to supply masts and spars for ships in the Spanish king's navy. The contract authorized him to draw an advance from the royal treasury for start-up funds for the project. Such authorization showed a great deal of trust on the part of the Spanish Crown. In May of the next year, Maria O'Brien recorded the first land transaction in the Baton Rouge area under the new Spanish regime, as she sold land and a house to Santiago Fuller. Situated on the frontier "lands of the dominion" (i.e., abutting vacant Crown land), the plot included 480 arpents (about 387 acres), a house complete with wooden floor, and "four negro cabins."[3] All of these transactions represent business and life as usual for the residents of West Florida under the recently installed government of Spain.

Several years earlier, in 1783, the Treaty of Paris, ending the American Rev-olution, officially recognized West Florida as a Spanish possession, and Spain took control of the area in 1784. The earliest records of the period, beginning in 1787, show a population with Spanish, French, and British surnames (and sometimes a corrupted mix of all three) going about the business of trying to live on the frontier. The everyday matters of living and dying—marriages, busi-ness contracts, slave and land sales, estate inventories, and the gaining and los-ing of wealth—all continued apace. The fact that the government in 1787 used a different official language from that which had controlled the area from the

Table 1. Shifting Governance of West Florida and Louisiana

European and American claims to West Florida	European and American claims to Louisiana
France, 1684–1763	France, 1684–1763
Great Britain, 1763–83	Spain, 1763–1800
Spain, 1783–1810	France, 1800
United States, 1811 onward	United States, 1803 onward

1760s through the early 1780s might seem the only significant change. Despite some similarities Spaniards were not simply Britons or Americans with a foreign tongue, and in any event the advantage of knowing at least two different languages was an everyday fact of life in frontier-borderland societies. As Catholics, the Spaniards owed fealty to the pope, and their king spoke for the pope in the New World. Theoretically, Spanish law required that subjects convert to Catholicism, or at least practice their Protestantism outside the public view, and Spaniards would, of course, try to convert Protestants to Catholicism.[4] Treatment of blacks, whether slaves or free people, would change under the Spanish, as would dealings with the Native American population. Most importantly, land policy would change, and the Spanish system of land grants—and the philosophy behind the system—did not exactly match that of the British.

The immigration that had begun several decades earlier continued, with the Spanish Crown replacing the British as the arbiter of land grants in the area. On the West Florida frontier, as in the rest of North America, the most efficient way to make a living was to own and work a piece of land using slave labor.[5] Despite the open frontier to the north in the Feliciana district, Baton Rouge was for the most part a stable area during the period from immediately after the transfer of West Florida to Spain in 1784 through the Louisiana Purchase in 1803. Residents bought and sold land, established businesses, got married, sued each other, and lived and died in the southern borderlands.

Understanding how West Florida came into Spain's possession is part of understanding the nature of Spanish West Florida. At the same time, understanding Spanish West Florida also requires understanding the U.S. South and the circum-Caribbean—the circular area including East and West Florida and the Gulf of Mexico, running along the Mexican coast through Central America to Brazil and back around to Cuba and the West Indies. This, in turn, requires a comparison of the Spanish system of land grants—and how Spanish officials and residents put this system into practice in a frontier society—with the emerging system of land grants in the United States. The specific contemporary example of Kentucky also provides a useful comparison in that the two systems of land grants helped drive the evolution of a unique frontier economy that was both on the outer fringes of European settlement and at the same time intimately connected to the expanding U.S. South, the Caribbean, and the Atlantic world. The Spanish system, especially in comparison with Kentucky, provided a stable means for residents and immigrants to acquire new land quickly and easily without favoring speculators, which in turn engendered loyalty among residents eager to engage in what Joyce Chaplin has called the "anxious pursuit."[6] (See map 2.)

France and the French

France's desire to prevent British control of the Mississippi River prompted French colonization of Louisiana in 1684. Ownership and control of this valuable waterway would allow the French, they hoped, to limit Britain's expansion to its already-viable coastal settlements on the Atlantic. The French approached the mouth of the Mississippi from the north, beginning in the Canadian provinces, working their way downriver, and eventually founding a colony on the Mississippi coast at Biloxi. As Gwendolyn Hall and others have noted, France could hardly bear the expense involved in maintaining the new colony. The wars of Louis XIV and the War of the Spanish Succession had bankrupted France and spelled poverty for French citizens. The nation could ill afford to send any more of its population to an uncertain colony half a world away. At the beginning of the eighteenth century, a few scattered soldiers and fur traders comprised the majority of the initial, tumultuous French inhabitants. The next six decades saw settlement grow from a few camps based in and around Indian villages to a coastal colony with connections throughout the Caribbean and the Atlantic.[7]

Immigration received a boost with the formation of the Company of the West in 1717. Because France had difficulty finding voluntary colonists, prisoners helped fill the billets from 1717 through 1721. An estimated seven thousand people set sail for Louisiana, including 1,278 criminals and 1,215 women, while some two thousand others died or escaped from the ships before reaching their destination. A census from 1726 lists 1,952 French settlers in the colony—a number that surely reflects both the high degree of mortality due to disease as well as the mobility of French traders into the interior and that also recalls the initial disastrous years of the earlier Jamestown colony. As Hall points out, "Louisiana had little to offer" European settlers, and this was undoubtedly true of nearby West Florida as well. Unhealthy, poor, and remote, Louisiana was off the regular trade lines, while sandbars constantly blocked the harbors of the few ports. The river flooded coastal farms, famine plagued the colony, and swamps rendered lower Louisiana exceedingly unhealthy in warmer months.[8]

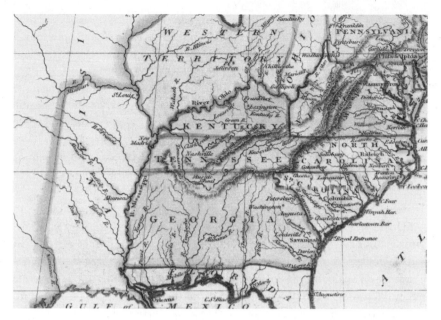

Map 2. General map of the west, from "United States" map by Daniel Lizars, 1806. Agee Map Collection, Birmingham Public Library, Birmingham, Ala.

The earliest men to drive colonization, Pierre Le Moyne, sieur d'Iberville, and his brother, Jean Baptiste Le Moyne, sieur de Bienville, brought settlers to the new land. They also stole from the French Crown, engaged in piracy, and stole ships and goods from nearby Caribbean islands. The lasting contribution of these men was to establish an alliance with the local Choctaw Indians against the British in South Carolina. These Choctaws, intentionally or otherwise, provided for the continued existence of the fledgling colony. Knowledge of boatbuilding (especially the classic one-piece pirogue common to the Mississippi waterways), local plants, medicine, and crops all helped the colony survive. More immediately, during times of famine French settlers moved into Indian villages. The relationship between the French and the Indians was complex.[9] Although the French depended on the Choctaws to provide warriors against British South Carolinians and their Chickasaw allies, France itself was never in a position of sufficient power to control Indian tribes. For a time the French colonies seemed to exist only at the sufferance of the most powerful of the local tribes, the Natchez. In the 1720s French relations with that tribe grew steadily worse, until in November 1729 the Natchez decided to strike under the cover of a trading mission; they killed 237 French men, women, and children and captured nearly 300 African slaves imported to replace Indian and French convict labor.[10] Because of this raid the French set out on a series of campaigns designed to remove the Natchez from the lower Mississippi Valley. As Gary Nash and others have argued, the Choctaws and other minor tribes in Louisiana maintained their alliances with the French as part of a strategy to contain the British and play the two European empires against each other.[11]

By the late eighteenth century, after long decades of disease and warfare, most Indian resistance in Baton Rouge was a dim memory. A shift in the economic structure of lower Louisiana, including Baton Rouge, from an informal trade or barter system to a more structured plantation economy relegated the more powerful and organized Indian tribes to the fringes of the economic system. A series of cessions and treaties, beginning with British control of West Florida in 1765, steadily reduced the power of the area's Native American tribes. With the Treaty of San Lorenzo, completed in 1795, Spain accepted American claims to land in the heart of Creek Territory. In West Florida, as in other parts of the empire, Spain followed a policy of playing tribes against one another and against foreign powers. At the same time a more sinister policy encouraged Indian dependence on Spain. In 1786 Spain's famous "Instructions" called for a deliberate policy of "peace by deceit."[12] This act decreed that "those Indians who had no acquaintance with alcohol be introduced to it and encouraged to acquire a taste for it."[13] Indian tribes friendly to Spain but not to the new United States received guns and ammunition. But Spain intentionally constructed the weapons such that Spaniards would be required to perform maintenance on them. This policy, the Spaniards hoped, would create a class of dependent Indians unable to fend for themselves.

In Baton Rouge, where from 1785 to 1810 there was no significant Indian economic or military activity, this policy seemed to succeed. The nearest large Indian village, about forty miles from Baton Rouge, was called "Vne" in the records.[14] Although Indians most likely came to Baton Rouge to trade, the records make little mention of them, and their part in the frontier economy of the district did not reach a level meriting much note. Where they do appear, the references are sparse. During an 1808 murder trial, Dane, a slave, testified that she had just returned to the murder scene from "an Indian camp located immediately next to the plantation of her master."[15] Her declaration hints that she traveled freely to and from that place and that such travel was common enough to, for the most part, go unnoticed. The lack of specificity in many records with regard to the location of Indian camps makes the Indian encampments extremely difficult to locate and study. However, the reference raises the possibility that otherwise undescribed "camps" in the lower Mississippi Valley might be small, and highly mobile, Indian settlements. In other records Indians appear as laborers and farmhands performing labor for which planters hired them by the day, the week, the month, or the task.

The French and Indian War squelched the French plan to populate Louisiana with smugglers, deserters, and other criminals, and after the loss of Canada, the eight-hundred-thousand-livres-a-year cost of Louisiana became too much for the French to bear. The 1763 Treaty of Paris gave Canada and East and West Florida to England, and the remainder of Louisiana west of the Mississippi as well as recently captured Havana to Spain.[16] For the British, West Florida represented a colony from which they could guard the Gulf of Mexico and trade with the Spanish. For Spain, Havana had both historic and strategic value as a traditional Spanish port and along with Saint Augustine served as both guard and way station for South American fleets returning to the Iberian Peninsula. Beginning in 1763 the British promoted migration, using the headright system, to encourage loyalists and their slaves to enter West Florida en masse.[17]

Great Britain

The immigration into and settlement of West Florida by Britons is perhaps as confusing as the political and geographical wrangling that gave them control of the area.[18] Loyalty to the empire received a boost in November 1775, when Peter Chester, the British governor of West Florida, declared the area a refuge for loyalists. Between 1775 and 1781 some 1,312 to 1,643 immigrants entered the West Florida area, with the largest proportion hailing from South Carolina (between 262 and 357) and Georgia (278 to 339), although between 115 and 232 came from the British Caribbean islands.[19] According to some estimates, the entire West Florida area in 1783 contained between seven and eight thousand residents, about a third of whom left after Spain acquired West Florida in 1783.[20] As J. Barton Starr has pointed out, the loyalty of these British immigrants cannot be viewed in the same light as that of Tories in the rebellious colonies.[21] In what would serve as an important model for the 1810 revolution, several residents of British West Florida joined the colonies in revolution, but in general the loyalty of British residents stemmed more from political isolation from the colonies than from political association with the Crown. Starr notes that correspondence between West Floridians does not even indicate an awareness of the colonial troubles until 1778, when American raiders entered the territory in a failed attempt to ignite the area into revolt.[22] In short, inhabitants of West Florida seemed more concerned with surviving on the frontier than with upsetting the political applecart. This theme would reassert itself again and again over the next three decades as issues of land, trade, and regional stability trumped issues of national loyalty.

A number of factors other than geographical isolation from the American Revolution helped cement the political leanings of these residents prior to the return of the Spaniards in 1783. First, West Floridians never exhibited any revolutionary sentiment to which the disaffected might turn. The colonial governor and assemblies provided sufficient avenues for resolving grievances. Second, the stabilizing effect of a high proportion of British troops in the colony also helped ensure loyalty. Finally, when West Floridians went to war with Spain in the early 1780s, the conflict presented them with a choice between a Protestant or a Catholic monarch—an easy choice for a population that was still mostly Protestant. The loyalty here was "loyalty by default."[23]

When Spain began an invasion of Mobile in January 1780, West Florida's loyalty was tested again. Troops taken from Louisiana and Havana regiments arrived at Mobile Bay on the tenth of February and began a siege of the fort and the city. By March 14 Spain had captured Mobile, and the Spanish commander, Bernardo de Gálvez, turned his sights on Pensacola; he took it in May 1781, thereby laying all of West Florida open to Spanish forces. Captured British troops boarded a Spanish ship for Havana, to be repatriated and eventually sent to New York to fight the Americans. The Treaty of Paris in 1783 confirmed the cession of the Floridas to Spain, and when the British abandoned the territory, many settlers migrated from East to West Florida.[24] Those loyalists who did not vacate the Floridas at the end of the revolution remained most heavily concentrated in western West Florida near the Mississippi, where the British themselves sowed the seeds of West Floridian loyalty to the Spanish Empire.

Spain

West Florida loyalists suffered tremendous losses in land and personal fortune during the war for American independence and the war with Spain. Raids by banditti and the exigencies of war helped destroy the personal fortunes of many British subjects. After ceding West Florida to Spain in 1783, Britain subsequently refused to compensate West Floridians for their losses. When residents turned to the United States for compensation or confirmation of their British land grants, the newly independent country similarly rebuffed the West Floridians. Loyalty then shifted by default to the Spanish, simply because Spain provided what Britain and the United States could or would not: a centralized government willing to act in residents' interests as long as those residents displayed a reciprocal loyalty. This loyalty was cemented by the Spaniards' willingness to accommodate the Anglo-Americans' quest for the main chance—to obtain and cultivate land through a liberal system of grants. Given that the same processes were at work in the British colonies during the same period suggests that for Americans, including those who migrated to West Florida, land and national loyalty went hand in hand.[25] Also, and perhaps more ephemerally, the Spanish

Crown was just that—a Crown. Loyalists fled the revolution in part because they believed in royal governance. Spain could provide a system of government with which they would be comfortable, as long as the religious impositions of the Spanish Crown did not weigh too heavily on them.

With these changes western West Florida was, in the mid-1780s, ready to begin the process of expansion, settlement, and construction of a national loyalty under Spanish rule. The settled areas between New Orleans and Baton Rouge, already sparsely settled, expanded under the British and the Spanish. In 1785 the town of Baton Rouge had a population of 68 whites, 2 free people of color, and 100 slaves, while settlement of the frontier north of Baton Rouge, in Feliciana, resumed after the Spanish occupied West Florida.[26] By way of comparison, New Orleans in the same year boasted more than 4,400 whites, 9,500 slaves, and 900 free people of color.[27] Spanish officials faced a dilemma in the early 1780s not unlike that which confronted France in the early part of the century: how to populate West Florida. They could attempt to populate the area with Spaniards by bringing them in from other parts of the empire. But faced with already-increasing numbers of U.S. citizens in Kentucky and the Cumberland regions, Spanish officials could envision clashes with the United States in the not-too-distant future. In August 1787, by royal order, Spain formally allowed Americans to settle in West Florida in order to establish a buffer between the two countries.[28] Americans would, of course, be required to take a loyalty oath, but honor would hopefully prevent them from taking action against their new king.

Early Settlement

Europeans first permanently settled what would become the Feliciana district, which includes Bayou Sara, in 1785, even though Europeans had resided in Iberville and other parts of lower Louisiana, including Baton Rouge, for the previous fifteen years.[29] A river stop along the Mississippi fifty miles north of Baton Rouge formally "founded" by John Mills, David Ross, and John O'Connor, Feliciana served as a way station for flatboats on their way from Natchez to New Orleans.[30] This was Mills's second business venture, the first being a failed sawmill in the Natchez area. A small village grew up around the post, and legends suggest that Feliciana took its name from Félicité de Saint Maxent, the wife of Don Bernardo de Gálvez, governor of Spanish Louisiana. The fundamental components of the economy in Feliciana changed little from the 1760s through the 1790s, although the prosperity of the colony certainly grew.[31] Plantations produced cattle, chickens, upland cotton, and other marketable crops on land that was just becoming well settled. Residents could sell these products locally, to government officials and troops, or downriver in New Orleans. At the same time, indigo, pitch, and tar provided other marketable goods, and established planters both planted crops and engaged in a household economy by producing items such as barrel staves—one of the earliest items exported in large quantities from West Florida.[32]

But in order to plant crops, settlers had to obtain land. Two principal methods of acquisition existed in the Baton Rouge area: land grants and private sales. Spanish surveyor Carlos Trudeau began surveying land after Spain took possession, though in the period immediately after 1783, the distance from government centers to the frontier north of Feliciana would have made it difficult for residents to obtain surveyors' services. Nonetheless, it makes sense to examine land ownership and settlement by both period and type—private sales before 1800, south and west of Baton Rouge, and private sales and land grants from 1800 to 1805 north of Baton Rouge in Feliciana.

Grants

Detailed maps commissioned in 1799 are the best source for determining some patterns of land grants in the Feliciana district prior to 1810 and help demonstrate the effectiveness of Spanish land grant policies in preventing large landholdings through government grants. Although maps exist for other areas in and around Baton Rouge, the Feliciana records present the best picture of Spanish land grant policies in West Florida because the area had not been extensively settled under the British or the French. Land distribution had already occurred in almost every other part of the Baton Rouge district and West Florida, under a mix of French, British, and Spanish systems and had then been subject to secondary sales, rendering any hope of analyzing the process in those areas within a Spanish context nearly impossible. Likewise, in both 1804 and 1810 residents of Feliciana played an important role in fostering regional instability, making land distribution in that area of particular interest.

Partially incomplete, the Feliciana maps nevertheless detail 182 plots of land in the district, which began at the northern border of the Baton Rouge district and ran north to the thirty-first-degree line separating West Florida from Mississippi. In a letter showing how seriously Feliciana residents took both their laws and their borders, Richard Devall wrote to alcalde and surveyor general Vicente Pintado regarding a hog thief named Daniel Waltman, who had stolen and slaughtered several pigs. Devall could not immediately capture Waltman because he had "gone above the line," a common reference to the border separating Mississippi from Spanish Florida.[33] For some unknown reason Waltman recrossed the border a week later, and Devall arrested him.

To the east, the Amite River bordered Feliciana and ran east into Lake Mau-

repas, forming a river basin that produced fertile cropland, potentially dangerous flooding, and a strategic lifeline to the Gulf. Plantations gradually faded
away as one moved toward the eastern portion of the district furthest from the
big river.[34] Plots in the district ranged in size from 31 to 2,000 arpents; the size of
21 of the plots listed was not indicated. Of the remaining 161, only 39, or just under 25 percent, were larger than 800 arpents—a limit on initial grants imposed
by Spanish law—104 plots, or 65 percent, measured less than 800 arpents, and
18 measured exactly 800 arpents.[35] Of the 39 plots that exceeded 800 arpents, 22,
or 56 percent, measured exactly 1,000 arpents. Women held title to at least 12 of
the 161 plots of land. Spanish regulations, of course, did not prohibit a person
or a family from accumulating more than 800 arpents of land through private
purchases; the largest single landowner who appears on the maps in Feliciana
prior to 1803 was John Turnbull, who held two separate 2,000-arpent plots. John
Mills, David Ross, and Juan O'Connor retained an interest in the area, with
combined landholdings of 1,490, 1,000, and 2,600 arpents, respectively.[36] While
several landholders did own more than one plot of land, only a few managed to
accumulate more than 1,000 total arpents before 1799. The average plot was 644
arpents, or about 519 acres. These numbers show that in Feliciana up until 1799,
and most likely for at least the next three or four years, the Spaniards were fairly
rigorous about their policy of not creating a class of large-estate landholders.
Also, most residents of the area could expect to amass enough land to engage in
profitable plantation agriculture. The nature of the Spanish land grant system
ensured this.

The Spanish system of land grants in Feliciana, as in the rest of the empire,
was quite simple. Any person who swore loyalty to the Spanish Crown could apply for a land grant. Spanish land policy operated under the principle that every
person deserved enough land to sustain a family, and that the way to govern or
to hold the land was to populate it. In theory, Spanish law required petitioners
to profess the Catholic faith, although in the Baton Rouge area during the early
nineteenth century there is no record of Spain enforcing this requirement.[37]
This lack of religious enforcement can be attributed to several factors. No doubt
it partially represented a concession to the nature of the West Florida frontier,
and the various nationalities and denominations present, as well as a recognition of the need to populate the land at any cost. The lack of a well-established
presence of the Catholic Church in the Baton Rouge borderlands was also a
factor.

All vacant lands in New Spain remained the legal possession of the Crown,
and the king retained the exclusive power to distribute lands for a fee.[38] Anyone
who received a land grant had to inhabit and cultivate a part of the land for
four years, after which that person would receive title to the property. Failure

to fulfill these terms resulted in loss of the title. Even so, in West Florida from 1785 through 1810 there is no record of any person forced to return unused land to the Spanish Crown, probably because officials ignored failure to improve the land in an effort to prevent unrest among residents and to encourage settlement from the United States. After all, if West Florida acquired a reputation as a place where the government confiscated settlers' land, the flow of immigrants would cease. At the same time the average plot size of 644 arpents promoted the influx of already-established planters and their slaves, who could begin to clear and cultivate the large tracts of land immediately. The large grants also provided nonslaveholding settlers with an immediate source of collateral that they could use to borrow the money needed to buy slaves and work their way up the economic ladder.

The size of a family usually determined the amount of land granted, as long as the grant did not exceed eight hundred arpents.[39] This did not limit an individual or a family to eight hundred arpents total. After the owner improved the land, he could petition the Crown for an increase in the size of the holding.[40] Thus cultivating and improving the land was an avenue to receiving extra grants. Daniel Clark used this practice to his benefit in January 1799 when he wrote to inform the Spanish governor of a bridge that Clark had built one league from the fort in Baton Rouge.[41] The construction of the bridge would allow him to petition for extra land either adjoining the already-existing grant or in some other place where Clark might want to begin a new farm. Despite the extra land due him because of improvements, Spanish policy still held firm to the notion that settlers should receive only as much land that they could realistically use. If the grant bordered a river, Spanish law required the owner to construct levees, canals, or bridges as needed. Squatters who occupied and cultivated a portion of land for at least ten years could make an outright purchase of the property after a government assessment, although liberal land grant policies meant that squatting occurred infrequently in the Baton Rouge district.

Under Spanish land policy, acquiring land was quite easy as long as the claimant could prove the ability to cultivate the land and improve it. This promoted two results. First, the policy discouraged rampant land speculation of the type seen in the Virginia and Kentucky portions of the British and later American territories. Second, it actively encouraged settlement, as the landholder had to live on and work the land in some fashion.

Secondary Sales

From December 1792 through November 1799, fifty parcels of land changed hands on the eastern side of the river in Baton Rouge, out of a total of ninety-five transactions in the records.[42] The size of arpentage sold ranged from 40 arpents, bought for five pesos, a horse, and a plow, to several transactions of 800 arpents. Twenty transactions at 240 arpents represent the median size of land purchased.

Of the fifty-eight land transactions with sufficient data for analysis, forty-six contain enough information to permit an estimate of the average price of land in the area.[43] Residents sold a total of 11,010 arpents for 10,706 pesos, or an average of about .97 pesos per arpent. The averages of the value of plots ranges from a 240-arpent plot sold for 50 pesos, or about one-fifth of a peso per arpent, to a 440-arpent plot sold for 1,500 pesos, or about 3.4 pesos per arpent. The price of the land, of course, depended on improvements and location (which itself indicated fertility), although Spanish customary law tried to ensure that all residents had river access of some sort—which could result in very oddly shaped plots. Because of improvements to the land, for instance, the plot purchased by local plantation owner and entrepreneur Marie Decoux from another woman, Marie Nivet, contained a house, storerooms, outbuildings, and 50 arpents under fence (presumably either to keep her cattle in or to keep neighboring cattle out). The land cost Decoux 1,500 pesos. The most common improvements that might increase the value of the land included the aforementioned items, but also levees, slave cabins, tobacco houses, sugar and mills, cotton gins, animal pens, kitchens, and wooden floors in the house. Although trees were not an improvement in the sense that the owner of the land constructed them, the records often listed them under "improvements."[44]

The language of a property sale varied little from record to record—the Spaniards used language quite consciously in all transactions. The bill of sale generally established the residence of the buyer and of the seller—necessary if the buyer perhaps owned property elsewhere in the district, and a handy means of keeping track of residents on an ever-expanding frontier. The residence of the seller would establish that person as an already-present member of the community or as an outsider trying to gain entry. For instance, a fairly typical document detailing the 1801 sale of a tract of land by the Bossler brothers lists the buyer as "Antonio Gras, a merchant of this city of Baton Rouge," then goes on to define the size and boundaries of the land, its exact location, and its physical attributes. This particular property was one mile north of Fort San Carlos in the heart of Baton Rouge; an artificial boundary, perhaps a pile of stones, marked the northern corner, while a gum tree set off the south corner. More important than the physical boundaries it delineated, a land sale document also identified the owners of the neighboring plots of land. This information not only fixed the land geographically but also located its owner physically and socially within the community. This was particularly important because an owner new to the area would be expected to serve in the militia, help pay for levees and other improve-ments, and perhaps act as an alcalde.[45] In short, land ownership brought with it a variety of commitments to civil society that placed the owner in service to the community and the community in service to the landowner in a very tangible way. It also established the new owner within the neighborhood.[46]

After verifying the location of the parcel, the document listed any improve-ments to the land such as a house, barns, slave quarters, other outbuildings, gins, and levees. The remainder of a land sale document generally detailed the financial dimension of the deal by naming a price and the terms of payment. The seller also promised that no mortgage existed on the land and then relin-quished any and all rights to it. The buyer agreed to make payments—usually half immediately and half within a year—or the land would revert to the owner. Finally, the governor of the Baton Rouge district, Carlos de Grand-Pré, along with the buyer, the seller, and at least one witness, would sign the document. Secondary sales for Feliciana do not appear in the records until 1801, though clearly some transactions had already occurred. Still, this is about the length of time one would expect, given that most residents would not have lived in the area long enough to have made improvements to their property. This pattern of land acquisition appears in virtually every secondary land sale document in the northern and southern portions of West Florida from 1785 through 1810. The first secondary sales in the Baton Rouge district reflect some of the ear-lier secondary sales from the southern parts of the district in the 1790s, in that Spanish officials tried, to some degree, to establish the lineage of the property. In February 1801, Jesse Munson sold to William Lemon, a man of indeterminate residence, a five-hundred-arpent piece of land. The document recorded the lo-cation and the neighbors, as usual, and the outbuildings. However, it also noted that Munson had obtained the land as a royal grant from the king on October 2, 1787, making him one of the earliest settlers under Spanish rule.[47]

Local Officials

In 1798 power to distribute lands rested with local officials, who collected the land grant fees and forwarded a percentage to the Crown. Spanish officials ex-tended this policy to require that any person living in Louisiana for fewer than two years who could not produce legal title to his land must surrender it.[48] Lo-cal Spanish officials, fearful of American reaction to the edict, replied with the well-known policy of *obedezco pero no cumplo*, or "I obey, but I do not comply."

In the Baton Rouge district, of which Feliciana was a part, Governor Carlos de Grand-Pré was responsible for land grants under this system. A Frenchman who had offered his loyalty to the Spanish Crown after West Florida became Spanish in 1783, Grand-Pré became thoroughly a part of the Baton Rouge community.

After serving in the Spanish colonial army throughout the lower Mississippi Valley, Grand-Pré received a promotion to governor of the Baton Rouge district in 1799—although he had already acted in an administrative capacity in nearby Iberville and Pointe Coupee. Nonetheless, by the time of his appointment to the governorship, Grand-Pré had already established himself in the district. He had held power of attorney for innumerable residents and served as godparent to residents' children, and residents in turn had named children after him, sometimes giving them the middle name of "Grandpré."[49] The governor also acted within the local network of lending and assistance, and his eleven children had married, or would soon marry, within the community. Five sons served in the Spanish Army of Louisiana, and one, Louis, was a sublieutenant at Fort San Carlos in Baton Rouge. Three daughters were married to local men—two to Frenchmen, the other to an Anglo.[50] Three other daughters were still minors in 1810, and the other two boys lived in New Orleans, where they attended school.[51]

As related to land grants, the governor operated through his surveyor general in Feliciana, Vicente Sebastían Pintado. Not much is known about Pintado's early life. Born in February 1774 in Santa Cruz de la Palma in the Canary Islands, Pintado served as surveyor general of Spanish West Florida from his base in Baton Rouge from 1799 until 1817.[52] He also held the position of alcalde and served as captain in the local militia. His prior military experience included command of a sloop on Lakes Borge and Ponchartrain for then-governor Baron Francisco Luis Héctor de Carondelet of Louisiana.[53] When he assumed the position of surveyor general for West Florida in 1799, Pintado came to an area that was well settled but at the same time part of an expanding frontier.

One way in which a land claimant might first acquire land was by introducing a letter testifying to his good character. Alternately, settlers who wished to obtain a grant of land from the Crown could first petition the governor for a specific parcel, stating the nature of their needs. In West Florida, Baton Rouge governor Grand-Pré then authorized Pintado to go to the area and make a survey, a process usually executed by one of Pintado's assistant surveyors. Established landowners—the local elite—could identify a plot they wished to obtain, make the survey on their own, and then present the survey to Pintado for verification. At some point, as his schedule permitted, Pintado would send an assistant to verify the boundaries. In the meantime, the claimant could begin to clear the land and work it.

Kentucky

Compare the process of land settlement in West Florida, then, with what was occurring several hundred miles to the north in Kentucky. The territory-cum-state of Kentucky provides a useful comparison with West Florida in regard to U.S. expansion for several reasons. On the one hand, Kentucky, along with Louisiana, represented for Americans the far western North American frontier in the late eighteenth and early nineteenth centuries. Moreover, both Kentucky and West Florida, as options for westward migrants, drew American settlers from Virginia and North and South Carolina. Finally, both West Florida and the Kentucky borderlands had recently changed from British control of land distribution.

In Kentucky the British law of 1705, like its Spanish counterpart, required claimants to settle on their land in a house, and to clear and plant at least an acre of land; a second law in 1779 reiterated the earlier requirement. Yet land speculators in the late 1700s easily evaded this stricture by hiring land jobbers to make a claim to a piece of land, build a cabin, and then plant a token crop, as the law did not actually require residence in the cabin, only its construction. Moreover, many settlers who moved to Kentucky acquired a piece of land by simply registering a description of a piece of land with the state auditor or the county clerk. In turn the settler received a certificate of claim to the land, and at a later time the county surveyor officially noted the boundaries. After a state official completed a survey, the governor would then ratify it by issuing a patent or a grant. At that point the claimant owned clear title to the land and could sell the property via a deed. In reality, as Christopher Waldrep has pointed out, Kentucky settlers traded the claim certificates in place of cash, using land certificates as a substitute for currency.[54]

Although in theory the ease of requesting a piece of land should have ensured that anyone could settle in Kentucky and make a living, in reality speculators gobbled up the best land in enormous tracts. The Ohio Land Company, the Loyal Land Company, and the Transylvania Land Company, for instance, acquired millions of acres in the Ohio Valley prior to and during the American Revolution.[55] Moreover, land jobbers in the late eighteenth century took much of the best land, traveling in groups to build dozens of cabins on vacant land and then clearing a few token square yards. They in turn sold the land at inflated prices to legitimate settlers, the effect of which prevented migrants from home-steading the land through settlement and cultivation.[56] One historian has noted that thousands of Kentucky migrants, drawn there in hopes of acquiring land, failed, "los[ing] their dreams in a morass of title disputes."[57] In one county fewer than one in five heads of household owned land in 1795. By 1800, presumably as a result of a series of legislative initiatives in the mid-1790s, progress meant that slightly less than half held clear title to a piece of property. Thus while Kentucky was certainly a land of opportunity from the 1750s onward, it was mostly such for speculators and those in need of farm laborers. Whereas much of North America's colonial period and the period of westward expansion was marked by high land-to-labor ratios, the reverse instead characterized early nineteenth-century Kentucky, leading to increasing tenancy.[58]

The unequal distribution of land forced settlers and lawyers into the state-house to battle for the soul of Kentucky's political economy, and Stephen Aron argues that rampant speculation undermined the unity of homesteaders by pitting them against one another in their efforts to obtain land.[59] At the same time, that unity suffered from a series of external threats at the hands of the British during the American Revolution and from Indians throughout the period of settlement. Compare this situation to that of West Florida, where an orderly land policy, absent speculation, engendered unity among the planters.

From the point of view of the actual settlers, settlement in Kentucky (and for that matter Tennessee) can best be described as semicontrolled chaos as speculators snapped up much of the best land, in quantities that sometimes reached hundreds of thousands of acres. The process marginalized small settlers and took the power of long-term settlement away from the settlers themselves. Land speculation also placed the largest plots of land, and therefore the economic, political, and social power networks, in the hands of a few elites. For settlers in West Feliciana prior to 1803, the nuts and bolts of the settlement process—and the effects thereof—was vastly different. First, although the Spanish took control of an area that was settled to some extent, large areas of West Florida included a great deal of available land, most of which had not been settled. Second, the Spanish process of distributing and ensuring the settlement of land actively discouraged speculation, though it did not prevent speculators from amassing large parcels through secondary sales. Nonetheless, whereas the British and the American systems theoretically required residence by those purchasing the land, very few control mechanisms, or the political will to enforce such mechanisms, existed for the enforcement of these policies. In northern New Spain, ordinary settlers had a much better chance of acquiring land through grants than almost anywhere else on the North American frontier in the early republic.

The remoteness of the frontier and the autonomy of corrupt authorities who disbursed the land heightened the problem for Great Britain and then for the United States. At the same time, officials tended to look the other way when dealing with land speculation. Unlike Kentucky, the government of Spanish West Florida required permanent residence in order to obtain a grant and withheld title to the land until the resident showed proof of improvement. Also, unlike in other parts of the emerging U.S. South, land certificates never served as a form of currency for West Floridians, and settlers did not battle one another for new, open land. After the transfer of West Florida from Britain to Spain, Spanish officials simply recognized existing claims obtained under the British government and continued to encourage steady settlement by small landholders who would live as residents.[60] Those living in West Florida after the transfer in 1783 and those who moved in afterward took full advantage of the opportunities available to them in their new land by settling, improving the land, and building ties to their community and government. While western migrants from the British colonies, and later the United States, could certainly be expected to understand the circumstances of land distribution in Kentucky versus those in West Florida from rumors, letters home from family members, returning migrants, and newspaper and government accounts, they also needed to understand the frontier itself and the ways in which profit could be extracted from the land.

Opening the New Frontier

The writings of one of those western migrants, William Dunbar, provide an illuminating account of the ways in which settlers extracted wealth from the borderlands and serve as a guide to the ways in which settlers in and around Baton Rouge could make a living. A Scottish immigrant to Philadelphia and eventually West Florida and Natchez, Mississippi, Dunbar left a diary rich in details of everyday life on the Spanish-American frontier. In many ways, Dunbar was a southern Benjamin Franklin, who made his fortune in a partnership with original settler John Ross (another Scotsman) raising cotton, indigo, and slaves.[61] He then retired to a life of scientific observation, introducing the square-bale style of cotton packing to the Deep South, making astronomical observations, conducting experiments, and exploring the frontiers of what would become Arkansas and Texas, first for Spain and then for the United States.[62] On a number of occasions, he corresponded with Thomas Jefferson, who recommended Dunbar for membership in the American Philosophical Society. Dunbar eventually wrote twelve entries in that society's publications.[63]

As a surveyor for the Spanish government, Dunbar took on the job of ascertaining the thirty-first degree of latitude boundary between Spanish West Florida and the United States in 1798. His report to Manuel Gayoso de Lemos, governor of Spanish West Florida, depicts a rich land full of potential—both for profit and for danger. The danger came first in the form of "innumerable swarms of Gnats, and a variety of other Stinging and biting insects" that plagued his survey party. But the "inconvenience arising from the Winged insects was easily removed by the smoke of a few fires placed around the encampment and a curtain of gauze secured [the party] . . . from the attack of these minute though troublesome creatures."[64] The party saw panthers "of a very ferocious nature," black bears, and wolves, but it was "the thundering Crocodile, all of hideous forms," that most fascinated the group.[65] Ever the scientist, Dunbar spent several pages of his diary discussing the mating habits and diet of the alligator.

The American alligator as described by Dunbar provides an excellent symbol for the relationship of Europeans to the "unsettled" wilderness environment of the South. On the one hand, the alligator, like the frontier, was "hideous in all its forms"—wild and foreign. On the other hand, settlers could conquer both animal and frontier. Dunbar describes the alligator and his relationship to it in quasi-military terms, noting: "It has been asserted that their skin (resembling a coat of mail) is impenetrable to a musket ball, but I never found any difficulty in piercing them with small rifle bullets unless the stroke [i.e., the shot] was made too obliquely." The ferocity of the alligator, like the ferocity of the frontier, also changed with the season, as "during the cold of the Winter Season they often become torpid and may then be cut to pieces with an Axe without their exhibiting any powers of motion. People have been known to sit down upon them in this state supposing them to be logs of wood."[66]

Dunbar speaks in similar terms of subduing the land north of Baton Rouge, and alligators in some ways represent the sometimes combative relationship between Europeans and the southern frontier—and the ability of Europeans to eventually tame and alter their environment. Dunbar's crew began to affect the frontier land immediately on their arrival, as one of his men accidentally started a fire that burned out of control for many square miles. Ever the settler, Dunbar saw this fire as a beneficial precursor to settlement and understood the accident within the context of taming the land and making it useful for settlers.[67]

Trees provided an initial means of income for settlers, and Dunbar describes more than twenty species, including oaks, ash, and two species of elm. Daniel Clark wrote to Thomas Jefferson describing abundant pecan trees growing wild and orange trees cultivated by planters.[68] The abundance of trees in West Florida enabled residents to produce a variety of wood products. The rot resistant cypress tree seemed the most versatile, and residents used it for housing materials in the form of shingles, planks, beams, posts, and rails. Inhabitants also used poplar for boat decking, and deciduous trees provided the raw material for making potash. Residents felled white and black oaks to use in a number of products. The lumber output of the area had been marketed to the West Indies since the 1770s, when a Jamaica newspaper featured an advertisement for West Florida barrel staves and headings.[69] Residents could also trade wood in a variety of places, but settlers sent a great deal to Havana, where after centuries of deforestation a dire need for wood of all types existed.[70]

One fascinating aspect of barrel stave production is that a resident, William Dunbar, for instance, could cut down trees and produce the staves in the forests, then move the finished staves from the cypress swamps back to his plantation. Because the slow-moving rivers in West Florida did not provide enough power for wheel-driven sawmills, Dunbar owned portable mills; female slaves hefted the saws, turning trees into logs, while male slaves transformed logs into staves.[71] The natural, untamed land, then, could provide many useful products. Residents above and below Baton Rouge consciously set aside tracts of forest for cultivation, and the resale value of a piece of property could be greatly enhanced by the presence of cypress and other trees. Once the settlers began planting crops and establishing a farm economy, they raised cattle and chickens, grew sugar, cotton, rice, and indigo, and manufactured pitch and tar to sell as staples. But Dunbar also describes a mélange of cultivars, as planters grew everything from squash, pumpkins, and melons, to tomatoes, eggplants, almonds, and four varieties of fruit trees.[72] In addition to using these crops for food, residents could also sell them in nearby Baton Rouge city or at the local docks along the Mississippi.

Although some residents like Philip Nolan led expeditions to Mexico and brought back wild horses to sell in Baton Rouge and New Orleans, cattle served as one of the main paths to wealth for many residents.[73] As Christopher Morris has shown, cattle ranching promoted "the first small step in the rise of commercial agriculture" among Mississippi Valley farmers.[74] It served as an entry-level occupation and enabled farmers to increase their wealth relatively easily. Settlers in Kentucky and Ohio who shipped their products downstream to the New Orleans market ran into trouble when it came to shipping beef. While crops such as corn could be dried and put in barrels without the threat of rot, curing beef required large amounts of salt, something to which Ohio Valley farmers had no easy access. The demand in New Orleans for fresh as opposed to cured beef presented a problem for Ohio Valley farmers; cattle herders in the Baton Rouge district had a distinct advantage in that they could simply walk their stock to market and sell the beef directly to local consumers or slaughterhouses.[75] As Morris argues, "the first commercial farmers . . . were cattle herders who sold their steers" to local Spaniards, and residents in the Baton Rouge district had an additional advantage because of their proximity to New Orleans.[76] Also, Susan Parker has observed that cattle ranching in East Florida helped settlers establish themselves in the local society, and that cattle and livestock "provided the capital to acquire slaves necessary for the transition to cotton."[77] Cattle in Baton Rouge presented a similar opportunity for non-slave-owning landholders to embark on the path to slave ownership.

Growing Local Wealth

Records from West Florida and Baton Rouge provide historians with a picture of up-and-coming farmers attempting to break into the ranks of the planters through cattle ranching. A 1795 census of the Bayou Sara frontier indicates that within ten years of its initial settlement the area had 287 inhabitants, 158 of whom were slaves. Sixteen children were born that year, and women endured two stillbirths. Residents owned 162 horses, 1,075 cattle, 194 sheep, and 1,099 pigs, making livestock in West Florida, as in other areas of the U.S. South at this time, a large component of the frontier economy. That same year plantations and wild gathering produced 1,600 pounds of indigo, and 61 barrels of processed indigo waited the market. Planters grew 10,000 pounds of cotton and more than 12,000 pounds of corn on 22,000 arpents of land.[78] Clearly, frontier residents enjoyed a two-tier economy of livestock ranching, on the one hand, and agricultural production, on the other.[79]

Two men at the opposite ends of the economic spectrum provide a glimpse into residents' emerging wealth. One cattle rancher, Louis Ricard, died in April 1793, leaving his property in the care of his brother-in-law, Jean Baptiste Bienville. Ricard did not own any land in the Baton Rouge area, although he may have had holdings in Pointe Coupee across the river. His estate inventory, however, lists no land ownership; cattle made up the bulk of his possessions. Ricard owned seven bulls, sixteen cows, one calf, three mares, one foal, and one ox. Judging from his succession inventory, he grazed his herd either on his brother-in-law's land or in the common pastures. The total value of his estate was 186 pesos, making him a relatively poor man by Baton Rouge standards, and his debts placed a negative value on his estate. However, Ricard's debt was actually a sign of his acceptance in the community, as residents would not lend money to someone they did not think capable of repaying it. His potential wealth was another part of his link to the community, as was the wealth of his brother-in-law. He could hope to breed the cattle and increase his wealth, thereby allowing him to purchase land and slaves.[80]

When Jean Baptiste Bienville died five years later, he left one of the wealthiest and best-connected estates in the district. Bienville had been intimately tied to the upper echelons of Baton Rouge society, occasionally holding power of attorney for locals, serving as a witness to mortgages, as a borrower and a lender among residents, and in a variety of other important capacities. Like many wealthy residents, he was occasionally late in repaying debts and sometimes came to the aid of his less-well-off neighbors. At one point one of Bienville's white female neighbors who apparently had no domicile went to Bienville's farmhouse to die.[81] In the half dozen or so documents in which Bienville appears from 1785 until his death in 1798, he always signed his name with the "Ordinary Mark" of an X, signifying his inability to write, and which required a second witness to vouch for him. However, in the estate inventory his son Julien could sign his own name.[82]

His estate went to his two sons, Basile and Julien, and his daughter Françoise, while some of the leading men of the district sat as witnesses and appraisers of the estate. Bienville's will divided the estate equally into thirds, and the succession documents show that Bienville owned four bulls, fourteen cows, nine calves, nine oxen (all with names), ten horses (also with names), two foals, a riding horse, twenty slaves, a 480-arpent plantation, and 180 pesos in cash. The total value of the estate was more than 13,000 pesos, one of the largest in the area before 1798.[83] If Bienville's farm mirrored that of his neighbors, and if the size of his slave holdings is any indication, he probably also grew some sort of crop, such as sugar, cotton, or corn. Cattle ranching should not require twenty slaves, no matter the size of the herd, and Bienville's estate inventory listed plows, grindstones, and scales with weights as part of the farm equipment.

But cattle and slaves formed the basis of Bienville's wealth, as it did for other residents, and allowed him to "grow" his wealth along two different lines. The cattle multiplied while grazing his land, and the chattel multiplied while working it. His twenty slaves included eight described as mother-daughter pairs, and seven of the twenty were under twelve years old—the age a slave typically went to the fields.[84] Bienville, with twenty slaves, could retire from working the fields himself and concentrate on plantation management, leaving one to wonder what he, a former slave emancipated in the 1770s or 1780s, thought when he watched his own slaves working in the fields as he once did.

Bienville and other residents of his stature concentrated on managing the processing of crops: indigo production, cotton ginning, sugar milling, and industries related to the cattle business. Indigo grew wild in Louisiana, and residents began to process the plant into dye in the 1720s. Gwendolyn Hall has speculated that slaves familiar with the same plant in Africa introduced whites to its production.[85] The lure of indigo, of course, was in the easy profits. Because it grew in soil where rice would not, farmers could easily "marry" it with rice production.[86] Farmers planted rice in the spring, and the crop required very little attention until the summer months. During the intervening time they could begin to plant indigo. Joyce Chaplin describes the indigo harvest in South Carolina as beginning in July after the first blooms and the fullest leaves appeared. At that time workers harvested the upper sections of the plant. Over the next few weeks new growth would appear, and planters could harvest again in August and possibly again in September. After the third harvest the major work of the rice season began. Lower Louisiana seemed to follow a slightly different pattern of harvest from South Carolina, and the growing season might have been a bit longer because of the more southerly latitude.

In 1776, the only year he really describes indigo harvesting, William Dunbar cut his first plants on June 22. His next cut occurred on August 5 (and meanwhile the cutting of the earliest of the ripe rice), another on August 19; he discusses no more indigo harvests until November 19, when he cut indigo for its seed.[87]

It is instructive to note that Dunbar both worked planted indigo crops on his plantation and gathered wild indigo as he went about the business of turning cypress trees into barrel staves. For Dunbar, who cultivated tobacco, rice, corn, and sugar, in addition to making barrel staves, indigo seemed to be a "target of opportunity" crop, in part, possibly, because of the early time period in which he was working. Manchac, where Dunbar lived, in the southern part of the Baton Rouge district, was established but not well settled. Wild indigo still grew in enough quantity to make a small crop on the side when paired with his usual plantings. However, even after regular settlement wild indigo could serve as a way for new, poorer residents to gain wealth by harvesting seed and selling it to planters. The circumstances in South Carolina during the same period suggest that indigo in West Florida played the same role as in South Carolina—that of a "fill-in" crop in times of need. That is, in years when the rice or sugar crop failed, indigo production might soften the economic blow.[88]

Although many, if not most, West Floridians engaged in simple plantation agriculture to earn a living, other, more complex, industries grew up in the Baton Rouge area during this period. In June 1790, John Buhler entered into a three-year contract with Robert Ory to establish a dairy—the first on record in the district.[89] The terms of the contract shed light on the nature of business contracts on the early frontier. The records suggest that Ory entered into the agreement with nothing more than his skills as a blacksmith, while Buhler stood to receive little revenue from the agreement. Buhler, a cattleman by profession, agreed to put up several arpents of land and supply fifty cows, four horses, and two barrels of salt each year. In addition, Buhler would furnish Ory with corn for the animals until he could grow his own. Ory would then reimburse Buhler for the loss of any animals to other than natural causes. Finally, Buhler would rent to Ory some blacksmith tools for a substantial forty pesos per year. For his part Ory would manage the dairy, to be called Saint Peter's Vacherie in Saint John's Plains, milk the cows, and receive "the fifth part of the calves which the cited fifty cows [would] produce."[90] Ory would also receive all the revenue from the milk. At least on paper, Buhler did not stand to make any money from this contract, and nothing except the possibility that he would receive the other four fifths of the calves might explain the odd arrangement. After all, John Buhler incurred all the risks, while his partner was only to manage the dairy. However, one possible explanation could be that the dairy side of the venture was a new industry, and the cows would also be slaughtered for beef. Perhaps Buhler was to profit from the unstated, but already established, slaughterhouse portion of the business, while Ory would profit from the newer, and as yet untested, dairy operations. As West Florida progressed from a newly settled frontier area to one with more-established plantations and profit ventures, residents could effectively circumvent the lack of specie and expand the economy by pairing skills in unusual arrangements profitable to all parties.

Whatever the case, the establishment of the dairy shows that the inhabitants of Baton Rouge and its environs had begun to produce more than simple plantation goods even at this early stage of settlement. As the settlements in West Florida grew, the region became tied to the outside world through commerce. Residents shipped products from West Florida's plantations and farms out of Baton Rouge, down to New Orleans, and out to the Caribbean, Europe, and the United States. Perhaps just as important was their connection with the expanding northwestern United States. Both New Orleans and Baton Rouge shipped goods upriver to settlements in Tennessee, Kentucky, and Ohio.[91] While some of the upriver commerce such as gunpowder, sherry, tea, and chocolate could not have originated in either Florida or New Orleans, other products, such as sugar, cheese, indigo, and cotton, could have originated in Baton Rouge. From 1799 through 1802 the value of goods imported from the Floridas and Spanish Louisiana nearly doubled, from more than 500,000 dollars in 1789 to more than 1 million in 1802. Perhaps more importantly the variety of goods expanded as well, from sixteen to thirty-three different types of cargo. Floridians and Louisianans, for their parts, also received a staggering amount of commerce. In large part this reflected the place of New Orleans as a center of Caribbean and Atlantic world commerce. U.S. ports sent to New Orleans and the Florida ports ninety-six different types of merchandise, the value of which fluctuated from 2 to 3.5 million dollars between 1799 and 1801. However, this value included only goods shipped from the Atlantic states from Massachusetts south to Georgia, excepting New Jersey.[92]

Compare this with the trade between the Floridas/Louisiana and Spain and its New World colonies. Merchants in New Orleans sent unprocessed items, including wood, tar, wheat, cotton, and sugar, to Spanish colonies throughout the Old World and the New. New Orleans ports also shipped an incredible variety of refined items such as harnesses, chairs, cigars, munitions, hammers, chests, lace, and distilled liquors. The presence of butter, calfskins, and meat confirms the persistence of the cattle industry in the Mississippi Valley.[93] The variety of goods passing through the Floridas and New Orleans to and from Spain and its colonies far outstripped what the United States could offer. Nonetheless, while New Orleans was important to the economy of Baton Rouge and the Mississippi Valley, the city played a minor role in the economy of New Spain.[94] Although the value of commerce through Havana in 1803 totaled more than 20 million pesos, only 500,000, or 1/4 of 1 percent, passed through New Orleans. Out of a total of 491 ships that left Havana in 1803, only 44 sailed to New Orleans, bringing 241,875 pesos worth of goods to western settlers, for an average of 5,497 pesos of trade per voyage. On the reverse trip, 77 ships sailed from New Orleans to Havana, bringing 329,056 pesos of goods, for an average of 4,911 pesos per voyage. This was a signal that the colony was producing a number of products that could be sold in Cuba, the New World, and Europe by Spanish merchants. Compare this, however, to other, wealthier ports such as Veracruz and Montevideo. For example, 17 ships sailed from Havana to Veracruz, bringing 401,102 pesos of goods, or 23,594 pesos per voyage. On the return trip, 42 ships left Veracruz for Havana with 2,077,790 pesos in goods. This represented a staggering 49,471 peso per voyage average. New Orleans, then, was a small drop in the bucket of Spanish trade in the New World.[95]

This set of relationships with the outside world would place settlers in the position of struggling to live in the borderlands and begin the process of creating a farm economy, while at the same time having to maintain some awareness of the markets in the outer world. Further, it tied them into American markets to a much greater degree than to Spanish markets, a set of relationships that as of 1803 did not test their loyalties. However, for West Floridians this would change with the transfer of Louisiana to the United States.

DESPITE A HISTORY that seemed to foreshadow nothing but confusion and a North American context that suggested corruption, West Florida progressed somewhat easily from French to British to Spanish rule, as wars and geopolitics determined the political fate of the area. The British presence brought with it the first serious attempts to settle the region, using the same headright system that had worked well in the rest of the American colonies. However, most of the early settlement in the Baton Rouge district occurred in the southern part of the district, as some residents moved upward from New Orleans while others came down the Mississippi and bypassed the northern frontier to live closer to the big city. While Britannia ruled the province, settlers arrived and began to establish plantations and engage in a variety of agricultural pursuits. The land in and around Baton Rouge furnished settlers with natural resources that they could sell on the open market, and as in other parts of the borderlands, residents used cattle ranching as a means of earning money to buy slaves and move on to better-paying staple crops such as sugar, tobacco, and cotton.

In 1783 the Spanish took control of the province, and by 1803 their administration in the Baton Rouge district provided residents with a means of gaining land and engaging in plantation agriculture. Almost anyone with the means of working the land and improving it could gain land grants in the area fairly easily. Furthermore, in comparison to settlement north and east of the area, land distribution policy worked quite equitably. The result was a system that begat a fairly even distribution of the land—and an adherence to the Spanish rules of land settlement—on the Feliciana frontier. It also saw the resale of lands well within the maximum acreage allowed by Spanish law for initial grants. The overall effect of these patterns of settlement, combined with the land the settlers inhabited, was a widely varied economy based on a society in which few land-holders in the district "outweighed" their neighbors by a wide margin. Where wide margins did exist, residents could reasonably expect to surmount them through hard work that would bring additional grants of land.

These small farms also led to a more dynamic economy of the type usually associated with colonial New England. As in the New England merchant and fishing communities of Boston, Providence, and elsewhere, Baton Rouge farmers produced such a variety of goods, including cattle and lumber, that the failure of one of them could be balanced by the abundance of another. As in Natchez and Spanish East Florida, cattle ranching and lumbering could, to some extent, assuage the occasional economic setback caused by crop failure. Many residents engaged in both, as well as in growing sugar, cotton, and tobacco. Continued prosperity for the Spaniards and the American, British, and French inhabitants depended on the promise of continued stability in, and ease of access to, land sales and land grants.

Simply working the land to survive, however, was not the ideal to which borderlands migrants aspired. Many came to improve their "station" by increasing their wealth through the large-scale growth and marketing of some type of staple crop. Those kinds of aspirations in the Atlantic world required a considerable labor force that could be coerced, either through wages or by the tip of a whip, into performing plantation-style agricultural work. In Spanish West Florida circumstances developed along the lines of those in the Chesapeake region, the Carolinas, the Caribbean, and parts of South America as local planters turned to slave labor to satisfy their desire for wealth.

CHAPTER TWO

Working the West Florida Frontier

Slavery and the Accumulation of Wealth

As Anglo-Americans and British expatriates moved into Spanish territory between 1785 and 1806, they encountered and helped modify a unique system of slavery in an area of foreign laws, social mores, and political culture. The Siete Partidas—the foundation of Spain's slave law—gave rise to a system of slavery that recognized many more freedoms for slaves and allowed for the transition from slavery to freedom much more readily than did British and later U.S. law. This created a system in which the place of blacks and mixed-race peoples was much more fluid.[1] Despite a more rigid system in the British colonies, immigrants who came to West Florida from the mainland colonies and later the United States brought with them a surprisingly fluid notion of the place of blacks in a slave society—a society where economic realities and racial control nonetheless helped create a system that placed slaves firmly outside the social order. This dualism created a unique set of assumptions regarding the role of slaves in the social and legal system.

Immigrants also entered an area where slavery seemed particularly threatened: the ideology of the French and American revolutions seemed on the verge of spreading to West Florida; after the Louisiana Purchase, the United States debated the prohibition of slavery in the new territory; and a series of revolts also rocked the circum-Caribbean region, from Saint Domingue to nearby Pointe Coupee to more than fifty other places in the Caribbean from 1785 to 1806. The area from which the immigrants came was also not immune to revolt, as Gabriel's attempts to spur a slave uprising in Virginia in 1800 demonstrate. It was within this context of competing slave systems and uncertainty about the future of slavery that West Florida planters built their wealth—on the backs of African slaves. Moreover, the majority of slaves living in West Florida between 1785 and 1810 originated in Africa, which created another potential threat to the stability of the institution. Thus planters in the Baton Rouge area faced a unique set of problems as they sought to establish their wealth in an area where the institution that supported the main source of their prosperity, plantation slavery, was subject to laws outside the scope of their Anglo experiences and therefore could be perceived as unstable. The context of those problems would have great significance for West Floridians.

Background and Legal Culture

For the most part, we can discount the role of the French legal system in shaping law in West Florida. Of more lasting impact was the social inertia fostered by the French residents who remained in the Baton Rouge area after French occupation ended in 1763. The Code Noir—a much harsher version of slave law than that governing Spanish slaves—influenced French assumptions regarding slavery.[2] Although the code forbade the sale of children away from their mothers, gave slaves a day of rest on Sunday, and recognized slave marriage as long as the slaves and the masters agreed, French law, as with its Anglo-American counterpart, concerned itself more with restricting slaves' freedom. Slaves could not testify in court in a case involving whites; slaves could not own property, nor could they engage in a contract or sue in a court of law. Manumission required government permission and could only be completed under extraordinary circumstances. When Spain acquired Louisiana in 1763, the less rigid Spanish system, embodied in the Siete Partidas, slowly replaced the French slave code.[3]

The social and legal status of slaves in the Baton Rouge district under the Spanish government presents historians with something of a conundrum. On the one hand, the Spanish government operated under the aegis of the Siete Partidas as administered by the king's agents in the New World.[4] Heavily influenced by Catholic doctrine, the Partidas, written in the thirteenth century by Alfonso X of Castile, formed the theoretical basis for all Spanish law on the peninsula and in the New World and could trace its lineage to Roman and canon law.[5] On the other hand, these laws made up only the third tier of what Charles Cutter has termed "peninsular law," as opposed to *derecho indiano*.[6] *Derecho indiano*, or law of the Indies, came about as a result of "New World distinctiveness" and a recognition of the need for a strong body of law formulated to apply only to the Indies.[7] Although *derecho indiano* allowed New World lawmakers to customize Iberian Spanish law, the Partidas remained the foundation of the Spanish legal system in the New World and informed Spanish legal and social relations with their slaves.[8] A body of law that included provisions for the protection of slaves, the Partidas recognized the slave as a human being with certain rights, provided for manumission in a number of ways, and tried to protect the slave family from abuse at the hands of either the master or any other freeman.[9] The Partidas also allowed slaves to testify in court against their masters in cases of murder involving the master and the mistress, in cases where either the master or the mistress stood accused of killing the other, and in a variety of other murder-related cases.[10] Also, slaves could sue their masters "in cases of ill treatment," as was the case of two slaves who testified against their master in 1807 when their master was accused of whipping another of his slaves to death.[11] The Partidas also allowed slaves to testify in cases of all types in the Indies.[12]

More importantly, the Partidas engendered a system of social relations between master and slave unknown in either the French or the U.S. territories and provided "social devices [that] narrowed the gap between bondage and liberty."[13] The Partidas permitted a slave to marry a free person as long as the other party knew the status of the slave. Slaves did not need their masters' permission to marry, as long as they continued to work as before.[14] Myriad laws governed the ways in which slaves might become free. However, *coartación*, the right of self-purchase, was perhaps the most important component of the Spanish system. The concept had its roots in Roman law, where freedom was the natural state of a person. Under Spanish law, slaves who so desired could purchase themselves out of slavery using what we might call an installment plan. Slaves could exercise this right either with or without the consent of their masters; if the master refused, a court would arbitrate the matter. The opportunities for self-purchase occurred most often in larger cities where a slave could earn the money needed to buy freedom, but areas like Baton Rouge and nearby New Orleans before the Louisiana Purchase made this action feasible in West Florida as well.

For instance, in 1787 Marie Decoux, a resident of Pointe Coupee and a property owner in West Florida, set her Indian slave Jacob free conditionally so that he might work to purchase himself from her for the sum of four hundred pesos.[15] A few years later she acknowledged the freeing of another slave, Poival, by her husband as part of his will.[16] In short, slavery under the Spanish system functioned as a nearly contractual arrangement under which the state could function as an intermediary between master and slave. The implications for African slavery in Louisiana under this system are varied, but for Spanish society slavery did not carry the same stigma as it did for Anglo-Americans. More importantly, residents in these borderlands accepted the Spanish legal culture through extensive *coartación*. Though Thomas Ingersoll reaches the opposite conclusion with regard to the meaning of the Spanish slave system, even he notes the disparity of self-purchase cases between the French, the U.S., and the Spanish regimes. Under the French, Ingersoll notes, "only a handful of slaves were permitted to buy freedom."[17] Under the Spanish, however, residents (slaves and others) in Spanish Louisiana spent a total of $511,254 to free 1,496 slaves between 1770 and 1810.[18] Ingersoll notes that when owners refused to agree to the *coartación*, slaves took the matter to court and experienced a high degree of success in their claims. That the majority of the slave-owning population in Spanish

Louisiana during this period were Anglo and French residents suggests that no-tions of race and the institution of slavery were not yet as fixed as others have suggested is the case in the eastern portion of the United States. The flexibility that Anglo residents, in particular, demonstrated with regard to *coartación* may have been due to the particular mentality that allows someone to uproot himself and travel hundreds of miles into the unknown in order to eke out a living.

The Spanish concept of *derecho vulgar*, or the local interpretations and vari-ations on Iberian and New World law, certainly had more impact on locals. Judges needed to distinguish between *ley*, or written law, and *derecho*, what might loosely be termed "justice." *Derecho* could be found in a mixture and meeting of written law, the experience of judges, customs, and local community sensibilities. Local customs and customary laws were possibly more relevant to the everyday life of West Floridians, because customary laws derived from local practice—practices that eventually gained the force of law. Customary law also allowed slaves to test the boundaries of their enslavement. Witness, for instance, the example of *coartación*. Exercising the right of *coartación* in the borderlands reinforced its presence as a condition of slavery in West Florida and connected Spain's legal periphery to its legal metropolis. In smaller ways slaves could also use the reliance on customary law to their advantage. They could own horses, sell produce, work on their own time, own firearms, and roam the county with-out a pass, all of which slaves did in the Baton Rouge area with some regularity. After a time, planters could not violate this customary law without incurring consequences.[19]

Occasionally, the mechanics of slavery demonstrate something useful about the system of slavery. For instance, Spaniards and local residents used very un-ambiguous language to describe both freedom and slavery. When William Dun-bar bought ten African slaves from Pedro Lartique, the bill of sale followed a very particular pattern. After establishing the identities and the residences of the two men, the contract described the slaves themselves—"seven negroes and three negresses, untrained and lately imported of ages from sixteen to twenty-five years." The contract then noted where Lartique obtained the slaves (from a slave dealer in New Orleans named Biran), the date, and their origin (the Gold Coast of Africa). The document also established that the ten Africans were slaves according to Spanish law and permitted Lartique to sell them—"they are sold as captives subject to serve, and in the form and condition that they are accustomed to sell lately imported negroes and also according to that which relates to infirmities, but free of mortgages." The men agreed on a price and the type of payment (3,950 "hard Mexican milled dollars") and that Dunbar would pay one half of the money the following month and the next half one year later.

Intricate language followed, transferring the ownership of ten human beings from one man to another: "I [Pedro Lartique] separate myself from the right of ownership, possession, use, seignority and other real and personal actions which I have and had in said negroes, and I cede, renounce and transfer them all [to] the buyer and in which he may have his cause in order he may possess them as his own property and the payment fulfilled he may sell or dispose of them at his will."[20] Of particular interest is the reference to "seignority"—a throwback, perhaps, to the idea of lordship and the responsibilities that it entailed. In the remainder of the document Lartique renounced his claim on the ten slaves. All slave sales in the Baton Rouge district followed this same essential formula with very little variance. The importance here, of course, was to head off any future claims by Lartique to the slaves and to provide him recourse in case of nonpayment by Dunbar. At the same time, the bill of sale also clearly established the enslavement of the Africans, lest any questions of prior freedom be raised once they became familiar with Spanish law and the avenues to freedom.

The language of freedom was, if anything, even more precise and more instructive. Take the case of Josefa, emancipated by Alexandre Patin as part of a *coartación* in August 1791. Rather than María purchasing her daughter, as former slaves occasionally did in the United States, the Spanish system allowed her to purchase her daughter's freedom. This gave the girl a set of rights that her mother did not possess. The document notes that Josefa, the daughter of the slave María, was set free and therefore able to "agree, contract, purchase, settle, appear in lawsuits, grant deeds and testaments, and do all the other proceedings that all free persons [could] do, so that she [could] use all these at her own free will."[21] Josefa was eight months old.[22] In some ways the language describing freedom in the contract outlined what freedom meant for both blacks and whites in the Spanish borderlands—the ability to act within the legal system through contracts, lawsuits, deeds, and testaments. This would have been an important aspect of freedom except that under Spanish law slaves could already make contracts, purchase goods, appear in lawsuits, and do all the things listed in that statement and more. The document specifically recognized the more nebulous aspects of freedom in general—but of Spanish customary law in particular—by noting that she could exercise her own free will. Here the main difference between slavery and freedom under Spanish law is spelled out, with slavery regarded as a Lockean subjugation to another's will—heady stuff for an eight-month-old girl mostly unaware of her surroundings. Nonetheless, the legal culture of slavery extended to include both the technical aspects of defining freedom and the less definable attitudes of the free toward the enslaved. Of course, nowhere in the document were race and slavery linked in any way.

Thus Spain's flexible legal system, especially regarding slavery, begat a social system that might have been considered at best excessively permissive and at worst almost sacrilegious by the more restrictive Anglo-American standards of slave control. Because Spain's law did not firmly define race and ethnic status with regard to slavery, the social status of persons of color in the Spanish Empire, from an Anglo-American standpoint, was similarly flexible. The Spanish social hierarchy, naturally enough, placed Spaniards at the top; *castas*, or mixed-race people, in the middle; and pure-blooded Africans and Indians at the bottom. Thus it was that the middle section of Spanish society, the *castas*, occupied a netherworld of racial classification that allowed mixed-race peoples to move from class to class with few barriers, especially when compared to the Anglo-American system. Citizens willing to pay a small fee could have their baptismal records changed to move them up within the social hierarchy.[23]

Furthermore, children of mixed-race parents retained the option of claiming one or the other parent's lineage—in essence choosing to become a member of whichever *casta* race was more advantaged. Or if their skin was light enough and their fortunes well established, they could move up the ladder even above their parents. In some cases mixed-race adults might even claim Spanish heritage. For example, Domingo Velázquez discovered that his baptismal record in Mexico City listed him as a *casta*. To rectify the "error," he simply gathered three witnesses who testified to the local priest that he was a Spaniard. Officials then changed his record to reflect his status.[24] Race in the Spanish Empire, then, was a social label that could be changed with some degree of fluidity. This occurred more frequently in the large cities but was certainly possible in frontier areas like Baton Rouge.

As one historian has noted, "slavery . . . did not provide an unambiguous assertion of racial order" in the Spanish world.[25] "Most blacks were slaves" in New Spain, "but most mulattoes were not," and because no property restrictions existed to prevent a mulatto from owning another mulatto, "property rights prevailed over the racial order."[26] In the United States, by contrast, whites used property rights in part to help support a racial order that placed almost all blacks on the lowest social rung. Considered in light of the more relaxed racial strictures evident in the Spanish world, the historical record presents a picture not, to be sure, of racial harmony and equitable justice, but at least of a system that remained flexible during the Spanish colonial period in the 1700s and persisted into the early 1800s. While the empire, like much of the rest of the world, was feeling the effects of the American Revolution, little threat existed to the racial order, because fluid racial lines already characterized a Spanish social system that created and maintained slavery and race relations. Further, the slave system served less as a system of racial control than as a purely economic system that could be exploited by black, white, mulatto, or Indian, as long as the slave owner adhered to social mores and abided by the forms of the Siete Partidas.

For instance, in 1788 the recently free mulatto Jean Baptiste Bienville, a resident of Baton Rouge, served as the executor of the will of Pierre Avarc as well as the caretaker of Avare's estate—despite the inability of Bienville to read or sign his name.[27] Bienville's role as caretaker in this case required him to take possession of Avare's entire estate, liquidate it, and then remit the proceeds to Avare's brother, who lived in Quebec. In return, Bienville was to receive all the buildings, tools, and furniture of the estate. After a lengthy inventory and auction, Bienville instead claimed two horses and a young slave named Bosilo, who was eleven years old at the time.[28] For Bienville, who also owned slaves, his status seemed secure because neither Spanish officials nor, more tellingly, the Anglo-Americans helping to handle the estate questioned the propriety of a mulatto handling the legal affairs of a deceased white man.

The immediate impact of this type of system for slaves of Spanish subjects was a small degree of comparative freedom. Slaves like Bosilo living on the Spanish frontier might be apprenticed out and work in the cities, earning money for themselves and their masters as peddlers or street vendors; they could own property, including horses, giving them a source of income independent from the master. Because he might find work in the town, Bosilo would have had more opportunity than slaves living further out in the country. While the master would receive most of what a slave earned, slaves gained some measure of status among their peers by working outside the plantation. More intangibly, slaves who could earn money and work for themselves, particularly as artisans, clearly demonstrated to all classes the simple fact that *castas*, blacks, and Indians possessed the capability to function within, and as a part of, Spanish society.

The ability to work on one's own and to live within the otherwise normal strictures of urban slavery was a bit more common on the Spanish frontier than in the cities. This was true because of the inherent weakness of frontier racial colonial institutions but also because Spanish attitudes rested on the assumption that a slave was still a person—essentially a person without freedom who nonetheless maintained what might be called a "judicial personality that came from Roman law."[29] Was this status prompted in part by the Catholic Church? Historians have debated this for decades and continue to do so. Yet the question does not hinge on the physical presence of the church or on the necessity of priests in residence. Baton Rouge and the surrounding districts contained a number of priests who could influence social thought, most of whom were Irish Catholic—in itself a factor that no doubt also affected how local Catholics viewed the status of enslaved peoples.[30] However, in a society where church and government found themselves so tightly bound together, the degree of influence would have been high. It is also probable that West Florida witnessed a mix of social mores that evolved out of the essentially contractual relationship between master and slave as outlined in the Siete Partidas. These combined with the strictures of the Catholic Church to produce a system in the Spanish borderlands that adapted to the realities of frontier life.

In practice, the Partidas and the social system it gave rise to could not mitigate the essential brutality of the system of slavery, which, like all other slave systems in the New World, could always fall back on terror, abuse, and punishment as a means of control. Witness the February 1789 restriction on the branding of slaves that officials in Havana felt the need to enforce.[31] During the same period, Spanish officials also sought to tightly control the slaves coming into the colonies from French and British possessions. Despite their awareness of the cruelty involved in branding human beings, officials nonetheless continued to debate the prohibition, arguing that branding was the most effective way to keep track of fraudulently introduced slaves as well as refugees from the various slave rebellions that had begun to rock the circum-Caribbean.[32] Yet this was the third time officials had issued such a decree. In November 1784 and again in May 1785, Havana had formally abolished the practice of branding, but apparently to no avail.[33] The use of branding as an easy way to identify slaves, combined with the fear of fugitive slaves from nearby islands, served to prolong the custom. Thus the illicit practice of branding continued for some time, indicating that even with the many avenues to freedom under Spanish law, slavery remained a cruel institution everywhere in the New World.[34]

Also, the Partidas could not assuage the reality of death and terror that accompanied slave labor in the mines, the cane and cotton fields, and other jobs in which slaves found themselves. But the process engendered by the Partidas and the basis they formed for the *derecho indiano* meant that in Northern New Spain in general, and Baton Rouge in particular, the forms and functions of Spanish law applied to slaves as well as to masters.[35] This places West Florida and by extension Louisiana in something of an exceptional position with regard to U.S. history. Thomas Morris has argued that "the sources of Southern slave laws lie deep in seventeenth-century Virginia," and that the "core of American slave law was the common law of England."[36] The South as it evolved out of Louisiana, with its complete absence of common law after statehood, and the South as embodied in the southern tier from West Florida/Baton Rouge/Feliciana to Saint Augustine does not fit this mold.

The Anglo-American system that existed across the Mississippi River by 1785, to the south in New Orleans, and north of Baton Rouge in the Mississippi Territory, was for all intents and purposes static in its assumptions about race and the place of blacks of whatever mixture in the social hierarchy, yet could not have been more different, socially, from its Spanish counterpart in 1800. The Anglo-American system has been correctly described as a biracial society in which white was white and all else was black. For mulattoes in America, inasmuch as "the social identification of children require[d] the self-identification of the fathers," it was clearly a society, when compared with New Spain, in which self-identification was not the requisite for social standing.[37] Historians describe Spanish society as one of "social hierarchy structured according to degrees of intermixture," a fluid society where *castas* could pass from one level to another with some ease.[38] In the United States by the time of the Louisiana Purchase, a mulatto was both de jure and de facto a black man and therefore assumed to be a slave. Further, as many historians have noted, the Anglo-American obsession with property rights always trumped any notions of government interference with a slave owner's right to hold human chattel, guaranteeing that any humanitarian concerns about the system would take a backseat to economic prosperity and racial control.

This was clearly not the same "trump" that existed in the Spanish world, because the Anglo-American system, from the early 1700s onward, assumed that anyone with dark skin was a slave and assaulted free blacks of any racial mixture with a host of restrictive laws designed to enforce the racial control maintained so easily through servitude. It would be more correct, then, to argue that property rights in the United States, as applied to white men, prevented interference with slavery where it existed. At the same time, for free blacks and mulattoes in the United States, there existed the tacit assumption that free persons of color would side with slaves if the always-dreaded racial upheaval ever came to pass.

In part this situation existed because slavery in America as an economic institution was in the process of tremendous change. The American Revolution brought with it a spate of manumissions that seemed to threaten the social order. The reality of slave owning in the United States belied the rhetoric of liberty and equality, and the impetus for emancipation found salt scattered in its fields within five years of the signing of the new Constitution. Whites responded to the manumissions that had occurred by tightening the laws restricting free blacks—on the one hand, to prevent miscegenation and, on the other, to maintain control over the free black population—except in northern states, which enacted post-nati emancipation laws designed to gradually phase out the institution after a few decades. Only the international slave trade had been brought to heel by revolutionary sentiments. As white Americans gained more rights in the immediate aftermath of the revolution, free blacks, paradoxically, lost them to voting and property restrictions. Meanwhile, slaves saw their avenues to freedom in the southern states narrowed by a variety of other measures set in place to ensure racial supremacy for whites.

More importantly, however, economic events conspired to give U.S. slavery a tremendous boost in the 1790s, ensuring its expansion for the next seventy years. The invention of the cotton gin in 1792 reversed whatever republican antislavery tide might have existed and guaranteed the expansion of the peculiar institution in the U.S. South. In the years after the introduction of the cotton gin, cotton production in the United States rose from 3,000 bales in 1790 to 178,000 bales in 1810.[39] Indeed, more than one million slaves moved west between 1790 and 1860, most of them after 1810.[40] The cotton boom that facilitated the expansion of slavery also ensured that slaves would remain under tight control in order to guarantee profitable crops from year to year.

Those slaves who became part of the American westward migration prior to 1810, along with those caught up in the economic expansion of the 1790s and early 1800s, likely encountered the same tightening system found in the East. In contrast to the Spanish legal system, which attempted to ensure some basic rights for slaves through an elaborate system of laws, slavery in the United States offered slaves certain legal protections yet retained a paternalistic system of master-slave relations that placed all legal authority in the hands of the master. So while Spain used the rule of law to protect and ensure slaves' rights, Anglo-American slavery rested on a less formal system of social and legal control. Americans and their British forebears considered slavery a private affair regulated by the property owner.[41] Common law and the emergence of market capitalism in America meant that "the interest of the individual rather than of society became the central assumption" of the law.[42] Therefore, no systematic slave law existed in the United States that might mitigate a slave's categorization as chattel; it remained to the states to determine the function of slave law. For at its essence U.S. slave law, with the exception of Louisiana's, derived from English common law regarding property, which, when modified in the colonial legislatures, transformed slaves into chattel. This made slaves "things" for Anglo-Americans in the United States, rather than persons, as slaves were for Spaniards. The social status of free blacks and slaves naturally followed, because if people with black skin, of whatever hue, were naturally slaves, then even free persons of color must be inferior. Not that people of color attained anything approaching social or legal equality in the Spanish Empire, yet a comparison of the two systems reveals that they nonetheless could still exercise a number of "rights" not conceived of in the expanding United States.

Some historians have argued that manipulation of the law by the masters caused an acceptance of paternalism on the part of the slave.[43] More importantly, slave law in the United States for the most part required enforcement not by de jure law but by a de facto master-class system of "plantation law."[44] As Douglas Edgerton has argued, "The law and their masters were thus one and the same."[45] This more individualistic system of slave control did not mean that slaves had no direct experience with de jure law. Indeed, slaves could be put on trial for any number of crimes, from rape and murder to arson, theft, and insurrection. However, it is most accurate to follow the observation of historian

Ariele Gross that slaves "were persons when convicted of a crime and property the rest of the time" in the United States.[46] Any other legal relationship between master and slave, for Americans, threatened the social order. Thus allowing a slave to testify threatened a white man's honor by allowing the possibility that a slave could deceive a white man. An acknowledgment of that ability would threaten the carefully constructed social order in which whites had power over all aspects of the lives of their black slaves. This meant that Anglo-American slave owners outside West Florida had little chance for contact with their slaves outside the master-slave relationship; therefore, formal contracts, as recognized by the state, between master and slave did not exist and would have challenged the social order. In the still-Spanish Baton Rouge district, though, the Spanish legal and social system reigned—regardless of how American its residents were becoming.

Witness the incident of Marie Decoux entering into a government-recognized contract with her Indian slave Jacob. Enslavement of Indians in West Florida, as in the United States, was the exception rather than the rule. That Marie Decoux set Jacob free is not unusual; that she had an Indian slave was. Spanish law forbade the enslavement of Indians, although French law did not. Ownership could be explained if she had acquired Jacob prior to 1769, after Spain had taken control of Louisiana and found that the French residents already possessed Indians slaves. The new governor, Alejandro O'Reilly, notified the Spanish king of the problem of Indian slavery and in the meantime allowed the slave owners to continue holding their property. Notwithstanding Marie Decoux, Indian slavery in West Florida by 1785 was for the most part a dead letter.[47]

The context of master-slave relations for West Floridians prior to 1803, then, is one of a Spanish legal system in an area populated mostly by British expatriates, under invasion by Anglo-American sensibilities. The question for both Spaniards and resident Anglo-Americans was whether those Americans could live under the more relaxed Spanish view of slaves as persons with rights, and whether Spaniards, and their legal and social system, could withstand the strain of Anglo-Americans operating under a wholly different approach to slavery. This would become more important over the years as a series of legal cases in the Baton Rouge district would test residents' understanding and application of Spanish law. At the same time, the situation also forced residents to explore a cultural understanding of slavery.

Regional Instability Involving Slaves

One thing both Spaniards and Anglo-Americans could agree on, perhaps, was the need to quash slave rebellions. And certainly looking at the world around them in 1800, the inhabitants of West Florida saw danger on the horizon. During the period under consideration here, David Geggus has counted fifty-two slave rebellions and conspiracies in the circum-Caribbean area.[48] However, three major slave revolts rocked the Western Hemisphere between 1790 and 1804 that had direct consequences for the inhabitants of West Florida. The French Revolution had begun in 1789 and initially produced divided loyalties in the United States. It also reverberated throughout the Caribbean world when the slaves of Saint Domingue revolted against their masters. The May 1791 decree of the French National Assembly that gave full civil rights to mulattoes who owned property in France at first also gave hope to the free colored population of Saint Domingue. However, the National Assembly sent mixed signals to the island by alternately giving and taking away the rights of free blacks. Enraged mulattoes revolted, but the rebellion was suppressed in 1791. In August of that same year, however, slaves rose up in a major revolt, turning the island into a charnel house. Americans reacted at first with sympathy in some quarters, but then with increasing horror. The revolutionary doctrine that had begun in America, spread to France, and then to Saint Domingue could, after all, make its way back to the United States and take up intellectual residence among slaves.[49]

Spaniards in Louisiana were no less worried. In 1793 refugees from Saint Domingue began to show up in South Carolina and Louisiana. Afraid that the "ideology of the Rights of Man" would cause free blacks and slaves to rise up in revolt, Spanish authorities tried to contain the revolutionary sentiment coming from France and the island of Saint Domingue by prohibiting free blacks and mulattoes from any French colonies from entering Louisiana.[50] It was to little avail. While Spaniards might hope to prevent the physical introduction of revolutionary ideology in the persons of freemen, the genie was out of the bottle. Given that newspapers and escaping slaves and their owners widely reported news of the rebellion in Louisiana, slaves in Spanish Louisiana knew of the events in Saint Domingue and knew of the French convention's abolition of slavery in the French colonies.[51]

In early 1795 slaves, free blacks, and several whites in the Pointe Coupee area of then-Spanish Louisiana, directly across the Mississippi River from Feliciana and Baton Rouge, plotted to overthrow the slave system through the murder of masters, uncooperative slaves, and free blacks. Because Spanish Louisiana was a large territory with places of escape and numerous targets for possible attack, a revolt there would be a more serious affair than revolts on the Caribbean islands. Spanish law permitted slaves to accumulate money and travel with relative freedom, and those slaves might ally themselves with free mulattoes, who could own weapons. Rather than a simple uprising designed to kill whites, the 1795 conspiracy, according to historian Gwendolyn Hall, was "a multiracial abolitionist movement supported by a large segment of the dispossessed of all races in Louisiana and throughout the Caribbean: a manifestation of the most radical phase of the French Revolution, which had spilled over from Europe to the Americas."[52] In short, it was, significantly for Spanish America, a revolt characterized by a lack of racial identification. The slaves discussed support for the new French government and hoped to aid the French should they invade Louisiana.[53] While the Saint Domingue revolution eventually ended with freedom for the slaves in 1804, the Spaniards put down the Pointe Coupee revolt. The unique Spanish approach to race and slavery manifested itself in various ways during the revolt. In a typical move, the Spaniards offered amnesty to runaways who would return to their masters. Problematically, armed blacks claiming free status wandered Pointe Coupee, declaring by action their intent to assert freedom and throwing into relief the problem of distinguishing between free and slave. In the United States, where laws prevented slaves and even free blacks from owning firearms, the spectacle of free blacks carrying guns would have been inconceivable. Yet for Spain, which for nearly three hundred years had dealt with revolts and uprisings among Indians all over the empire, this latest event was merely another in a long history that had a simple and effective solution: execute or imprison those who would not return to their masters and then exile the rest.

Another slave rebellion in the early nineteenth century that must have weighed heavily on the minds of West Floridians began on a Sunday in August 1800, as word spread through Richmond of a plot by Thomas Prosser's slave Gabriel to incite a slave uprising. As many as five to six hundred slaves may have joined the revolt.[54] As it was elsewhere in the United States, slavery in Virginia was in a state of upheaval due to economic expansion and revolutionary rhetoric. Fueled once again by the liberalism of the American Revolution and with their anger sharpened by the Virginia assembly's move to tighten slave codes, Gabriel and his comrades tried to act.[55] Nonetheless, this plot, like many others, was revealed by several loyal slaves and put down by the white ruling class. The rebellion, however, was widespread enough to command fear in whites for miles around Richmond and across the state of Virginia. From 1801 to 1805 Virginia debated the end of the peculiar institution, although the discussion came to naught. In 1802 Virginia planters put down a second slave revolt, called the Easter Uprising. West Floridians, with relatives back in Virginia and Maryland, could not help but have heard of both these revolts.

The West Florida *mentalité* with regard to slavery, then, combined several powerful elements. The institution presented frontier settlers with a unique set of operational guidelines and assumptions regarding the nature of the institution and the slaves in their part of the world. On the one hand, the Spanish legal system, with regard to slavery, brought with it attitudes and produced assumptions regarding the place of blacks in society and the protections that a slave might expect from the legal system. This, in turn, required a more liberal view of blacks and mulattoes as persons deserving not only legal rights but some consequential human rights as well. At the same time, the circum-Caribbean region—of which West Florida, with its trade, social, and political connections was a part—experienced tremendous slave upheaval from 1791 to 1806. Slave owners entering the region and residents purchasing slaves must have been aware of the regional turmoil and therefore required greater control over their slaves. Finally, after 1803 but before 1806, for Anglo-Americans the West Florida area, despite the Spanish legal and social system, was actually more protective of slavery because there was no chance that the Spanish government might abolish it, and the system was stable in terms of its legal, social, and political evolution. On the other hand, slavery seemed particularly threatened in post-1803 American Louisiana, as rumors surrounding the closure of the slave trade and the prohibition of slavery swirled.

Slavery and Wealth

Slaves and slave owners in the West Florida borderlands built the peculiar institution in an environment like no other in North America. The wealth that slave owners accumulated rested, not surprisingly, on owning slaves. As in the U.S. South, the bulk of a slave owner's wealth was tied up in slaves. Thus the Spanish government was meticulous about conducting estate inventories. Whenever someone made out a will, died, was involved in a legal dispute, or needed to use his plantation as credit, the Spanish government would conduct an inventory. From 1785 through 1794 the government conducted twenty-two inventories of use to historians, for everything from death to lawsuits to a property estimation intended to establish credit.[56] Slaveholders comprised nine of the inventories; nonslaveholders the other thirteen. The distribution of wealth among slaveholding estates and the wealth disparity help describe the wealth distribution in the district. The thirteen nonslaveholder inventories during this period averaged 455 pesos in wealth, ranging from 19 to 5,925 pesos.[57] Of the thirteen nonslaveholders, eight owned land, three were artisans (one of whom owned land), two were farm laborers, and one was of indeterminate profession.

The nonslaveholding landholders were, on average, 230 pesos wealthier than the nonslaveholding nonlandholders, and their landholdings, including domiciles, constituted about 29 percent of their personal value. Livestock and personal items made up the remainder. None of the landless persons was worth more than 200 pesos, except for Claude Guidry, worth 614 pesos and carrying 233 pesos in French silver at the time of his death. The two farm laborers, as might be expected, possessed the least wealth, at 19 and 20 pesos each, at the time of their deaths. One of the men, Thomas Callahan, an Irish sharecropper from Cork who died when he fell out of a boat, drunk, into the Mississippi, left nothing but a trunkful of clothes.[58] Joseph Trahan, whose estate suggests that he was a merchant, died with his wealth tied up in land (30 percent), 300 gallons of wine, 260 pounds of coffee, and 300 pounds of sugar. It would seem, then, that for nonslaveholders the majority of wealth, if they had more than 200 pesos, would be in land and livestock.[59]

Nine of the slaveholding records for 1785 through 1794 are complete enough to use as a basis for analysis.[60] The slaveholders averaged 10,229 pesos of wealth, ranging from 2,182 to 25,500 pesos.[61] Land formed 18 percent of a slaveholders' net worth—only 2 percent less than that of the nonslaveholders, meaning that land as a percentage of wealth remained equal for slaveholders and nonslaveholders. The big difference between a middling and a wealthy landholder was cattle versus human chattel. As with the nonslaveholders, a great deal of wealth was tied up in livestock, although the slaveholders also tended to cultivate more diverse crops such as indigo, corn, wheat, tobacco, cotton, and sugar. George Proffit, one of the wealthier planters in the area when he died in 1790, and at forty-five slaves the largest slave owner on record during this period, grew five different cash crops on his 2,100-arpent plantation.[62] The buildings on his plantation, a far cry from the simple structures listed in the inventories of the nonslaveholders, reflected his status. Aside from a large house set on pillars, his property also contained a not-yet-completed grinding house, a separate kitchen, barns, slave quarters, and a pigeon house. Other planters possessed similarly diverse types of property, even when their wealth did not bring them large slaveholdings. The inventory for James Hillin listed among other things 90,000 shingles that he owned, sitting "on the edge of the river" and worth 270 pesos.[63] When John Fitzpatrick died, he was worth 6,200 pesos. The assessors valued his 440-arpent estate, with a house, at 2,000 pesos, and his livestock was worth 726 pesos.[64] He also owned an enormous book collection that included several histories of England, eleven volumes of Jonathan Swift, works of Milton and Pope, some general histories, and books on philosophy, among other things.[65] But it was his eleven slaves, valued at 2,590 pesos, who provided the bulk of his net worth. As in the U.S. South, then, not only were slave owners wealthier, but the wealth in West Florida brought the ability to profit from a diverse crop, underwrote a variety of leisure activities, and enabled slave owners to increase their wealth more easily by providing a means of obtaining credit. In short, owning a plantation and several slaves was a sure way to greater wealth on the West Florida frontier.

Samuel Steer would have understood this. An owner of thirty-nine slaves,

Table 2. Average Wealth of Baton Rouge Residents, 1785–94

	Slaveholders	Nonslaveholders
Average wealth in pesos	10,229	455
Land as a percentage of wealth	18%	20%[a]
Slaves as a percentage of wealth	59%	n/a

[a] Among nonslaveholders who owned land

Steer's 44,000-arpent landholdings spread over several districts, contained grinding mills, indigo warehouses, and more than a hundred head each of cattle and sheep, as well as hogs and horses valued at 25,500 pesos. Steer was more than two and a half times as wealthy as his average planter neighbor during this period. However, slave owning was not confined to plantation owners. Michael Mahier, variously listed as a surgeon and a doctor, purchased five slaves and sold one other between 1785 and 1792. No permanent land records appear for Mahier, although he lived in the Baton Rouge district and bought and sold parcels of land from time to time. Whether he was a petty speculator or a landowner, or both, is unclear. What is clear is that by the late 1700s slave owning in West Florida, as in the U.S. South, was a clear path to wealth for anybody who could afford the initial investment. In some cases this required bringing the slaves into the territory—in essence building on already-existing wealth. At the same time, the Spanish policy of land distribution, in which families could obtain up to 800 arpents based on need, provided even nonslaveholders with a means of establishing credit to set out on the path to slaveholding and greater wealth.

Slave Demography

The slave demographics for the Baton Rouge area tell a significant story. Of the 282 slaves who appear in the Baton Rouge records between 1785 and 1794, 222, or 78 percent, are listed with either their ages or some indication of their status as adults—a significant status in an area where, as it turns out, most adults came from outside the area, while most children were creole.[66] The adult population of 162 slaves, or 72 percent of the known total, included 94 males and 68 females, for a ratio of about 1.3 males per female. Their origins are more significant. While the birthplaces of 24, or 15 percent of, adult men are unknown, 100, or fully 68 percent, were Africa-born. Of the remaining creole slaves, 17, or 10 percent, came from the United States, 5 from Baton Rouge, and 5 from the Caribbean (3 percent each), and one man was from Portugal. The sex ratios, with regard to origin, remain in favor of Africans, who made up roughly 70 percent of the men and 64 percent of the women. Even if we assume that the "unknowns" are not African but rather hail from one of the other four places, the numbers still tell of an overwhelmingly African slave population in Spanish West Florida during the early period of settlement.[67]

The population of sixty children was composed of thirty-one females and twenty-nine males, for a roughly equal sex ratio. The adult sex ratio, then, was skewed toward males, while the child population was almost even. Of more interest for West Floridians were the origins of the slaves. In their attempts to ensure that all citizens received a classification by race or nationality, the Spanish tried very hard to note the origins of all slaves sold in the empire. Records from Baton Rouge list national origin for the slaves in 61 percent of the transactions.[68] Most of the slaves of unknown origin are also of unknown age, and the records contain very little information about them one way or the other. However, when broken down by age, no significant pattern emerges. The records list no origin for thirty-eight of the sixty children.[69] Of the rest, eight were from Baton Rouge (13 percent), five originated in the United States (8 percent), and nine were from Africa (15 percent).

The population statistics also provide insight into the nature of slaves as property on the Spanish-American frontier. For the most part all slave inventories list slaves by their age, name, national origin, and value. The usual exceptions in the West Florida records are the small children. The Spaniards usually listed the children along with their mothers as part and parcel of the mother-child package. Whether a small child belonged to its mother or to the slave owner is moot. The natural increase of a female slave was the property of the master. Most often, however, mother and child would be sold as a package, with an inflated price that the mother alone would not have brought. Spanish law prohibited slave owners from breaking up families except in extraordinary circumstances, and of 150 slaves sold in familial relationships between 1785 and 1800, no record exists of a mother separated from her under-twelve child. In one estate sale the buyers kept together three generations (grandmother, mother, son) of slaves.

However, at some point that slave child ceased to be an infant or toddler and acquired "value" as a commodity under the U.S. and Spanish conception of slavery—as a unit of property whose labor could produce income for the master. At what age did a slave child cease to be simply a child, with no intrinsic monetary value, and when did he or she become worth something as a valuable piece of chattel? This is no small question, and one that is difficult to answer, given the different ways in which an owner might try to place value on a slave. Samuel Steer, for instance, inventoried his entire estate in 1793 for the purpose of using it as credit.[70] Assessors gave every one of his slaves, then, a monetary value—even down to the one-year-old infants, priced at one hundred pesos each. Steer's motivation is clear: he needed to make his estate look as valuable as possible, and so he wanted the assessors to place a monetary value on everything. Other inventories and sales, however, provide a clearer answer.

Once a child on the Spanish-American frontier reached the age of six, that person became a slave unto himself, a valuable commodity apart from his mother.[71] This does not mean that he could be sold separately from his mother. But the West Florida papers contain no record of a child having any independent value assigned to him or her, except in the cases of property assessments for either credit purposes or a lawsuit, or when no parent was present on the plantation. It would seem, then, that by the age of six a slave could expect to at least begin to exist as a commodity, if not as an integral part of the labor force. When a person made the transition from childhood to chattel through the assignment of a monetary value, the master-slave relationship was forever altered, and the child started on the road to adulthood. This is not necessarily a legal definition but rather an economic and social one.[72]

These figures meant several things for the residents. On the one hand, the population statistics represent a startling contrast from the situation directly across the river in Pointe Coupee. In that area, historian Gwendolyn Midlo Hall has uncovered population statistics from 1771 through 1802 that reveal a more evenly distributed population, where Africans formed 39.4 percent of the population, local creoles 43.8 percent, imported creoles 5.3 percent, and unidentified slaves 11.5 percent. The African Baton Rouge slaves, then, made up more than one and a half times as great a percentage of the slave population as did the slaves in rebellious Point Coupee, also a Spanish-administered possession at the time. Of the 282 slaves, 64 lived in some kind of family arrangement, whether as children or as husband or wife, which could be an indicator of future growth. From 1785 through 1794, however, a high proportion of Africans in the population might indicate a high rate of mortality among the slaves; more likely it admits to a demand for slaves due to Anglo immigration into the area. Among the 101 slaves sold in Baton Rouge during this period, 49 came from slave dealers importing slaves from Africa, the United States, and unknown parts. An area sustained by a 50 percent import rate among slaves indicates a region experiencing growth and, therefore, economic potential, external and internal threats aside.

Africans imported legally into West Florida would have come from Havana via New Orleans, and many slave dealers brought slaves to Baton Rouge from that port city. At the same time, residents occasionally made the journey to New Orleans to pick up slaves. Other slaves came from the United States. The trade with Havana apparently went in both directions. In November 1803 officials in Havana approved a petition for a dealer to bring ten thousand slaves from the

United States, as long as the dealer also included five barrels of flour per slave in the trade.[73] Non-slave-dealing Baton Rouge residents conducted the remainder of the sales among themselves, indicating that while Baton Rouge did import a number of slaves, most of the slave dealing existed as internal trade. This also means that there was a dual social system for the masters and slaves. Although the masters might have had trouble verbally communicating with their African slaves, relying instead on third-party interpreters and force as a way to explain orders, no such barrier would have existed between masters and the creole children. The possibility exists, then, of a closer relationship between masters and slave children than between masters and slave adults.

Consequently, and more importantly, this high proportion of African-born slaves had the potential to be distinctly dangerous for West Florida planters, for whom slaves represented 59 percent of their wealth. Natives of a foreign part of the world, speaking foreign tongues and chafing under the bonds of servitude, slaves would naturally resent their station. While freedom for slaves in the Spanish Empire came more easily than it did under the French or in the United States, freedom nevertheless remained elusive. Also, area slaveholders had only to look at the world around them—at the rebellion in Point Coupee, at the Haitian Revolution that had driven thousands of slave owners and slaves to Louisiana from that island, and at Gabriel's Rebellion in Virginia, from which so many residents had come—to know that the planter's world was an unstable one. The revolutionary ideology that many planters fled during the revolution could infect their slaves. The plantation economy was changing as well; as planters converted to cotton and shifted further from indigo, future economic fortune was not assured.

The possibility of problems induced by the state system was easily preventable, though, as long as the Spanish government helped West Florida's residents retain tight control over their slaves, and as long as Spain itself retained tight administrative control over Louisiana and West Florida. Any threat to the residents' growing wealth, any signs of governmental weakness on the part of the Spanish, any serious tests of the master-slave relationship in this diverse but largely Anglo-American area—in short, any suggestions of a loss of control on the part of Spain—could have dire consequences for Spain. The question would be whether or not such tests, which would in fact begin in 1804 and then be followed by others in 1806, 1807, and then 1810, could shake the faith of West Floridians in the Spanish government and its administration.

CHAPTER THREE

Owning the West Florida Frontier

The International Microcosm of the

Louisiana Purchase

An unanticipated problem manifested itself for Americans living in Spanish Louisiana and West Florida when in 1800 the bulk of Spanish holdings in the area reverted to French control. Within three years that territory would become part of the United States, fueling an expansionist drive that would transform the lives of frontier settlers. In recent years historians have examined in great detail many facets of the purchase and what it meant to Louisianans. Less clear has been its impact on West Floridians, whom the purchase would set on a course toward incorporation with the United States. In the fifteen years from 1785 to 1800, West Florida had gone from a sparsely settled region to one in which a wide variety of crops supported a burgeoning population. Large-scale wealth in the area rested on plantation slavery, though slavery of a different type than that known in the United States. However, for West Floridians all was not well. A great deal of change was on the horizon—change that might threaten West Florida's development as well as the ability of plantation owners to prosper in a stable environment. The circum-Caribbean was rife with rebellion, and even the United States had seen a rebellion in Virginia. Also in 1800 ownership of Louisiana reverted to the control of a dictator seemingly intent on conquering all of Europe.

The consequences would be far-reaching. Americans in West Florida would no longer be isolated from the U.S. government. Scots-Irish-English immigrants would find a government aside from Catholic Spain with which to deal. At the same time, the immediate aftermath of the purchase brought confusion over ownership as Spain protested the legality of the purchase and both Spain and the United States argued over the boundaries of Louisiana and whether the two powers would trade Louisiana for West Florida.

Moreover, the Louisiana Purchase brought a major change in the Baton Rouge district's relationship with the outside world. By 1803 the population had grown to nearly eight times its 1785 count, reaching 1,513 people. This included 958 whites, 16 free people of color, and 539 slaves, an indication that the slave population was growing more slowly than the white. The area also had an economy that produced a wide variety of goods and enjoyed a stable relationship with the Spanish government.[1] An Americanized Louisiana could change that by introducing a new and different set of slave laws nearby. Furthermore, the election of Thomas Jefferson to the presidency in 1800 had a lasting effect on the Spanish presence in Louisiana and West Florida. Jefferson's statement in 1786 that the fledgling nation was the "nest from which all America, North and South, [was] to be peopled" and that control of the Mississippi waterway would be vital to American interests offered a prescient view of the future of Louisiana and West Florida.[2] Jefferson's administration was expansionist, successfully buying Louisiana from the French and then working to acquire Florida from the Spanish by any means.

In the 1790s Pinckney's Treaty had secured free passage on the Mississippi for the United States, but the retrocession of Louisiana to the French in 1800 caused Jefferson some worries over the threat to American rights of navigation. Despite French ownership, Spain continued to administer Louisiana and when Juan Ventura Morales, a Spanish official, closed the port of New Orleans at the behest of King Charles IV in October 1802, Jefferson and Congress prepared for the possibility of war with Spain.[3] In the meantime, Robert Livingston, the American minister to France sent to Paris to arrange either the purchase of New Orleans or a treaty guaranteeing more secure navigation rights, concluded one of the greatest land deals in U.S. history, the Louisiana Purchase.

Negotiated on July 3, 1803, the Louisiana Purchase set the tone for seven years of conflict between the governments of Spain and the United States over the exact boundaries of the agreement. The treaty also placed Baton Rouge's largest market, New Orleans, under foreign control and produced a great deal of instability in both American-held Louisiana and Spanish West Florida. The myriad problems created by the purchase ranged from the seemingly simple issue of determining what was included in it to assessing the boundaries of the new lands and then evaluating the loyalty of citizens in the new American territory, reigning in the self-interest of land speculators whose actions might destabilize both the American and the Spanish government, and then deciding what would happen to the growing institution of slavery in Louisiana.

What Was Included

Conflicts over the boundaries of the Louisiana Purchase stemmed from the Spanish cession of Louisiana to France in the Treaty of San Ildefonso in 1800.

That treaty created a problem that—for the Jefferson administration—remained unsettled in 1803: the exact boundaries of the French and Spanish possessions. Spain's government argued that the Louisiana Purchase did not include the territory of West Florida, land it had gained from the British during the American Revolution. At the same time, the Treaty of San Ildefonso contained a clause forbidding the French from selling any part of the ceded territories to a third party.[4] On these grounds King Charles IV of Spain declared the Louisiana Purchase null and void. Spain, however, could do little to prevent Napoleon's sale.

The reasons for the objection may not seem obvious. France was a declining power in North America; wars in Europe required the attention of Napoleon Bonaparte, and the Revolution in Saint Domingue demonstrated France's inability to maintain an overseas colonial empire. Merchants in New Orleans sent unprocessed items including wood, tar, wheat, cotton, and sugar to Spanish colonies throughout the Old World and New. New Orleans ports also shipped an incredible variety of refined items such as harnesses, chairs, cigars, munitions, hammers, chests, lace, and distilled liquors. The presence of butter, calfskins, and meat confirms the lasting presence of the cattle industry in the Mississippi Valley of 1803.[5] Despite this wide range of manufactured goods and raw materials, the port of New Orleans was more important economically to Baton Rouge and the Mississippi Valley than it was to the Spanish Empire. While the value of commerce through Havana in 1803 totaled more that twenty million pesos, only half a million, or 1/4 of 1 percent of Spain's New World trade, came and went through New Orleans. Out of a total of 491 ships that left Havana in 1803, only forty-four sailed to New Orleans, bringing 241,875 pesos worth of goods to western settlers, an average of 5,497 pesos of trade per voyage. On the reverse trip, sixty-seven ships sailed from New Orleans to Havana, bringing 329,056 pesos of goods, an average of 4,911 pesos per voyage. Although these data indicate that the colony was producing products that could be sold in Cuba, the New World, and Europe by Spanish merchants, New Orleans's importance to Spanish commerce was minor compared to wealthier ports such as Veracruz and Montevideo. For example, seventeen ships sailed from Havana to Veracruz in 1803, bringing 401,102 pesos of goods, or 23,594 pesos per voyage. On the return trip forty-two ships left Veracruz for Havana with 2,077,790 pesos in goods. This represented a staggering 49,471-peso-per-voyage average. New Orleans, then, was a small drop in the bucket of Spanish trade in the New World.[6]

For Spain the real value of New Orleans and Louisiana lay in the same strategic considerations that had brought France to the colony two centuries prior to the purchase. Instead of the need to contain the British, however, Spain by the early nineteenth century wanted to halt or at least slow American expansion across North America—an expansion that could threaten not just European control of the Mississippi and points west, but also northern Mexico and potentially all of New Spain. Thus while the Americans desired control over the Mississippi River to ensure open access to New Orleans for farmers in the Ohio and the Mississippi valleys, the purchase of all of Louisiana would be a grave threat to Spain's empire. Moreover, as the British recognized in 1802, U.S. control of Louisiana also threatened the Floridas, making American expansion into those areas all but inevitable.[7] It was for these reasons that Spain's King Charles declared the Purchase void.

Of more concern and further confusing the issue of ownership was the fact that Jefferson had sent Livingston and Monroe to Paris to acquire New Orleans and West Florida, not New Orleans and points west. Hoping to acquire the strategic Isthmus of Florida, with its dagger into the heart of the Caribbean, Jefferson claimed—while probably knowing otherwise—that the Louisiana Purchase included West Florida. So the situation arose whereby Spain ceded territory to France in 1800 without clarifying the exact locations of the borders. France then sold a large portion of that territory to the United States with a similar lack of clarity on the issue of borders.[8] The United States maintained that the purchase included all lands east to the Perdido River, while Spain set the eastern borders at what is present-day Louisiana west of the Mississippi. Newspapers in the United States took up the thread, with some stating that the Floridas—sometimes East, sometimes West, sometimes both—were part of the purchase.[9]

The West Florida "question," as U.S. newspapers were beginning to call it, had also by 1803–4 become part of the Federalist-Republican debate over Jefferson's conduct with regard to the Louisiana Purchase. The *Washington Federalist*, in a statement typical of other Federalist newspapers, celebrated local filibustering and played up the supposed pro-U.S. sentiments of West Floridians, trumpeting that the United States "ought never to own an inch of ground beyond the Mississippi" and "the annexing of Louisiana to the United States" would "produce the INEVITABLE DESTRUCTION OF OUR UNION" (emphasis in original).[10] The *Washington Federalist* also cataloged the alleged abuses of the inhabitants at the hands of the Spanish and noted, inaccurately, that a group of bandits called the Kemper Brothers had captured the fort at Baton Rouge.

In a series of letters published in New York's *American Citizen* in September and October 1804, two writers, one signed "Graviora Manent" ("The worst is yet to come") and the other unnamed, went to great lengths to outline the history of European possession of Louisiana and the Floridas going back to the early eighteenth century, noting—correctly—that the Floridas had always been regarded as separate from Louisiana by the British, the Spanish, and ultimately the French.[11] The most compelling and detailed account of what was included in the purchase appeared in early October, when an unknown author used more than six columns of newspaper space across two pages to write a history of the Floridas from their discovery until the time of the purchase. The *American Citizen*, it should be noted, was a Federalist paper looking to condemn Jefferson at any possible turn. Thus, Jefferson's argument for the inclusion of the Floridas as part of the Purchase, whatever its merits, would naturally be open to attack. Nevertheless, the historical arguments outlined in the *Citizen* followed a logical path and, whatever the political bent of the author, give a rough idea of the historical reality of the possession of the Floridas.

In any case, Jefferson needed to confirm the boundaries. At the time of the French transfer, Daniel Clark Jr. served as the U.S. consular agent in New Orleans and maintained commercial and political connections throughout the United States.[12] Clark had been one of the original American merchants to settle in New Orleans and first received a land grant of five hundred acres from the British in 1770.[13] Subsequently, Clark bought a plantation in Natchez, Mississippi, just north of Feliciana, and maps of Feliciana list him as the owner of a 1,000-arpent plot of land in 1799.[14] He counted himself among the aristocracy of New Orleans, having, among other things, introduced the first cotton gin to the city after reading a report of Eli Whitney's design in a local newspaper.[15] His writing hints at a well-educated and wealthy man who spoke of an annual income of some eight thousand dollars in the 1790s and who littered his prose with Latin phrases when he corresponded with those he felt above his own station.[16] Following a pattern common to New Orleans at the time, Clark did not specialize in any single business, serving as director of at least two banks and owning a cordage factory situated on Royal Street.[17] He also helped James Wilkinson manage Wilkinson's Spanish-guaranteed monopoly on goods shipped from Kentucky through New Orleans.[18] This potential for conflict of interest, where a man like Clark might find himself on two international sides of a business dispute, remained fairly common during the early American period and caused friction among planters and merchants.[19] Meanwhile, throughout 1795 and 1796 Clark played both sides off against each other. On the one hand, he worked closely with Spanish officials Manuel Gayoso de Lemos and Baron de Carondelet to help maintain the Spanish government in Louisiana and Florida.[20] On the other hand, he encouraged American settlement in Louisiana and West Florida, writing to Gen. James Wilkinson: "I love America, I have long ate her bread: She adopt'd me easily in life as a son—she furnished me with a wife whom my son adores, and I shall ever retain for her a strong national Gratitude."[21]

So when Jefferson and Madison began to inquire into the initial controversy over the inclusion of West Florida and wanted someone with knowledge about the area, they wrote to Clark—one of the most geographically knowledgeable Americans in the area and in the employ of the United States—and several other local planters. Madison's letters, especially, reveal the depth of confusion surrounding the administration's understanding of what was included. Asking for "all the information [Clark might] be able to give" regarding the exact boundaries of Louisiana, Madison also asked Clark to serve as a liaison between French and American officials.[22] With regard to the boundaries, Clark concluded that the line of cession conformed to the Treaty of 1763, in essence telling Jefferson that the boundaries claimed by the Spanish were valid and that West Florida was firmly a Spanish possession. This conclusion made Clark, who owned a great deal of land on both sides of the Spanish-American border, subject to two very different methods of land distribution and administration.[23] Clark had a great deal to gain if West Florida became an American territory. He already owned land in Feliciana and was a well-respected and wealthy merchant in New Orleans. American control of West Florida would certainly open the area up to land speculation, a venture in which he would have no small influence and would be ideally situated to exploit.

At the same time, controversy over the boundaries could bring conflict between the United States and Spain. As a merchant with wide interests in the city, Clark could expect to profit handsomely from any problems. He chose, however, to adhere to a strict legal interpretation of the boundaries, while Jefferson chose to ignore him. In all likelihood Clark was merely hedging his bets, not wishing to alienate either national power until one gained complete control over the borderlands.

With regard to the issue of what was included in the purchase, one boundary alone seemed clear to those living on the ground in Louisiana and West Florida and to those with an understanding of the territorial history. The line north of thirty-one degrees latitude outlined the 1795 border between Florida and Mississippi and set off the Mississippi territory from the West Florida district. Just north of Baton Rouge and south of the thirty-first-degree line sat the Feliciana district, right in the middle of what the U.S. government considered disputed territory.

Surveyors under direction from President Jefferson, who was eager to find out as much as possible about the purchase, crossed Louisiana and West Florida, checking boundaries.[24] In August 1803, Jefferson received a detailed report from the new territorial governor, William C. C. Claiborne, who answered several questions regarding the territory included in the purchase. Claiborne told Madison that, first, there were no dependable large-scale maps of the entire area, though he was working to obtain copies of smaller, detail maps. Although the Spaniards had made a few maps, they had, unfortunately for the Americans, never published them.[25] More pressingly with regard to the "West Florida question," Claiborne informed the government that according to the 1763 Treaty of Paris, and confirmed by "the authority of the oldest settlers in this territory," "New Orleans was the only tract of Country east of the Mississippi included in the Province of Louisiana as then ceded by France to Spain."[26] Claiborne went on to describe the various features of the new territory as he understood them, the nature of the Spanish militia, the disposition of local Native American tribes, land grant issues, the code of laws and the character of Spanish justice, any system of education that might be found in Louisiana, the monetary and tax system, and the state of trade.

Exploration and Control

In December 1803 France formally transferred control of New Orleans to the United States and withdrew its troops from the city. Scarcely one month before, the French had assumed control of the city from the Spaniards, who had exercised a kind of institutional inertia by governing the city and territory in the absence of any other formal power. One historian describes Claiborne as both a "neglected American statesman" and a "dictator of Louisiana."[27] Whatever his merits or faults, Claiborne had previously served as a congressman from Tennessee and then territorial governor of Mississippi and so maintained interest in the Baton Rouge area. In late 1803 he found himself administrator of the largest territory the young United States had known—a territory with unknown boundaries to the north and contested boundaries to the east and west. When he came to New Orleans, Claiborne brought with him a contingent of Mississippi militia under the command of Gen. James Wilkinson—Daniel Clark's old business partner in the Kentucky tobacco trade. Claiborne, fearing the reaction of the local free black militia after the French and the Spaniards vacated the city, begged Washington for troops and weapons to counter a perceived threat. His call became more strident when the black militia, a common sight under the Spaniards, held a parade during the transfer ceremonies. Although the Spanish governor of Louisiana, Juan Vicente Folch, remained in the city during the transfer period to assist with the bureaucratic exchange, no Spanish help would be forthcoming, nor did the Americans want any.[28]

In the absence of any regular U.S. troops in the city and with the Mississippi militia needed back home, Claiborne chose the previously mentioned merchant Daniel Clark—a man with whom he did not get along, and with whom he would fight a duel in 1807—to organize the first militia in New Orleans under American control. His force consisted of more than 350 men and included both Americans and French creoles, but no blacks or resident Spaniards. He chose as his militia colonel a local New Orleans resident, fellow merchant, and friend Reuben Kemper, who maintained business connections in New Orleans and, through his brothers Samuel and Nathan, had land interests in the Feliciana district.[29] This connection to Baton Rouge was typical. Many people who owned land in the Baton Rouge district also owned land across the river in Pointe Coupee, in Mississippi above the thirty-first-degree mark, in other parts of Florida such as Mobile or Pensacola, or in New Orleans itself. The next task for the American government, then, was to determine what had been included in the purchase and then set about exploring that territory.

The Lewis and Clark expedition remains the most famous of the U.S.-sponsored explorations of the new territory; however, it was only one among many. Although Lewis and Clark certainly gathered a great deal of information on their journey through the northern reaches of the purchase and beyond, Spain viewed other explorers, such as Zebulon Pike, as clearer threats to their national sovereignty over lands from Texas to California.[30] Jefferson required information not just about the vast territory of Louisiana but also about Spanish strength along the western boundaries of the recently acquired land. That made William Dunbar the perfect choice to head an expedition into the lower part of Louisiana known as the Red River area, and he received two letters from Jefferson proposing an expedition up the Arkansas and the Red rivers.[31] Although Spain also had an interest in Dunbar surveying the Louisiana-Texas border, the Mississippian instead accepted his old friend Jefferson's proposal—though he persuaded the president to confine the initial Anglo-European expedition to the Red River.[32]

Dunbar was a logical selection to head the expedition for a number of reasons. A longtime resident of the area who had lived in both Natchez and Baton Rouge, he still owned land in Spanish territory and remained on friendly terms with the Spanish government (and probably on their payroll). Whereas Lewis and Clark could evade the Spanish by going deep into territory largely unexplored by Europeans, Dunbar could hope to use his connections with Spain and knowledge of Spanish culture to avoid problems. He set out on October 16, 1804, and worked his way up the Red River, cataloging species of birds, making astronomical observations, taking temperature measurements, sounding the river, and conducting scientific experiments. This "Lewis and Clark of the South" forwarded his information back to Jefferson, who cataloged it with the findings of other expeditions. Dunbar finally returned to Natchez in January 1805, three months after setting out.[33] The significance of his expedition has long been overlooked. While Lewis and Clark opened the northern area of the continent to American expansion—in essence paving what would become the Oregon Trail—Dunbar's expedition, though much shorter and more limited, nevertheless announced the intention of the United States to continue its southern expansion across Louisiana and Arkansas, thereby directly challenging Spain's holdings in Texas and by extension New Spain out to California.

Trading Louisiana for West Florida

While the United States set about exploring its new territory, and the problem of what was included in the purchase swirled, rumors to the effect that the United States might trade Louisiana for West Florida also spread through West Florida, based in large part on ongoing negotiations between the United States and Spain. In late 1803 William Dunbar, who had served as a surveyor for the Spanish government and had determined the thirty-first degree of latitude boundary between Spanish West Florida and the United States in 1798, wrote to his long-time correspondent Thomas Jefferson regarding the need to establish the boundary line between Louisiana and Spanish territory.[34] While the Spanish had an interest in Dunbar surveying the Louisiana-Texas border, Dunbar noted that local officials had not made any firm plans because of the widespread belief that Spain would give the two Floridas to the United States in exchange for the western side of the Mississippi.[35] Likewise William Claiborne noted that the "general received opinion" of Louisianans and Floridians in 1803 was that James Monroe would acquire the Floridas through negotiation.[36] Such rumors, coming in 1803, could be expected to follow such a momentous transfer of land. Perhaps they even delayed slightly U.S. efforts to implement a new administration in the territory. Certainly the rumors provided Spain with an excuse to delay the departure of its own administration. Meanwhile, the Spanish government, perhaps also thinking that such a trade might occur, conceded royal land in Matanzas, Cuba, to residents of Florida who did not wish to remain in the area.[37] There they could join the already-settled evacuees from East Florida who had arrived in Matanzas in 1763.

However, two years later, in 1805, the story was strong enough in Louisiana and West Florida that Claiborne again stated: "[M]any persons here yet believe that the Country West of the Mississippi will be receded to Spain."[38] Detailed rumors concerning the negotiations between Spain and the United States flowed through New Orleans, and Claiborne received at least some of these reports from the former governor of Spanish Louisiana, the Marquis de Casa Calvo. In what must have been an attempt to either confuse the governor or perhaps demonstrate intellectual superiority, Casa Calvo chose to deliver the news to Claiborne in French, a language the governor only barely understood.

Spanish agents in Natchitoches, near the Texas border, used the possibility and prevalence of the rumors to weaken residents' loyalty to the U.S. government, highlighting the problem of defining the extent of the western boundaries of the purchase and then keeping that area under control.[39] That Indian chiefs and Spanish Catholic priests had also been spreading this information, according to Claiborne's informants, suggested that the rumor had enough currency to resonate widely, and that a multitude of cultures had gotten involved in what Claiborne had in another letter called "the sport of foreign and domestic intrigues."[40] Moreover, Spanish agents used their knowledge of Native culture to play on the Indians' fears of American treatment, telling them that the United States "offered no protection to religion, and that an association with Infidels (meaning Americans) would dishonor the shades of their ancestors."[41] These efforts were intended to produce two results. First, as Claiborne noted, Spanish agents wished generally to destabilize the frontier along the Natchitoches area. Months of tension between the United States and Spain over the exact boundaries of Texas and the United States culminated in a meeting at the Sabine River. There the two sides struck the Neutral Ground Agreement of 1806 whereby they agreed to a sort of "demilitarized" zone between Texas and the United States, which they hoped would prevent war. At the same time, however, the agents also continued to use the possibility of a Louisiana–West Florida trade to weaken residents' loyalty to the U.S. government in the eastern portions of Louisiana.

In 1806 negotiation between France, Spain, and the United States for the purchase of the Floridas collapsed. Although Jefferson had gotten Congress to appropriate two million dollars for the sale, hoping to persuade Napoleon to pressure Spain into ceding the territory, both Spain and France refused, leaving the United States to search for other ways to obtain the territory. In April of that same year, and on the heels of a Spanish withdrawal from the Sabine, Claiborne wrote to Madison concerning a report: "[O]ur differences with Spain are settled; . . . the Floridas are ceded to the United States."[42] Two months later Claiborne reported that in New Orleans Casa Calvo "principally employed himself in persuading the people that all [that] side of the River Mississippi would soon again return to Spain either by negotiation or Force."[43] In short the rumors, true or not, demonstrate a wider Spanish effort to undermine U.S. interests not just on the Louisiana-Texas border but also across Louisiana and even to head off potential trouble in West Florida. Claiborne described the results of these rumors as leaving Louisianans unsettled and unsure of the permanence of the American government.

Land Sales in West Florida and Louisiana

The intrigues to which Claiborne referred seemed to receive confirmation in and be furthered by the actions of Juan Ventura Morales—the man who has received the blame for the closure of the port of New Orleans.[44] Further, given the nature of land sales in West Florida and the lengths to which Spain seemed to go to ensure an adequate distribution of land, the problems created by Morales struck at the heart of governmental stability in West Florida. In 1804 Morales held the title of paymaster general and intendant pro tempore of West Florida. Described by Claiborne as a man with "more information, but less principle than any Spanish officer," Morales had already been in trouble with his own government for diverting money from the Crown and failing to account for a number of transactions under his responsibility.[45] In light of those actions Claiborne suggested that Spain put Morales on trial under the American court system, though no records exist of this actually occurring.[46] According to Claiborne, Morales had also been at the heart of a plot—along with Daniel Clark—to remove Claiborne from his position as governor, was also rumored to "command in cash five hundred thousand dollars," paid regular bribes to speculators in the city, and was perhaps working with Daniel Clark to further land speculation in West Florida.[47] How much of this is true cannot be determined, but Claiborne's letters discuss the issue in a manner that suggests he felt he was reflecting a widespread belief.

What is certain is that sometime before June 1805 Morales set up a land office in New Orleans and began selling large tracts of Crown land in eastern West Florida near Pensacola. The rumor in New Orleans was that he had been "instructed by the King of Spain to dispose of all the vacant lands in East and West Florida" and therefore acted under the authority of the Spanish government.[48] Given that the Spanish government had been giving land grants to Americans in West Florida through 1803 but had then halted them, Morales's actions smacked of profiteering. Also, to Americans it must have appeared that Crown officials, thinking that the United States and Spain would trade West Florida and Louisiana, were trying to profit from land sales prior to handing over the territory. Finally, as Claiborne asserted to James Madison, rumors that some of the land had been purchased by Spanish officials who intended to engage in speculation began to circulate through New Orleans.[49]

A suspicious Claiborne asked for clarification from Casa Calvo, who initially professed ignorance of the order, then stated that he believed the Crown had issued it. Casa Calvo then promised to halt the sales until he could undertake an investigation.[50] Reflecting American attitudes, the tone of Claiborne's letters indicates a sense of possessiveness regarding East and West Florida, as if the Spanish Crown did not have the right to sell its own land. Claiborne explained this attitude as being consistent with the fact that the United States claimed West Florida as part of the Louisiana Purchase, that Spain and the United States were engaged in negotiations to resolve that dispute, and that selling the disputed land would be improper and would harm relations between the two countries.[51] Casa Calvo, for his part, stated that Morales was acting without authority by misinterpreting a royal order regarding the survey of Crown lands in West Florida for new immigrants.[52] Though Morales did claim to be acting on a royal order, no local governors seem to have been informed of it.[53] The land sales, as Morales stated, were an effort by the Crown, to gain "all profitable advantages in favor of the Royal Chest," and the order had come straight from the Crown, circumventing the local governors.[54]

Part of the marquis' responses were classic Spanish bureaucratic obfuscation of the type seen everywhere in the empire. But land sales resumed for a time, despite Claiborne's requests that they halt, that Morales's office be closed, and that the intendant be expelled from the territory as per the provisions of the treaty of cession.[55] Claiborne reported to James Madison that many leading New Orleans citizens visited Morales to purchase land.[56] A note in late August from Morales to Claiborne explaining his actions reveals that Morales had taken a rather liberal interpretation of his duties "to regulate and conclude the affairs of interest belonging to Spain in the Province of Louisiana."[57] Under pressure from Spanish and American officials, Morales finally agreed to stop selling Crown lands, though he had already sold off more than one million acres in the area east of Baton Rouge extending to Mobile. Apparently Morales sold no land in or around Baton Rouge, including the Felicianas.

Some Spaniards—unauthorized or not—selling Crown land in West Florida while others simultaneously bought land had potentially grave effects on the Louisiana–West Florida issue and the development and maintenance of national loyalty in West Florida. On the one hand, these land deals, when paired with Spain's offer of refuge in Matanzas, created the perception that Spain intended to abandon claims to West Florida, especially given that rumors to this effect already flowed freely throughout Louisiana and West Florida. Claiborne argued such to Madison in August.[58] In fact, the Crown had no intention whatsoever of abandoning its remaining holdings in North America. In the minds of American officials, these problems reinforced the already-extant stereotypes regarding Spain's corruption, inefficiency, and inability to control its overseas empire. This issue contributed to the instability in the Gulf South, as residents could not be sure of the long-term tenure of their parent government. However, Morales was not alone in his efforts to profit from the transfer of power, as New Orleans and West Florida elites who had bought land from him and from one another then turned around and sold their holdings to newcomers, some of whom were intent on becoming the area's new elite.[59]

One example, not surprisingly, was Daniel Clark. Sometime in 1803, after news of the purchase had reached New Orleans and West Florida, but while the territory was still under French and Spanish control, he purchased a 208,000-

acre tract on the Ouachita River in present-day north central Louisiana. Clark capitalized on the fear of possible chaos following the change, purchasing as much local land as he possibly could, and quickly turned himself into one of the largest single landholders in the Mississippi Valley. From Thomas Urquhart, Clark purchased nine separate plots in and around the Baton Rouge/Feliciana area. The land totaled more than 96,000 arpents in size, with the largest plot at 50,000 arpents and the smallest at 602 arpents. These sales placed Clark in a position to capitalize on settlement in West Florida by reselling land to incoming Americans.[60]

While Urquhart was selling his land to Clark, other large landholders similarly divested themselves of their holdings. Emanuel de Fausos sold 35,000 arpents, and Jaime Jordia sold 40,000 arpents.[61] These plots were located on the western side of the Mississippi River, at a time when that area was considered part of the Baton Rouge district. A flight of the landed elites could have had serious consequences for the social order had settlement not already been occurring on such a large scale, and had not such settlement already been creating a new landed elite (albeit with less land but a great deal of wealth) in the area. Other landowners hedged their bets by making new claims under the Spanish system but at the same time registering those and older claims in the U.S. Land Office in New Orleans.[62]

The issue of land sales, land surveys, and how each government would honor surveys struck to the heart of residents' potential bonds with their respective governments on each side of the Mississippi. When the United States initially agreed to honor land surveys conducted by France and Spain, it signaled some stability in the main currency of frontier fortunes. Sensing a chance to profit, Louisianans in 1804 began to survey land on their own, hoping to be able to make claims before the United States could gain bureaucratic control over the region.[63] Although such activity may have taken place in other parts of Louisiana, it occurred mainly along the coastal Mississippi-Louisiana border. There, residents of Adams County in and around Natchez crossed the river— never really a serious physical or psychological barrier—made surveys, and then cleared and partially improved land. Similarly Spanish civil and military officials began to make claims on larger bodies of land, with the expectation that they could either sell them to incoming Americans or perhaps retain those parcels if the territory reverted to Spanish control.[64]

Sensing the problem, Claiborne partially reversed course, stating that he had no intention of honoring land surveys made by the Spanish after the cession date, that he considered surveys conducted by planters themselves after the cession of date "as conferring no title either in law or equity," and that he therefore regarded the land vacant.[65] This policy stood in stark contrast to the previous

Spanish policy of allowing locals to conduct their own surveys and then have them confirmed later by an official of the government. Spanish officials believed that allowing such surveys meant that settlers would begin to live on and cultivate their land sooner, while the Americans, fresh from land problems in Kentucky, Tennessee, and Mississippi, most likely wanted to prevent corruption while advancing their own fortunes. No method exists for measuring how many surveys were affected by this policy, but the notion that the United States might disregard existing land claims must have alarmed residents in both Louisiana and West Florida.

Problems of Loyalty

Finally convinced that the Louisiana Purchase did not include any part of the Floridas—or at least dropping any public pretense of such—Jefferson and his secretary of state James Madison asked both Daniel Clark and the new American governor, William Claiborne, to assess the region's loyalty.[66] Any kind of national loyalty in the Mississippi Valley in general, and Louisiana and West Florida in particular, had always been a difficult problem. People such as William Claiborne, Daniel Clark, William Dunbar, and James Wilkinson frequently worked for both governments, whether as spies, casual informants, explorers, or translators. Their loyalty for the most part hinged on their paychecks, though some did have deeper patriotism toward one or the other government. Aside from the loyalty to state, men such as Clark developed deep personal friendships with—and, it should be noted, serious animosity toward—men in both governments. Nowhere is that example clearer than in a series of letters from then-governor of the Natchez district Manuel Gayoso de Lemos to Daniel Clark in 1796. Writing to Clark after a journey from Pointe Coupee to New Orleans, Gayoso states that Clark's "effectionate [*sic*] friendly letter" and its sentiments are "not greater than the attachment" Gayoso has for Clark.[67]

Correspondence between the two men, going back as far as 1792, runs the gamut from demonstrative assurances of mutual friendship and affection to the more mundane recounting of a demonstration of Clark's cotton gin.[68] Each man also knew that the other might help fulfill private ambitions. In the case of Gayoso, it meant that Clark, and through him perhaps Clark's friend Wilkinson, might help the governor realize his plans of causing havoc with the United States by separating the western United States, including Tennessee and Wilkinson's Kentucky, from the mother country. For Clark, Gayoso represented both friendship and a path toward greater wealth through access to Spanish lands. Clark gave Gayoso information regarding Lower Mississippi Valley politics, introduced the Spaniard to a more efficient cotton gin, and provided Gayoso's acquaintances with an entrée into American immigrant society; the Spanish governor reciprocated by resolving legal disputes, helping Clark financially during crop failures, and generally serving as Clark's entrée into Spanish society.[69]

Where, then, the loyalty—even prior to the Louisiana Purchase, when the United States had not yet become a full-fledged power in the Mississippi Valley? The correspondence of the two men suggests a deep sense of mutual personal loyalty that may have transcended national ideology, and Clark's actions in this and later periods more than hints at his lack of anything resembling national loyalty. He was as friendly and devoted to the interests and people of the United States as to those of Spain.[70] Gayoso, who worked to cleave the western United States from the country east of the Appalachians, was nothing if not a Spanish patriot. Yet though his first wife was a Spaniard, his next two—whom he married in Louisiana, where Spanish women generally did not settle—came from the United States. More importantly, one can see the substance of Gayoso's loyalty in a letter he wrote to an Indian chief, stating: "If I am anything else than a Spaniard, I am an American as I have married one."[71] Gayoso, unlike Clark, retained a high degree of national loyalty. But he also came from a country with hundreds of years of national history, and where one's position in the government, and therefore one's easiest path to honor, social status, and wealth, depended on loyalty to a sovereign.

In late 1797 Gayoso penned a letter to the king of Spain shortly after taking an extended trip through Tennessee, Kentucky, Virginia, Pennsylvania, Illinois, and Michigan. The stated purpose of the trip was to allow the Spanish government to follow up on Citizen Genet's attempts to separate parts of the west from the United States and allow Spain to assess the loyalty of Americans west of the Appalachians. In the main, Gayoso described the loyalty of western frontier Americans as up for grabs, allowing for certain circumstances. Though he received a hostile reception in Louisville, Gayoso met with General Wilkinson in Detroit and delivered a letter from Baron de Carondelet. Wilkinson sent a reply to Carondolet back with Gayoso. Wilkinson also informed Gayoso that President Adams had ordered the governor of the Northwest Territory to arrest the Spaniard and send him to Philadelphia. Despite the official position of the U.S. government, the general provided a security guard to accompany the Spaniard back to Spanish territory.[72]

Notwithstanding the apparently hostile reception, Gayoso gave a frank assessment of American loyalty in the Tennessee and Kentucky borderlands. On the one hand, he spoke against any hopes of disaffection with the United States that Spain might have entertained, noting in 1797 that "the dissatisfaction existing among the people four years ago had quieted down" and that Wilkinson felt that western inhabitants had no motive or desire to separate from the United States. Further, Wilkinson declared that Kentuckians had promised to gather an army of some three thousand men to invade Louisiana should the United States and Spain go to war. In part, Wilkinson was trying to provide himself with political cover. But Wilkinson also told Gayoso that he might be named governor of the new territory around Natchez, and from there he could more effectively execute their shared schemes.[73]

One the other hand, Gayoso presented his king with the observations of Benjamin Sebastian, a court of appeals judge in Kentucky.[74] Sebastian believed that war with the United States would provide Spain with an "effective way of turning [Kentuckians] against the States of the East." Here Gayoso's opinions and those of Sebastian become indistinguishable, as Gayoso argued that elites in Kentucky, Tennessee, and the Northwest Territory supported Genet and that given the current climate of hostility between France and the United States, "they [were] enemies of those that [were] enemies of the French." Gayoso then outlined three conditions that either he or Sebastian thought might impel the western states to secede from the Union. First, an outbreak of war with France would inflame what he believed to be pro-French sentiment among westerners. Second, any attempt by the United States to either settle in Spanish territory or close navigation of the Mississippi River would raise ire. This last clause is fraught with the irony that the closure of the Mississippi River to American navigation by a Spanish official in 1803 would drive the United States into the Louisiana Purchase, thus destroying any plans Spain might have had with regard to halting American expansion. Finally, Gayoso felt that if the United States forced the issue of tax collection in the West, settlers might respond with force and then be receptive to Spanish overtures. Moreover, the United States maintained negligible forces in the West, and those that did exist were poorly trained and lacked "all the qualities (except bravery) that a good soldier should have."[75]

In general, the American Claiborne's 1804 assessment of Louisianans' loyalty to the U.S. government was not negative, though it also was not glowing. Most district officials took loyalty oaths without question, while a few Spanish officials "graciously" declined to serve the new government, and the United States replaced them without trouble. Claiborne believed that most elites transferred their national loyalty to the United States, especially after U.S. assurances of maintaining the status quo vis-à-vis their local power.[76] Claiborne also noted that Louisianans retained what he called a "great partiality for France as their Mother Country" as well as for the Spanish system.[77] More ominously for the United States, Claiborne could not guarantee that Louisiana creoles would side with the United States in the event of a war, though he thought it possible. A final problem for the U.S. assessment of residents' loyalty was the state of the free blacks and the free black militia, about which many historians have written.[78]

All these fears were reinforced by the continuing presence in New Orleans of several high-ranking Spanish officials, despite persistent U.S. requests for them to leave—a seeming echo of the events just after Pinckney's Treaty in 1795, when Spanish troops delayed withdrawal from the Natchez district until 1798 while at the same time stirring up anti-U.S. sentiment among local Indian tribes.[79] In fact, while the French withdrew from Louisiana fairly quickly, Spanish officials remained in the city for years. As Philip C. Brooks has argued, this may have been in part because of a perceived need to ensure the continued defense of Spain's Gulf Coast possessions.[80] Also, a continued Spanish presence in the area would allow Spain to maintain its protest against American possession of Louisiana and to keep a close eye on American activity. In New Orleans, Claiborne worried not only that the Spanish troops and officials "weakened the attachment of [the] Citizens" to the government of the United States but also that their presence reinforced the belief that the U.S. government was only temporary, and that the area of Louisiana west of the Mississippi would soon be returned to Spain.[81] In the course of discussions with Claiborne, the Marquis de Casa Calvo of New Orleans and Governor Folch of West Florida apparently expressed surprise that the United States would try to expand west of the Mississippi. The Spaniard Folch, for his part, neatly played on some of the Federalist debates of previous decades when he "introduced the hackneyed argument that a Republican form of Government could not long exist over extensive territories."[82]

Claiborne also emphasized the fact that not everyone in New Orleans, even two years after the purchase, had shifted loyalty to the United States, and he worried that Spanish officers in the city might combine with the "many adherents to the Spanish interest" who might unite against the United States. These soldiers of the Crown also had the potential to stir up discord, at least according to American officials. Claiborne's letter to Madison in February 1804 described a near riot between Spanish troops and residents of New Orleans but also contained a warning about the "great share of national pride" evident among the American, French, and Spanish soldiers in the city. Those feelings created resentment between the various soldiers, and Claiborne saw in those troops the seeds of broader problems for U.S. administration of its new territory.[83]

More problematically, the U.S. legal system and legal culture brought concerns to Louisianans. A pair of lengthy letters from Claiborne to Thomas Jefferson and James Madison designed to educate the U.S. administration on various aspects of Louisiana's political, geographical, cultural, and legal situation dwelled at some length on the legacy of the court system in Louisiana. Claiborne noted that the court system generally favored the wealthy, ironically suggesting that this might make the U.S. system a good replacement. He also noted that the province contained no lawyers in the sense the term was understood in the United States, but rather that the Spanish government employed lawyers as administrators.[84] Madison's inquiry into the situation in Louisiana was matched by the residents' musings about the U.S. system. Three years after the purchase, residents remained upset by the introduction of the English language, which went along with the new government. That might have been expected, however. More vexing for them was the trial by jury and the perceived legal wrangling that went along with it. Claiborne informed Madison that many residents, accustomed to trial by a judge, considered trial by jury as "odious—and the lawyers as serious nuisances."[85]

The issue of loyalty and the repercussions of the purchase were not strictly the province of whites. The Louisiana Purchase had a deep effect on slaves and Indian tribes. Longtime actors occupying the "middle ground" in the power struggles between Spain, England, France, and then the United States, Native American tribes used their geographic position, their knowledge of the terrain, and their abilities as traders to influence the course of larger nations in what Jane Landers has termed "racial geopolitics."[86] Prior to 1763, when Spain took possession of Louisiana, Indians in Louisiana had been firm allies of the French and enemies of the Spanish. After Pinckney's Treaty, Wilkinson in 1798 accused Spain of trying to stir up anti-American sentiment among the Choctaws in and around Natchez. Although Manuel Gayoso de Lemos vehemently denied having any hand in the effort, he did not deny that such efforts had been made.[87]

The following year rumors percolated out of Natchez that the Marquis de Casa Calvo had told the Choctaws that any who remained loyal to Spain after the American takeover would continue to receive Spanish gifts and protection, despite U.S. control over the area.[88] More threatening was the attendant rumor that Casa Calvo was attempting to arrange a pan-Indian conference with the intent of broadly organizing an alliance among the disparate tribes.[89] In a manner suggestive of U.S. attitudes toward its place in the borderlands, the American response to the problem of loyalty here was twofold. First was the problem of a foreign power trying to subvert so-called Indian loyalty in American territory. But the letter writer also, paternalistically, seemed just as perturbed that the Spanish offer to clothe the Choctaws amounted to an accusation of negligence on the part of the United States.[90] The marquis and other Spaniards of course denied any attempts to engage in "tampering with the Indians" by organizing the tribes into an anti-American alliance, but local Americans in Mississippi were nonetheless wary of such a possibility.[91] Meanwhile, the arrival of some seven hundred Choctaws in New Orleans at the same time that the rumors were circulating and coinciding with the beginning of an expedition of Spanish gunboats for what the Spaniards called, but Daniel Clark did not believe was, exploration must also have given some pause to Americans in Mississippi.[92] The fact that Americans believed the rumors possible speaks to probable continued attempts by the Native tribes themselves to play the two powers off against each other.

The period after the Louisiana Purchase held some promise for Native Americans, and Todd Smith argues that tribes in the western portion of Louisiana favored the U.S. purchase of the territory.[93] Even here, though, Spain held some advantage over the United States, having maintained long-established trade contacts with tribes across the area from the Floridas to California and generally having established solid alliances with tribes throughout the region. Though rumors of Spain instigating a war between Spain, Indians, and the United States floated around Mississippi, Louisiana, and the Floridas, nothing ever materialized.[94] To some extent the rumors and conflicts that occurred in Mississippi after Pinckney's Treaty replayed themselves in 1804, but with Texas as the setting. This time Governor Claiborne and the Marquis de Casa Calvo parried accusations that Spaniards were trying to foment disruption among the tribes along the Louisiana-Texas frontier.[95] Spanish officials, of course, denied the rumors, but they came at the same time as rumors that Indian chiefs and priests were spreading rumors of a Louisiana–West Florida trade. Whatever the case, Native Americans' place in between the two European powers certainly gave them some autonomy and power for as long as the two powers needed the tribes as proxies in their battle over the Louisiana frontier.

For slaves the purchase would have a more startling effect. In late 1804 Spanish officials in Nacogdoches, in Spanish Texas, spread news of a royal decree that offered asylum to any slave escaping from American-held Louisiana into the province of Texas. Officials in New Orleans, including Casa Calvo, confirmed its existence.[96] Within weeks rumors of insurrection spread through the lower part of the Louisiana district, and slaves began fleeing American territory for Texas. More frighteningly for whites, some of the slaves took powder and shot with them, raising the specter of armed rebellion. Other slaves told whites that they knew that if they fled to Spanish territory the Spaniards would free them, having been told such by Spanish officials and Spanish agents living in and around Nacogdoches.[97] This was a policy Spain had used to great effect in East Florida in the late seventeenth and early eighteenth centuries in an attempt to destabilize the British colony in South Carolina.[98] By late 1804 Claiborne described "a spirit of insurrection" among the slaves at Pointe Coupee—site of the 1795 rebellion—and noted that slaves in that area carried copies of the Spanish proclamation.[99] The decree seemed to have its intended effect, for a much-angered Claiborne dispatched troops to Pointe Coupee, occupied himself with trying to reclaim slaves who had fled to Spanish Nacogdoches, and pleaded with Casa Calvo to rescind the decree. Louisiana governor Claiborne could do little but beg. Through 1808 the fugitive slave policy was still in effect, and slaves continued to escape to Texas.[100] Perhaps reflecting its more unstable position with regard to U.S.-Spanish relations as well as intercommunity relations between West Floridians and merchants in New Orleans, West Floridians promptly returned fugitive American slaves who had escaped to West Florida.[101]

As noted in chapter 2, the French and the Spanish legal systems differed greatly from whatever the Americans would institute, and the same held true for slavery. When the United States took control of Louisiana west of the Mississippi, it at first tried to institute Spanish law in the territory and may have assumed that the Anglo-American forms of race relations would follow. The first territorial legislature, composed mostly of native-born Louisianans, tried to retain most of the Spanish system of law through an act of the legislature. As opposed to France, Britain, and the United States, Spain operated under the principle of civil rather than common law. As noted, Louisianans in 1803 wanted no part of the U.S. courts, or common law, with its system of precedents. The fear among inhabitants was that Jefferson would ban slavery in the new territories, citing as a precedent the actions of the Continental Congress with regard to the Northwest Territories. Indeed, the United States had banned new slave importations into the Louisiana territory, and Jefferson endorsed closing the foreign trade into Louisiana altogether.[102]

William Claiborne vetoed the act of the Louisiana legislature; he agreed, however, to a compromise in 1808 based on Spanish law but which put in place the more stringent measures of the French Code.[103] The compromise solidified Louisiana's Black Code of 1807, which had negated or weakened several components of Spanish law. Slaves could no longer purchase themselves, owners wishing to manumit slaves needed government permission, and removal from a cruel master became next to impossible.[104] Thus although the Code contained a few forms of French slave law, it seemed directed toward establishing something similar to the U.S. system of racial and social control that had evolved over the previous two hundred years, and which succeeded in erasing what Americans found as "the objectionable aspects of Spanish slave law."[105]

What does all this mean for West Floridians as well as for Americans looking to West Florida as a possibility for migration? Between the time of the Louisiana Purchase in 1803, when the Baton Rouge district remained part of Spanish West Florida, and 1807, when Louisianans firmly protected slavery through the Act of 1806 and the Black Code, slavery in the southwest, ironically, was more secure for Anglo-Americans under Spain's rule in West Florida than under the United

States in the territory of the Louisiana Purchase. Louisianans believed that the U.S. government might abolish slavery in the Louisiana territory, while the Spanish system of slavery, in place for more than three hundred years, seemed secure and unlikely to change to any great degree.

The Louisiana Purchase, then, had serious consequences for people in both West Florida and Louisiana quite apart from the mere transfer of land. Regional instability in the form of unauthorized land sales, confusion over who would control the Floridas and Louisiana, and U.S. maneuvering to gain control of the Floridas ensured that West Florida would be at the center of U.S. efforts to control the continent and Spanish maneuvering to resist that encroachment. More importantly, the Louisiana Purchase created a "surrounded borderlands," with West Florida surrounded by U.S. possessions to the north, south, and west, and by mostly unsettled frontier immediately to the east. This placed West Florida in a unique situation—occupying the space between an expanding power with aspirations to empire. What would this mean for American residents living under the Spanish Crown when the government that many of them had so recently left then returned so suddenly at their doorstep, nearby and available?

The problem of national loyalty in Louisiana was no doubt mirrored in West Florida, though due to a lack of sources on the subject, historians must extrapolate. It is safe to assume that West Floridians felt the same uncertainty with regard to their national government just after 1803 as did Louisianans. Which territory would fall into the hands of which government? How would the issue of slavery play out, given the increasingly tight controls on the American side of the border and the relatively lax, by American standards, on the Spanish side? What about land surveys and the easy availability of land? Finally, how would Spain's government maintain stability and the rule of law in its surrounded borderlands? These would be the questions requiring an answer in the coming years.

While the full import of this geographical anomaly would develop over the course of the next few years, some sign of the problematic nature of Spain's position in the Floridas came before the purchase had been announced. It was James Madison who, perhaps unintentionally, best expressed one indication of what a surrounded borderland would mean to West Floridians. In 1805 he wrote to William Claiborne about a proposed mail route that would run from Washington, D.C., to New Orleans through West Florida.[106] That road would be paired with another U.S. mail route between Natchez and New Orleans. Though the proposal came within two years after the United States took possession of Louisiana, it is symbolic of the American perception of West Florida as a place that should have been included in the purchase, and as one that would, inevitably, become part of the expanding nation soon enough. At the same time, Madison's words show the already-porous nature of the West Florida borderlands, which despite being under Spanish control was subject to American machinations. The proposed road and Madison's sense of inevitability regarding its path through Spanish territory symbolize the precarious situations for West Floridians after 1803.

The surrounded borderlands that emerged after 1803 would mean that to an ever-greater degree West Florida would be populated by people who owned land in both nations and who might have an interest in seeing one or the other country lose control over its frontier territory. Another precarious situation for West Floridians in the surrounded borderlands would be the ease with which people could cross national boundaries. While much of this traffic would be legal, a great deal of it would not. Petty thievery would certainly annoy residents, and the escape of these thieves across national boundaries would pose a legal challenge. However, the Lower Mississippi Valley was no stranger to organized raids by armed gangs—filibustering. It remained to be seen if the newly created surrounding borderlands would encourage those activities and how those activities would challenge the residents' loyalties.

CHAPTER FOUR

Strains on the System I

Filibustering

The Louisiana Purchase brought confusion and disorder to both the new U.S. territories and Spanish West Florida for the next several years. As rumors swirled regarding the disposition of each area, some locals attempted to take matters into their own hands, forcing the United States into action. Others took advantage of the confusion to pursue criminal agendas. Still others saw that the two might go hand in hand. The Kemper raids, or Kemper Rebellion as it is sometimes called, have long been regarded as a symbol of growing Anglo-American dissatisfaction with Spanish rule in the late colonial period. The Kemper brothers—Reuben, Samuel, and Nathan—themselves helped to shape much of this thinking through their efforts to proclaim a "West Florida Republic" in 1804 complete with flag and a declaration of independence reputedly authored by Edward Randolph. The Kempers owned land in both the Feliciana district in Spanish West Florida and nearby Pinckneyville, Mississippi, just over the line. Beginning in June their gang terrorized the area for several months, crossing and recrossing the border into U.S. territory as a means of escaping the Anglo-American-staffed Spanish militia. The goal of their raids, they declared, was to bring about the overthrow of Spanish rule by the residents of the district and invite what they termed a more stable American government into the area. In reality the raiders stole slaves and other property and in their wake left burned buildings and residents and a Spanish government determined to run the Kempers to ground.[1]

Historians have long argued that Anglo-Americans in West Florida were unhappy with Spanish rule, and that Spain maintained an ineffective presence in the New World in general and in West Florida specifically. Although a seemingly minor event in the history of Louisiana, the Kemper Rebellion was the central event that led to a change in Spanish land policy and Spanish colonial administration of the region. Given the number of armed bandits roaming the American and Spanish countryside during late 1804, it could also have been the catalyst for a local takeover by pro-American subjects of the Crown. Yet the inhabitants of Feliciana did not rise up to support the border ruffians, choosing instead to work in large numbers with the Spanish government to combat the raids and eventually track down and arrest some members of the gang. In part this was because of the nature of the raids and the raiders themselves. Intent on stealing slaves and cattle, the Kemper gang seemed less like a revolutionary vanguard and more like the leaders of a group of land pirates intent on plundering the district. The Kempers, despite their attempts to sow discontent among Spanish subjects, instead serve as a symbol of the residents' continuing loyalty to the Spanish regime.

For their part West Floridians had already experienced their share of the kind of filibustering in which the Kempers engaged. This makes the Kemper raids an excellent case study for loyalty in West Florida specifically and the borderlands in general. When examined within the context of the Baton Rouge district, the raids can help us gain insight into the ways in which the larger Spanish governmental apparatus reacted to the threat of a possible rebellion, the ways in which middling officials handled the local aspects of the raids, and the ways in which residents themselves responded. At the same time, when the raids are placed within the larger context of filibustering across the Florida/Louisiana/Texas frontier, they lose much of their significance. Along with the James Willing expedition of 1778, the Aaron Burr conspiracy of 1805, Gen. James Wilkinson's Texas raids in 1805, and other ventures, the Kemper raids were less about protorevolutionary sentiment among West Floridians than about the nature of the people attracted to the borderlands. Beyond that, Col. George Nixon's 1814 gulf coast filibustering raids, Andrew Jackson's invasion of Florida, and other incursions point to a broader string of raids that in many ways were simply part of the borderlands existence.

On the part of resident Anglo-Americans, the story of the West Florida raids by the Kemper gang is one of political loyalty to the Spanish Crown. In part this might have been due to the strength of the Spanish in West Florida—especially relative to what it would become five years later. For the most part modern historians have accepted the thinking of earlier counterparts who argued that in 1804 the Spanish military presence in West Florida and the Baton Rouge district was fairly weak, the militia unreliable, and the general populace disloyal. However, resident Anglo-Americans had good reason to remain loyal. The Spanish land policy attracted migrants from various places in the United States, many seeking a more lenient and open policy of land distribution. West Florida drew settlers not only from different areas but also of various backgrounds. Along with the previously described William Dunbar and Jean Baptiste Bienville, Reuben Kemper could serve as one of several "archetypes" of borderlands settler. Dunbar arrived in West Florida with moderate wealth and used his connections within the government and his position of power to engage in extremely lucrative pursuits. This allowed him to retire to a life of science and writing. Bienville, on the other hand, gained his freedom and began at the bottom of the economic and social ladder. Using cattle ranching as a path to wealth, he amassed a plantation, slaves, and eventually a small fortune. A mulatto, his social and economic position nonetheless mitigated his racial status in the eyes of his neighbors. Reuben Kemper apparently came to West Florida with little and left with even less. Though he had begun to build his fortune, by 1804 he had lost both his position within the community and his lands when he and his brothers engaged in cross-border raids against the people of Feliciana. Kemper, then, represents the failed frontier settler who turned to crime as a means of existence. In fact, the Kemper Rebellion itself is best viewed within the larger context of American expansion, filibustering, and rebellions occurring all along the southern tier, from East Florida to Texas, and from the time of the American Revolution through the second decade of the nineteenth century.

The James Willing Expedition, William Augustus Bowles, and Philip Nolan

For Baton Rouge residents the Kemper filibustering was not even the first series of raids in their area. That honor belonged to the raids led by James Willing.[2] In a diary entry dated May 1, 1778, with the note that a "Grand Revolution hath taken place on the English side of the Mississippi," William Dunbar described the raid that had occurred three months previously. In February, Baton Rouge residents first heard of a nearby attack by Americans against a merchant ship, and the residents prepared for an attack on their city and plantations. Planters with the ability to do so moved their slaves and other possessions across the river to Pointe Coupee. After following his slaves to that area, Dunbar heard rumors that the Americans intended to "rob & plunder Every English subject who had property of any value."[3]

He later learned that the leader of the expedition was James Willing, originally from Philadelphia and a former resident of the district who had left the year before. Willing, according to rumors, had drawn up a list of specific people and plantations that he intended to target and probably carried something resembling a letter of marque from officials in Philadelphia authorizing him to seize British property.[4] Dunbar later discovered that Willing had obtained a commission and left Fort Pitt (in present-day Pittsburgh) with twenty-five men and orders to sail downriver to New Orleans and take on provisions, then return up the Ohio capturing British property along the way. Willing had also persuaded Americans in Philadelphia that loyalists on the lower Mississippi would close that river to all traffic, including that carrying American war supplies, and that he could ensure that the province would remain neutral.[5]

Table 3. Selected Filibustering, Exploration, and Military Movements in the Floridas, Louisiana, and East Texas, 1776–1817

Who	Where	When	Type
Bowles	West Florida	1788–1803	Filibustering
James Willing	West Florida and Louisiana	1778	Filibustering
Francisco de Miranda	Louisiana and the Floridas	1781	Filibustering
Dunbar	Red River Expedition	1804	Exploration
Kemper	West Florida	1805–6	Filibustering
Aaron Burr	Louisiana/West Florida	1806	Filibustering
United States/Spain	Natchitoches	1806	Military movements
Pike	Texas and Southwest	1807	Exploration
Various	Natchitoches	1807	Military movement
Various	East Florida	1811–14	War
Gutiérrez-Magee	Texas	1812–13	Filibustering
British Army	Louisiana	1814	War of 1812
Nixon	West Florida	1814	Filibustering
Jackson	West Florida	1814	Filibustering
MacGregor	East Florida	1817	Filibustering
Aury	East Florida	1817	Filibustering

William Dunbar seemed surprised that Willing had taken up arms against his former neighbors. Although he had no kind words for Willing—noting that the man had a "natural propensity [for] getting drunk"—Dunbar did complain that this was the same man who had "been often entertained in the most hospitable manner" and "who had frequently lived for his own convenience for a length of time at [their] houses." Willing had been very much a part of the community in Dunbar's recent past. In the year before he left the district, Willing had apparently lost his entire fortune, perhaps because of a series of bad crops, or perhaps he had simply never been able to make it in the first place, which would explain why he lived at the houses of various people in the area prior to returning to Philadelphia. By the time Willing's expedition arrived in the Baton Rouge area, his force had grown to about two hundred (mainly "vagabonds and rascals, of which kind the river [was] always full"), and Dunbar estimated that that number would be enough to accomplish Willing's goal, considering that "perhaps one half of the Inhabitants [of the Baton Rouge district in 1778] were in the American Interest."[6]

Willing, however, followed many of the same patterns that the Kempers would sixteen years later as "the temptation to loot overrode his promise" not to disturb any residents who had declared themselves neutrals.[7] After securing oaths of neutrality from Natchez residents, Willing moved south into the Baton Rouge district, where he captured a ship and raided plantations from Bayou Sara to Manchac.[8] His men looted and burned the major plantations and stole cows and pigs. The party also searched for plantations with slaves that the gang might steal. Finding none "on the English side, they pass[ed] over to the Spanish Territories & Seize[d . . .] Negroes," then proceeded to steal everything from sugar to silverware to shirts to bed and table linen, looting the major plantations in the district. The Americans then burned the cotton gins and indigo works, as well as houses, cabins, and barns. Dunbar called them "Villains" and "Rascals" and wrote that to call them "Americans" would "be a prostitution of the name of Americans."[9] After the raids Willing eventually sailed to New Orleans, where he sold his booty, including one hundred slaves, for tens of thousands of dollars.[10] Anglo-Americans serving in the Spanish and British militias soon caught a number of Willing's men and returned some of the plunder to the rightful owners. In the long run Willing's raid had almost no effect on the district outside of the slight economic hardship brought on the inhabitants. The local militia offered little resistance, and for the most part residents simply fled Willing when they could.[11]

This pattern repeated itself across the borderlands from 1778 through 1803 as discontented residents found outlets for their unhappiness in banditti raids, and legitimate military officers from the United States tried to either provoke a conflict with Spain or foment an uprising by supposedly nationalistic resident "Americans." Even the filibustering and political and military machinations in faraway Texas had implications for the residents of Baton Rouge. Though the United States did not pose a threat to Texas before the Louisiana Purchase, Spanish officials readied themselves for what they thought was a planned invasion. In late 1800 Philip Nolan, a friend of and former bookkeeper for James Wilkinson nominally in Texas to gather and trade horses, had agreed to map and explore parts of Texas for Thomas Jefferson and the United States. Since 1794 Nolan had, under a Spanish passport, made forays into Texas, bringing back thousands of wild mustangs to sell in Natchez and New Orleans. Afraid that Nolan was in Texas to pave the way for U.S. settlers and stir up Indian hostility against Spain by making alliances between local tribes and the American government, the Crown responded to his trip in 1800 by sending a force of about 150 regulars and militia to capture Nolan's men. Whether they viewed it as such or not, the Spaniards termed his mission an "invasion," and they eventually killed Nolan and captured his men to put an end to the possibility that his "information gathering" in the Texas borderlands would aid American interests there.[12]

However, not all the raids involved American citizens looking to displace the Spanish in favor of the United States. From 1788 until his capture and death in Havana's Morro Castle in 1803, William Augustus Bowles conducted filibuster raids in Spanish West and Central Florida as titular "director of affairs" of the Creek and the Cherokee nations. Bowles had been an ensign in a Maryland unit of Loyalists, though he was discharged from the service for disciplinary reasons while stationed in Pensacola. A party of Creek Indians took him in, and Bowles married into the tribe, learned the language, adopted Creek customs, and eventually became a chief. For his help against Spain, the British by 1781 had restored his commission, and after the Spaniards captured Pensacola, Bowles was sent to New York with other British prisoners. After his return to the Floridas and his home among the Creeks, the British then sent Bowles to New Providence in 1785. On that island Bowles went to work for a local trading firm, Miller and Botany, with the idea of breaking the monopoly over Indian trade in the Floridas held by Panton Leslie and Company. Whatever plans Miller and Botany had in this regard, Bowles had a grander scheme: to evict Spain's forces completely from the Floridas. Here Bowles's connections with the Creeks put him in an excellent position to remind the various tribes of the end result of white encroachment on Indian lands. His connections with the British allowed him to travel first to Nova Scotia and then to London in search of British support.[13]

After his return to Florida in 1791, Bowles began negotiations with the Spanish governor, hoping to parlay Spanish fears of American power into recognition of a Creek and Cherokee nation in Florida that would serve as a buffer between the United States and Spain. However, his subsequent attack upon and capture of a Panton and Leslie store in San Marcos convinced Spain that Bowles was too dangerous to bargain with. In 1793 he was arrested in New Orleans and spent the next five years in Spanish jails, first in New Orleans, then in Havana, Madrid, and Manila, in the Philippines. During transfer from Manila back to Madrid, Bowles escaped and again tried to drum up British support for his plans to drive Spain out of the Floridas. In 1799 he returned to Florida, organized the Creeks and the Seminoles, and proclaimed an independent "State of Muskogee." Bowles then approached the United States asking for official recognition of the sovereignty of his new nation. At the same time he declared war on Spain and in May 1800 began attacking Spanish holdings. That same month, at the head of a group of Indians and soldiers of fortune, Bowles surrounded the Spanish fort at San Marcos and captured a ship sent to relieve the Spanish troops inside. Though the fort was constructed of stone, the ship carried a small cannon, which the commander of the fort mistook for a weapon of larger caliber. He surrendered the fort, giving Bowles's State of Muskogee its first victory against the empire of Spain. Nonetheless, Spanish troops recaptured the fort three weeks later with a large, heavily armed contingent of troops supported by waterborne artillery.[14] A subsequent attempt on Bowles's part to take the fort in 1802 failed.

Although British support for Bowles had waned by 1802, the director general had gained a great deal of influence over various Indian tribes—so much so that Vicente Folch, the governor of West Florida, made plans to arrest Bowles in 1803. Captured at a conference in New Orleans, the director was sent to the dreaded Morro Castle in Havana, where he died in 1806. Bowles's impact on West Florida is hard to quantify. Most of his operations occurred in and around Pensacola, and records from Baton Rouge make only passing mention of him. However, for nearly three years, from 1799 through 1802, his Indians attacked Spanish trading posts and facilities and in general helped to destabilize Spain's relations with other Indian tribes. However, Bowles's filibustering did not offer Anglo West Floridians anything to which they could attach their loyalty, presenting only the faint possibility of Spanish removal and Indian dominance over the Floridas. Certainly no property owner in West Florida would rally to that cause.

The Kemper Raids and "Rebellion"

In late 1803 the Feliciana district remained a part of Spanish Baton Rouge, and the governor of West Florida, Vicente Folch, exercised dominion over Carlos de Grand-Pré, governor of Baton Rouge. Any military protection required by the colonists would come from Baton Rouge or one of the nearby forts. Directly across the river from Feliciana, in Pointe Coupee Parish, Fort Punta Cortada guarded a bend in the Mississippi River.[15] Part of U.S. territory after 1803, Spanish troops in early 1804 nonetheless continued to occupy Punta Cortada until U.S. troops could take control of the area. Estimates of Spanish military strength and manpower in the Feliciana district vary. But the accepted studies disparagingly list "an uncertain militia"—assuming that local Anglos would serve reluctantly—and describe fifty-six regulars of the Spanish army available for military duty.[16] However, the Spanish records of the force at Punta Cortada show a fearsome array of weapons. The Spanish militia could supplement the unknown number of soldiers stationed at the fort, while Baton Rouge maintained its own fort with a contingent of men.

The strength, composition, and dedication of the regulars and militia in and around Baton Rouge have been of no small concern to historians. The 56 regulars, uncertain militia, and the poor condition of the fort have all been used as evidence of the weak Spanish presence, disloyalty (or at least apathy) on the part of residents toward the government, and the lack of commitment and funding by the Spanish government. All three points need revising. In March 1805 estimates by U.S. officials in New Orleans showed about 900 regulars in all of West Florida including Pensacola, with about 200 of those stationed at Baton Rouge. That same estimate claimed that the "Spanish government [could] place no reliance on the militia" because of a general pro-American sentiment among residents.[17] Later in the year Dunbar reported that about 120 men remained in the fort, and although the fort had been repaired, it was not well built or advantageously situated—"commanded by ground not more than a Quarter of a Mile distant."[18] What to make of this? The more concrete statement flatly contradicts historians' later claims regarding troop strength. On the surface it is also believable—William Claiborne had no reason to mislead Madison regarding military composition. If anything, he might have been tempted to underestimate it, given the difficulty of such counts. Also, given that he aimed to facilitate bringing West Florida under U.S. control, he might also have been tempted to forward an undercount to make the Spanish look as weak as possible. The fact remains, however, that contemporary American estimates of Spanish troop strength was nearly four times greater in Baton Rouge alone than historians have subsequently recognized, with more troops less than a week's march away. Claiborne's estimates regarding the state of the militia are less quantifiable and therefore more open to testing. How this "uncertain militia" would react when called upon stands as one test of the residents' loyalty to the Spanish government.

Spain's policy discouraging absentee land ownership required owners to live on and improve their claims, and the Spaniards evaluated additional land claims based on the ways in which residents had improved their already-existing holdings. This did not, however, prevent local residents from making private sales to individual nonresidents. Although rare, such sales did occur.[19] Because the Spanish government did not regulate private sales, except inasmuch as they maintained guidelines for recording such sales, nonresidents could make private purchases. The result was that while the rate of absentee landownership was extremely small, it nonetheless remained possible.

One such absentee landowner, John Smith of Ohio, found himself at the center of the 1804 disputes.[20] The date of his initial settlement in Feliciana is unclear, but on the map for 1799 a John Smith appears as the owner of a 720-arpent tract of land near the border of the Baton Rouge and Feliciana districts.[21] In May of that year Smith established a partnership with Reuben Kemper, the son of a Virginia Baptist minister, previously a bookkeeper for Smith, and a friend of Daniel Clark. Smith's venture with the Kemper brothers was a strange and knotted affair. A Baptist minister, Smith may have met the Kempers in Virginia, where they had all originated. As occurred in many frontier areas across the U.S. borderlands-frontier, wealthy men engaged in a sort of speculation by bringing hard-to-obtain items to wilderness settlements and selling the goods at a markup, and John Smith initially engaged in this sort of venture. The records suggest that he first came to Baton Rouge from Cincinnati in May 1799, with about twelve thousand pesos worth of merchandise. Reuben Kemper accompanied him as a bookkeeper, having purchased the merchandise on account in Philadelphia. Unable to sell his goods quickly, Smith established a partnership with Kemper but retained possession of the supplies in his own name.[22] With that, the Kempers opened a settlement store in Feliciana through which they would sell merchandise to residents and new settlers, while Smith returned to Ohio and served as a senator from that state.[23] The Kempers lived on Smith's land and used the settlement store to encourage migration from the United States. At the same time, the Kempers' residence on the land perhaps helped Smith evade Spanish residency requirements. The Spaniards might also have decided to let the odd arrangement stand because the purpose of the store dovetailed with their plans for encouraging American migration into Feliciana.

The Kempers and Smith failed miserably in their joint venture. In April 1800 Smith dissolved the partnership, blaming Reuben Kemper for the failure. Among other problems Smith cited Kemper's 4,882-peso debt to two local men as evidence of poor management.[24] Using language that provides some insight into personal and national loyalty in the borderlands, Smith also referred to his association with the Kempers as a "conditional partnership," while the U.S. senator also stressed that he should henceforth be considered a resident of Spain's Feliciana district and should not be "held responsible for any of [Reuben] Kemper's dealings" from that point forward. A two-day inventory of the store listed such finery as linens, silks, and rugs, showed 12,000 pesos worth of merchandise, a number of debts to local residents, and some debts owed the store. Government officials had sold everything at auction by September 1800 to help settle the accounts.[25] Despite the dissolution of the partnership and efforts by Smith to reclaim his losses via a lawsuit against him, Reuben Kemper apparently remained in the area employed by Smith, living on Smith's farm, and worked with Smith's local agents to manage the place. During the same period, on February 11, 1801, Smith sold two hundred acres of land to Reuben and his brother Nathan.[26]

The West Florida records reveal little concrete information about the Kemper brothers' activities apart from the details of the filibustering, but what does exist hints at a troubled relationship with the government and other residents. Aside from a land claim and the purchase of a slave from a local priest in early 1800, the Kempers in general found trouble in the district.[27] In 1802 Reuben Kemper petitioned Grand-Pré to post a notice regarding trespassers on Reuben's land, writing of unknown persons "in possession of [his] woodlands and other belongings."[28] In response Grand-Pré required the "individuals who [were] at fault to evacuate immediately all the buildings and lands which they might occupy without consent of the complainant."[29] The language of the documents speaks to the possibility of squatters or perhaps to residents cutting his forests for lumber, but do not indicate the location of this land aside from a general reference to the Feliciana district.

By June 1804 Smith had become unhappy with the agents running his farm and sought a ruling similar to that of the Kempers' in 1802. In this case, however, Smith took a different legal route by obtaining a "judgment against them from a committee of disinterested neighbors," which would signal both the community's and the government's approbation of the Kempers.[30] The suit listed Nathan and, for the first time, the third brother, Samuel Kemper, as agents for Smith. Such petitions occurred with some regularity in the Feliciana district and in the Spanish Empire and point to one way in which residents regularly obtained justice from local administrators. For example, in the same month John Smith himself had participated in a testimonial against a man named Teaker, who apparently beat his wife to such an extent that neighbors felt obligated to intercede. Also in early 1805, in connection with the Kemper raids, the residents of the Saint Helena district to the east also petitioned Carlos de Grand-Pré to remove Alexander Bookter as alcalde of that district, claiming that he had been a supporter of the Kempers.[31]

Spanish law extended to all inhabitants of the empire, including slaves and Indians, the right to directly petition the king or one of his agents in the New World for redress of grievances.[32] It was for this reason that Spanish subjects in Feliciana neither required nor agitated for a system of judicial review. The right of petition allowed every person access to the highest Spanish official in order to present his or her case. Should the judgment of a local alcalde not bring satisfaction, residents could submit separate petitions to higher officials—in effect allowing for a process of appeal in which the accused and the accuser would supply witnesses and testimony to bolster their cases. With over three hundred years to draw upon, "official members of the judicial bodies of Spanish Louisiana represented an accumulative wealth of experience in colonial administration" that allowed them to mitigate disharmony within the community through a system of hearings and trials.[33] As Derek Kerr concluded after careful examination of available court records, "charges of corruption and inefficiency in the Spanish Courts are more a product of black legend historians than of actual court evidence" in Spanish Louisiana.[34] In many ways this issue becomes two distinct questions: whether there was corruption and/or inefficiency, which most would accept as true of any government at any time, and whether that corruption and/or inefficiency made a difference to the local populace.

In early June 1804, Alexander Stirling, a local alcalde, attempted to expel Nathan Kemper from John Smith's property. The Kempers took the expulsion from the property personally, choosing to fight the eviction notice through force of arms. Nathan Kemper refused to go, prompting Stirling to gather a militia force of about twenty men, who chased Nathan and Samuel Kemper and "four other well-armed companions" into a nearby house.[35] Unable to take the Kemper brothers by force, Stirling and the militia remained in the area in a futile attempt to catch the Kempers as they tried to escape. Within a few days another group of local militia drove Kemper and his gang over the line into Mississippi territory.

On June 16 Nathan Kemper returned to Spanish territory with a vengeance. Appearing at a local home, he accosted longtime resident John Mills. According to a letter sent to Grand-Pré by Mills, Kemper approached the house "armed with a Rifle Gun & long Knife sticking at his breast, a Pistol sticking in the waistband of his Breeches, and a Dager hanging at his side."[36] Kemper accused Mills of "meddling in [Kemper's] business and injuring him" and subjected him to "much abusive language."[37] Kemper's anger found its source in a rumor that Mills had warned residents of Feliciana to stay away from Nathan Kemper in particular and the Kemper residence in general during the unrest, which Nathan took as an insult to his honor.[38] That incident ended without any true violence—only the sort of quasi violence by which one man might try to restore his honor without actually engaging in dangerous activity—and Mills continued to help the Spaniards in their efforts against Kemper's gang.

However, while conducting some prisoners from Bayou Sara to Alexander Stirling's residence three days later, Mills suffered an attack by members of Kemper's gang, who managed to free some prisoners taken earlier by the militia and steal guns from Mills and his men. On June 23 Samuel Kemper and a second man approached Mills at his house, stopping outside the fenced yard. For the previous several days members of the Kemper gang had roved the area at night, stealing guns from residents.[39] Only slightly less well-armed than his brother, Samuel carried two pistols, one cocked and pointed at Mills, while the second man sat on horseback with "a pair of Pistols and a cocked Rifle in his hand."[40] As Samuel Kemper threatened to carry Mills to the mouth of the bayou, Mills pointed "a double Barreled Gun" at Kemper and threatened to kill him if he stepped within the yard.[41] At this point Kemper confirmed the worst fears of the Spaniards—or he simply played on their fears—by claiming to have the protection and blessings of Orleans territorial governor William Claiborne for the entire series of raids. He offered to take Mills to the river to prove the claim. Mills wisely refused. Sitting in the yard, and witness to the exchange, was John Smith.[42] After the incident, in a letter to Surveyor General Pintado indicating that he had had enough of the Kemper brothers, Mills requested to "absent" himself from the area until he could "return home with safety."[43]

Brother Reuben Kemper, operating from New Orleans, wrote to William Claiborne, hoping to influence the outcome of Smith's lawsuit against Nathan.

Claiborne in turn appealed to Grand-Pré through Casa Calvo, who, unaware of the letter from John Mills claiming that American interests in New Orleans supported the Kempers, nonetheless argued to other Spanish officials that the "rebellion" had begun at the behest of American officials in New Orleans. Casa Calvo also discussed with Claiborne the disputed claims of their respective governments in West Florida and the best means of solving the crisis. At Casa Calvo's recommendation, Grand-Pré offered amnesty to the Kempers if they promised to vacate West Florida; the Kempers responded with threats to burn local plantations and incite the slaves to rebellion.[44]

Spanish reaction to the encounters, which the locals termed "raids," was swift, decisive, and indicative of how Spain viewed its relations with resident Anglo-Americans. On June 18 Pintado ordered roving, permanent militia patrols commanded by local planters to detain any suspicious persons carrying firearms.[45] On the twenty-fifth Grand-Pré ordered Pintado to apprehend the "bandits," to "make known to the honored neighbors of Feliciana the murders committed by the Kemper Brothers," and to dissuade the Anglo-Americans, both within the Kemper gang and without, from the "mistaken belief that the American government would protect them." Furthermore, his directive required all inhabitants to work for the "apprehension and destruction of the . . . vagabonds."[46]

Grand-Pré engaged in a two-pronged strategy that reveals a great deal about his attitudes toward and the loyalty of the residents under his jurisdiction. On the one hand, he sought to inform residents of alleged murders committed by the Kemper gang. Moreover, he wanted to be certain that none of the Anglo-Americans in Feliciana thought that American troops would enter the area to assist either the Kempers or the Spaniards. On the other hand, Grand-Pré and Pintado clearly expressed trust in Anglo-American planters by allowing them to lead militia patrols and investing them with the capture of the Kemper gang. At the same time, calling other local, lower-class Anglo-Americans to militia patrols instead of leaving the problem to Spanish troops demonstrated a deep and wide trust in the Anglo-Americans under Spanish jurisdiction.

Despite the belief that American officials in New Orleans had at least encouraged the raids, the Spaniards did not view the raids as a true rebellion. Therefore, Spain never filed formal complaints with U.S. officials. Also, Spanish officials treated the raids not as an Anglo-American–Spanish conflict but rather as simple banditry of the type common in the West Florida frontier. American officials apparently concurred. In a letter to James Madison, Governor Claiborne called it "nothing more than a riot, in which a few uninformed, ignorant men had taken part."[47] Up through late June the violence seemed mostly random, directed not toward any one individual or institution. In fact, rather than a rebellion against the Spanish government, as both Spanish and American historians have tended to classify it, the Kempers' actions during June were nothing more than random thuggery in response to an unfortunate lawsuit. The Kempers, along with their small group of followers, attacked various farms and stole guns, horses, slaves, and anything else they could seize.

In July, as a result of a series of events, the nature of the raids changed from disorganized criminal action to open rebellion against the Spanish government. On July 5 Pintado ordered the group he now called "bandits" taken "dead or alive."[48] Sometime in the course of the next week, a militia patrol led by Pintado chased an unknown number of the gang to the Mississippi line. Rather than allow them to escape, Pintado's men shot and wounded two of the men and took them into Spanish custody.[49] The capture and questioning of these two men, as well as an extensive network of spies in Pinckneyville, Baton Rouge, and Bayou Sara, allowed the Spaniards to compile a list of men involved with the Kempers and to classify them within the community.[50] A list of "El Quadrillo [sic] de Nathan Kemper" (Nathan Kemper's gang), written in late June or early July 1804, breaks the group down into the "Leaders of the Insurgents," "[t]he most determined Contributors," "[t]hose who have confessed," and a group of five men with marginal involvement.[51]

On July 17 two other events occurred that heralded a change in the conflict in West Florida. On a tour of Bayou Sara and Feliciana to assess the situation, Carlos de Grand-Pré issued a thirteen-point proclamation declaring the Kempers state criminals and listing their offenses—including extensive thievery—and disclosing that one of the Kempers' compatriots, Nathan Bradford, had used his father's residence as a base of operations to spy on Spanish officials. Grand-Pré also stated that Samuel Kemper and some men had occupied a neighborhood house against the will of the owner and stayed there overnight. The governor made no mention of the alleged murders but went on to implicate several other men in the actions and to state that Fort Punta Cortada had received a large contingent of reinforcements over the previous few days.[52] Although Grand-Pré's announcement sounds like a straightforward list of criminal charges, the proclamation had broader implications. In declaring Nathan Kemper a criminal, he revoked Kemper's right to conduct business within the Spanish Empire until the matter was resolved within Spain's legal system. Under Spanish law, the edict also allowed for the seizure of any property Kemper's gang might hold in Spanish territory. Unless Nathan Kemper and the other men listed in the notice surrendered to Spanish authorities, their days as subjects of the empire had ended.

Also on July 17—the same day that Pintado conducted the wounded prisoners to a port for transfer out of the area, and the same night Grand-Pré published his notice regarding the Kempers and their "Quadrillo"—two men attempted to burn Pintado's house, although Pintado's slaves and the overseer doused the fire.[53] Pintado attributed this action to attempts to expel vagrants from Bayou Sara as well as to the notice served by Grand-Pré. The next day, in a letter to Folch, Grand-Pré discussed events in Bayou Sara and outlined his plan of containment. By this time the Spaniards could identify the men involved, and Grand-Pré's letter and the list of the "Quadrillo" sheds light on the gang's demographics. Of the thirty-eight men involved with the gang, none were Indians or slaves; all had Anglo-American surnames except one man, the French-surnamed Enrique Sletté.[54] The gang leaders, Nathan and Samuel Kemper, owned property, and by 1804 Nathan possessed at least one 1,000-arpent tract, making him an above-average landowner in the area.

Espionage activities likely placed fathers and son Nathan Bradford and Enrique Bradford and William and Samuel Kirkland in the "most determined" category. The "most determined" group also included a Leonardo Bradford, of unknown relation to Nathan and Enrique. Two other groups of men shared family connections as well. Enrique and George Earnhart and Billy Cobb, Arthur Cobb, and a young boy also named Cobb all shared surnames.[55] Maps from 1799 list William Kirkland as the owner of eight hundred arpents in the Bayou Sara region, and he still owned property in July 1804. His continued land ownership and residence in the area was almost certainly due to his extensive cooperation with the authorities after his capture. Five other men are listed in Grand-Pré's letter to Folch as local property owners. Clearly this was no petit bourgeois rebellion led by landless residents, although Kemper's gang may certainly have attracted such. Instead, there emerges a picture of a band of men drawn from all levels of society, from the landowner Reuben Kemper, who led the raids, to middling landowners like Kirkland, to nonlandowning men who served as farmhands or hired themselves out for other work. Also, there was a strong family component to the gang, with twelve or thirteen of the thirty-eight men related to others in the gang.

Grand-Pré separated the men into "habitantes" and "those who [did] not own homes, nor good wives, nor children in [the] area," terming the latter vagrants.[56] Grand-Pré also listed some men, such as Kirkland and Kemper, as "those who [could not] be called habitants" and those to whom he could not "give this title"—although they owned land.[57] Grand-Pré, a Frenchman for whom Spanish was a second or possibly third language, wrote the document in Spanish, mixing the Spanish *habitantes* and French *habitants* freely. For him the Spanish *habitantes* took on the same social significance as the Spanish *vecinos*—neighbors who are part of the community—rather than simply the definition of someone who happens to own land or a house in the area. Not only did Grand-Pré confiscate the lands of some of Kemper's fellow rebels, but he also demoted them on the social scale by placing them outside the circle of *habitants*. His classification of some members of the gang as *habitants* as opposed to others may have been a tactic to break up the gang by dividing them into classes of insiders and outsiders. Certainly Nathan and Samuel Kemper could never return to their former life in the Feliciana district while Spain continued to rule the territory. On the other hand, for their cooperation William Kirkland and Enrique Bradford received pardons from Grand-Pré. Subsequent to the pardons Grand-Pré ordered that both men could "be called habitants" once again.[58] By the end of 1804 Governor Folch had extended amnesty to all the gang save the Kempers and two others. Those who received amnesty returned to West Florida and resettled their homes.[59]

Here the Spanish use of amnesty as a tool for maintaining order worked quite well. The pardons given to Kirkland and Bradford reestablished their reputations within the community and allowed them to begin farming and earning a living. Status translated into social acceptance in the Spanish and U.S. borderlands. Therefore, when several residents the next year accused Bradford of continuing to harbor anti-Spanish sentiments and chided him for his role in the Kemper raids, Bradford reacted with a petition to Grand-Pré requesting the governor to issue a statement that Bradford had again become a productive and accepted member of the West Florida community. Note the major difference between the Spanish system of maintaining order and dealing with dissent and that of Bertram Wyatt-Brown's southerners. While the Spaniards issued pardons and land grants to bring dissenters back into the community, in Wyatt-Brown's Old South "when dissenters or deviants called into question the premises of the social order, they had to be rendered powerless"—usually through "extermination or public humiliation."[60]

The tactic of issuing pardons for some of the gang, as well as including Anglo-Americans in the local militia rather than using troops from Fort Punta Cortada, was aimed at bringing a fast end to the uprising while retaining Anglo-American loyalty. Because both Grand-Pré and Pintado believed that the Americans in New Orleans had initiated the raids, they must have been concerned about what they believed to be a rebellion spreading throughout the district. When the need arose to reinforce Punta Cortada, Grand-Pré brought in men from outside Feliciana.[61] Yet for operations within the district, Grand-Pré relied wholly on the residents of Feliciana and Baton Rouge. In fact, if Anglo-American discontent with Spanish rule had existed, this would have been the time to express it. Unlike the Anglo-Americans who later filibustered in East Florida, however, those in West Florida in general, and Feliciana in particular, never raised the cry to the American government concerning a lack of Spanish protection, nor did they publicly voice concerns among themselves sufficiently to be documented in the surviving record.

In early July, William Claiborne's father came to Feliciana bearing a U.S. "pardon for all the delinquents of the uprising" should they return to American territory.[62] This, combined with John Mills's earlier letter outlining Samuel Kemper's boast of American backing, must have further confirmed the Spaniards' fears. Although Grand-Pré told Folch that the thought of a pardon for the rebels "frightened many of the inhabitants" and caused the leading residents to present him with a signed "memorial" outlining their commitment to "peace, harmony, and friendship," the possibility that other landowning Anglo-Americans in the area would take up arms must have been on his mind.[63] For Spanish officials this was a troubled and confusing time indeed. But at the same time they took quick and decisive action. Grand-Pré had reinforced the local fort, strengthened local militia patrols, and managed to drive a wedge between the Kempers and their gang through the judicious use of pardons. Meanwhile, the militia had captured several of the bandits and sent them off to trial in Mobile.

For Nathan Kemper victories by the Spanish caused him to again change the nature of the uprising. As a result of the July directives, Nathan and Samuel Kemper crossed the Mississippi line with thirty men on August 7, transforming what had been simple banditry into open political rebellion. First, the gang kidnapped Pintado, John O'Connor, and another local militia captain.[64] They then burned Pintado's house and cotton gin and proceeded to Baton Rouge in an attempt to kidnap Grand-Pré and seize the fort.[65] What on the surface might appear to be purely an act of vengeance was not—though vengeance certainly played some part. This time the Kempers carried a blue and white striped flag containing two stars in a blue field along with a "proclamation of independence." In it they called for the people of West Florida to "throw off the galling yoke of tyranny and become freemen."[66] Edward Randolph, then residing in Pinckneyville as a partner of Daniel Clark, apparently authored the proclamation.[67] His house, according to information received later by William Claiborne, served as the meeting place for Kempers' gang in Pinckneyville.[68] Yet one of Pintado's slaves had warned Grand-Pré, forcing the Kempers and their men to release their hostages in the face of a possible battle with the local militia. The strident language of the proclamation is not all that unusual when placed in the context of the revolutionary period of 1776 through the early 1800s. In a bit of ironic foreshadowing, the *Mississippi Herald and Natchez City Gazette* first published reports of the flag-and-proclamation stage of the raids in the same issue in which it reported Aaron Burr's shooting of Alexander Hamilton.[69]

In that same issue a letter writer noted that had there been U.S. troops at Fort Adams, the Kempers would never have been able to pull off their invasion "of a peaceable neighboring nation." This is an enlightening piece of information. One of the hallmarks of earlier scholarship on the Kempers has been the argument that the lack of a well-staffed fort in Baton Rouge indicates Spain's inability to hold on to its empire. Here the letter writer seemed to indicate that the U.S. fort just north of the border was in similar disarray and that the United States would have helped prevent the Kempers' incursions. Other evidence indicates that there was a longer-term problem. In 1802 U.S. secretary of war Henry Dearborn sent William Claiborne some eight hundred muskets for the garrison at Fort Adams, having been informed that the troops there were completely unarmed.[70] The next month, in response to an assessment of the defenses around Natchez, Dearborn sent an authorization for Claiborne to draw funds for the construction of a blockhouse and a fort, along with specifications regarding dimensions and materials.[71] Had conditions not changed much two years later when the Kemper raids began?

Several men who were caught and questioned by local alcaldes confirmed this shift in the nature of the Kemper raids. Some who had joined the raid later—and were released on a five-hundred-peso good-conduct bond—said that the purpose was to overthrow the government. Others who had been with the Kempers all along noted that at first there had been no specific purpose, but that the Kempers then changed their goal and decided to overthrow the government. One man claimed that at that point he tried to get out of the gang but was afraid. The two-stage nature of the raids argues against the classification of the whole affair as indicative of revolutionary sentiment among the residents. To the dismay of Nathan Kemper, no Feliciana residents joined the rebellion, instead regarding it as no more than a cover for further thievery. Two days later, on August 9, local militia forced Kemper's gang to retreat into Mississippi.

There are any number of reasons that might explain why the supposedly disaffected Anglos did not rise up against the Spanish government when Kemper issued his declaration. Past accounts of the Kemper rebellion have always emphasized the weak Spanish military presence and the high degree of political dissatisfaction among residents. Yet that particular combination was a perfect recipe for a widespread rebellion, which did not occur. Historians have maintained, rather vaguely, that perhaps the time was simply not right, or that Anglos might not have seen a chance for success. Such arguments seem internally inconsistent and improbable. Anglos staffed most of the militia, and most elites held some position of authority in the government. For all intents and purposes there were very few "Spaniards" in Spain's government of Spanish Baton Rouge; Anglo-Americans and a few French held most of the positions of power. Had widespread disaffection existed in combination with a weak military, a takeover could have been effected with relative ease. The possibility exists, too, that residents saw the Kempers as nothing more than a gang of thieves and had no intention of legitimizing their affair by mounting a broad revolt. However, the residents could have revolted against the Spanish government and washed the territory of the Kemper gang if disloyalty had been as widespread as has been maintained previously.

On the other hand, the records point to a very low degree of outwardly manifested hostility toward the government and to a relatively strong military. Did the strong military presence have the effect of muting potential dissent? Again, Anglos commanded most of the militia in the Baton Rouge district, giving power to the very people who might exercise it against the government. In the end we are presented with only a few hard facts: Aside from the Kempers and other filibusters, there was very little expression of dissatisfaction among West Florida residents prior to and during the Kemper raids. The strong military presence, outside of Spanish regulars stationed in West Florida and those marched from Pensacola to put down the filibustering, consisted of a well-armed Anglo-led militia. Finally, the simple fact is that no broad rebellion occurred when one well could have. The simplest explanation is that by 1806, although residents may have had complaints about the forms of their government—in the same ways that residents in American Louisiana complained about the new American government—those complaints had not yet reached a level or intensity that would incite rebellion.

After being chased into Mississippi, Nathan Kemper and his men crossed and recrossed the border during August and September, engaging in horse and cattle thievery. In early September their luck nearly expired when a party of armed men dressed in black crossed into Mississippi, snatched the Kempers from Pinckneyville, beat them, and then put them in a boat and began to take them downriver to Baton Rouge. At the river turn by Pointe Coupee an American force rescued the brothers and arrested the captors, who turned out to be a mix of men from both sides of the line. Grand-Pré, in a series of exchanges with Governor Williams of Mississippi, denied having a hand in the affair and demanded that Williams turn over the Spanish subjects as well as the Kempers. Williams demurred, eventually releasing the Kempers on a promise of good behavior and returning the Spanish subjects to West Florida.[72] The Kemper rebellion as a large-scale operation was at an effective end.

Spanish reaction was not, however. Grand-Pré stepped up militia patrols, garrisoned roads, and blockaded Bayou Sara, hoping to capture Kemper's men and prevent any further uprising.[73] Casa Calvo also requested help from Governor Claiborne in capturing the Kempers' gang. Upon hearing of the initial problems in Baton Rouge, Governor Folch immediately began construction of a military road to connect Baton Rouge and Mobile.[74] Then, hearing of the political rebellion, he led a force of some 150 men to Baton Rouge to help quiet the disturbances. When he arrived in Feliciana in September, the Kempers had long since departed. In late August, Grand-Pré entertained a visitor bearing a signed letter from Nathan Kemper and five other men. In the letter Kemper offered to lay down his arms and cease his criminal activities in exchange for a pardon. In a turnabout from Grand-Pré's earlier offer of amnesty for the rebels, the bearer of the letter, Daniel Clark, suffered a lecture from the governor, who accused both him and the American government of precipitating the entire affair in order to steal West Florida from Spain.[75] Grand-Pré's position makes sense when viewed in the context of disputes over navigation on the Mobile River—hotly contested by Spain and the United States. To some extent Grand-Pré's relative position of power allowed him to issue this rebuke. Kemper and his men had fled the province, and Punta Cortada had received reinforcements. Meanwhile, Grand-Pré could still call on Folch's men, and local Anglo-American planters had demonstrated that they would willingly staff the militias. Also, the nature of the Kempers' crimes had changed drastically since late June. What had been crimes of thievery against individual planters had become crimes of treason against the Spanish Empire.

Grand-Pré's refusal of amnesty sent Reuben Kemper packing for New Providence in the Bahamas—Bowles's old stomping grounds. For whatever reasons, the brothers thought they might find British support for an invasion of West Florida, or at least an English commission and the ability to raise a larger gang. According to rumors they planned to come back in a heavily armed vessel and sail into Lake Ponchartrain. Less clear was their intent. Claiborne's informant claimed that the Kempers had a particular grudge against Grand-Pré, Pintado, and the surveyor Ira Kneeland (the three most directly involved in land surveys) and had no particular fear, by this time, of engaging a combined force of Spanish and American troops and vessels.[76] The rumor of a retreat to New Providence occasioned some panic among Claiborne and American officials in New Orleans, who feared a newly introduced British dimension to the riots. In response to a stern letter from Madison stating that both he and President Jefferson wanted the offenders brought to justice, Claiborne promised both the secretary of state and Casa Calvo—and copied his promise to the new governor of Mississippi, Robert Williams—that he would go to every length to prevent the Kemper gang from returning to U.S. territory.[77] To Madison he downplayed the scope but not the content of the rumors. In effect he told Madison that although he thought that "the people of West Florida [were at the time] discontented" and would rally to any "well organized party" who would "rescue the province from the Dominion of Spain," he did not think that the Kempers could accomplish that goal, and indeed he was not even sure that they had gone to Providence (in fact, they had). Nonetheless, to the secretary of state he reaffirmed his promise, in response to Madison's November letter, that he would strengthen the forts below New Orleans, inform the captain of the revenue cutter on Lake

Ponchartrain to be on the lookout, and do everything he could to prevent anyone in his territory from aiding the Kempers.[78] He also relayed a diplomatic
conundrum to the secretary of state: given that the United States claimed West
Florida as part of the Louisiana Purchase, what were his obligations with regard
to the defense of that province should British troops invade? Claiborne awaited
instructions.

There has been a great deal of historical speculation as to whether the Kempers had the backing or blessings of the U.S. government. Although Spanish
officials certainly believed such was the case, no documents have so far been
discovered that would prove that anyone at the high levels of the U.S. govern
ment knew of the raids beforehand. In 1805 the United States was in the process
of negotiation for the purchase of West Florida for ten million dollars. The idea
that higher-up officials would sponsor or encourage such raids—with the likelihood of getting caught and thereby poisoning the negotiations process—was
unlikely, and as expected Claiborne vehemently denied any U.S. involvement
in letters to Spanish officials.[79] But such action was not, of course, impossible.
Given the lack of documentation, historians will probably never know, although
the two Cobb brothers maintained that they had acted out of their own sense
of "injustice and ill usage they had received from Grandpree" when he had confiscated their property.[80] The confiscation to which the Cobbs refer is unclear,
given that Spanish officials do not list any property as having been confiscated
after the Cobbs became involved in the rebellion.

There are, however, some clues in the reaction of American officials to the
raids. William Claiborne wrote several letters in the latter half of 1804 and
through 1805 to keep Madison apprised of the events in West Florida, and he
included copies of some of his correspondence with Spanish and other American officials. In their communications Jefferson, Madison, and Claiborne seem
as surprised as the Spaniards by the raids—and in fact the raids themselves
seem far too spontaneous to have been planned. During August Claiborne had
received requests from the former Spanish governor of Louisiana, the Marquis
de Casa Calvo (who in 1804 was still living in New Orleans), to order the governor of Mississippi and the relevant officials in other Louisiana parishes to turn
over any members of the Kemper gang who might have found haven in their
provinces.[81]

The greater portion of the gang had by that time retreated to Pinckneyville,
and Claiborne—having just recovered from yellow fever—did in fact write to
Cato West, then-governor of Mississippi, and Julian Poydras, commandant at
Pointe Coupee, asking them to "prevent the Citizens of the Mississippi Territory residing near the line from taking any part in the dispute."[82] He also
promised Casa Calvo that he would investigate Reuben Kemper relative to his

support of the rebellion from New Orleans. Casa Calvo wrote again in September asking Claiborne to give orders to West to "deliver up the bodies of the brothers Kemper, Abraham Baril, a certain Belly & his brother [and the] sons of Arthur Cobb."[83] The marquis maintained that the public order of both countries required it, and he had a good argument. Claiborne demurred, claiming—falsely—that his authority did not allow him to arrest any of those men within the limits of the United States. He did, however, promise to write again to Cato West, asking him to "take such measures as his powers and duties permit[ted]."[84] This was a fairly prudent course of action whether or not American officials had a hand in the raids: wait and see how things played out, neither helping overtly nor arresting the bandits and thereby ending the raids.

By December Claiborne's estimate of the scope of the raids had changed only slightly; he noted that the "Insurgents were few in number, and at no time exceeding thirty." Most, according to Claiborne, had come from West Florida, and any who had not received amnesty remained in Pinckneyville.[85] In April he claimed that most participants were "uninformed, ignorant men" and that the affair had burned itself out rather quickly.[86] By this time the Kemper rebellion was in fact at an end, and the Kempers would steer clear of Baton Rouge and West Florida until after it became a U.S. territory.

What do the Kemper raids mean vis-à-vis the loyalty of West Floridians? Undeniably the Kempers tapped into a vein of discontent that existed in West Florida, and some residents rallied to the Kempers' "cause" and joined their band for whatever personal reasons they might have had. The overwhelming majority of residents, however, did not. Several reasons present themselves. The easiest explanation is that most residents retained enough loyalty to the Spanish Crown that they did not see the raids as a necessary outlet for their grievances. A counterargument could be made that in fact disloyalty was pervasive, but the Spanish might have been too strong, and the Kempers—who after all acted more like cattle thieves than revolutionaries—were simply an inappropriate vehicle for rebellion. Perhaps the opportunity simply did not exist. However, if disloyalty had been as pervasive as historians have suggested in the past, the Kempers could easily have been the spark, rather than the intellectual vanguard, of a wider rebellion. That is, while the Kempers roamed the countryside waving a flag and reciting their declarations, other disaffected residents could easily have seized the moment and organized themselves into an effective force able to surprise the fort's defenders and take control from the Spanish Crown—had they been numerous enough and had the will. However, no such support emerged. Even when the raids became open political rebellion, the residents united to suppress the invaders. In part this resulted from an efficient policy of dividing the rebels among themselves. However, the placement of Anglo-Americans as militia captains and patrollers indicates a broader reciprocal trust between Feliciana residents and government officials. Local officials would repeat this practice even in the coming years.

The Sabine River

By 1805 and 1806 disagreements over the exact western boundaries of the Louisiana Purchase had come to a head, with the Spanish building up forces at Nacogdoches near the Sabine River in late 1805. Some Americans claimed that the purchase had included Texas, and those people clashed with French and Spanish Louisianans fleeing the purchase territory ahead of the incoming American government. The Spanish garrison of 141 men increased its patrols, occasionally crossing the Sabine eastward into American territory—ostensibly on the heels of smugglers and horse thieves. More ominously for West Floridians, on February 5, 1806, a group of armed Americans, unsanctioned by the U.S. government, rode to the Spanish encampments east of the Sabine and demanded that the Spaniards recross the river westward. War seemed inevitable, even though both sides would rather have avoided it. Troops in New Orleans assumed a defensive posture, and the naval commander in that city wrote to the U.S. secretary of the navy communicating his fears that a Spanish military victory on the Sabine would leave New Orleans open to the Spanish. However, in November Gen. James Wilkinson, in command of the Texas troops, offered to withdraw to a place near the Red River in return for a promise by the Spaniards to pull their troops back across the Sabine. This settlement left open a vast "No Man's Land" that would be filled by filibusters and ruffians from both sides of the border.[87] In 1807 the U.S. Army marched toward the Sabine, prompting the Baton Rouge militia to send a force to Texas in response. Although Spain certainly could have fielded an army from Havana or even Mexico, Anglo-American residents of West Florida comprised the majority of that militia, again demonstrating the trust Spain placed in its local subjects.

And on it went for Texans and the western boundaries of Louisiana. In 1806 Spanish troops, acting on orders, arrested Zebulon Pike on suspicion that his expedition intended to scout lands for settlement. In 1810 Father Miguel Hidalgo y Costilla led a widespread revolt in central New Spain that, even though it eventually failed, by 1811 had nearly succeeded in gaining independence for Mexico. Revolts and filibustering continued to plague Texas through the war in 1846.[88]

Aaron Burr's Conspiracy and Later Filibustering

Perhaps one of the most famous filibustering raids, Aaron Burr's conspiracy, occurred within the context of the West Florida controversy of 1805. Global politics, always lurking in the background, came to the fore once again in that year. President Jefferson and the American government had always taken the position that the Louisiana Purchase included West Florida. Meanwhile Jefferson tried to buy the land from Spain. The Spanish Crown, of course, regarded West Florida as a Spanish province and responded to American efforts at acquisition with alarm and suspicion. As relations between the two nations collapsed, an eager Napoleon saw his chance to gain both power and gold for his war-depleted treasury. He offered to mediate the Spanish-American dispute and in return told the American minister to France that he would persuade the Spaniards to sell West Florida and parts of Texas to the United States for ten million dollars—money that would make its way from the Spanish treasury to the French via annual war subsidies. With the United States seemingly on the brink of war with Spain, Jefferson both requested troops in the case of war and asked for the money to purchase the territory. Although Congress gave Jefferson the money he needed to make the purchase, the deal fell through nonetheless, and Spain still controlled the area.

During this time, Aaron Burr plotted to establish a new republic west of the Mississippi. His partner, Gen. James Wilkinson, commanded the troops at New Orleans and maintained a Spanish-sanctioned monopoly on Kentucky tobacco shipped through New Orleans, and Spain had earlier paid him two thousand dollars per year for his help in trying to bring about secession in the American Southwest.[89] However, the admission of Tennessee and Kentucky to the Union in the 1790s had put an end to most scheming in this regard. Nonetheless, Daniel Clark, a voice for creole culture in Louisiana, helped keep talk of secession bubbling with the creation of an organization called the Mexican Association, dedicated to the possible takeover of northern Mexico from Spain. As political trouble between Burr and Jefferson heated up in 1804–5, the former met with Wilkinson in Philadelphia, where they likely discussed the seizure of Texas and northern Mexico. The political confusion surrounding the Kemper raids provided an opportunity for them to implement their plan. Burr tried to obtain British support, but by late 1805 it had become clear to him that none was forthcoming. Undaunted, Burr determined to go ahead with his scheme anyway and had in the meantime, in July 1805, sent a letter to Wilkinson outlining his ideas.

Wilkinson, on the Texas frontier in September dealing with the previously mentioned trouble on the Sabine River, received Burr's letter, made peace with the Spanish commander, and promptly forwarded Burr's letter to President Jefferson, minus the portions that showed his part in Burr's conspiracy. The letter gave Jefferson little choice but to order Burr's arrest on November 27. Wilkinson then proceeded to New Orleans, placed the city under martial law, arrested

Clark's Mexican Association creole dissidents, and then waited to arrest Burr. In the meantime, Burr had arrived in Nashville, Tennessee, gathered some men, and set out for Natchez, Mississippi. In Natchez, Burr learned of the arrest warrant and promptly turned himself in.

The Burr conspiracy, insofar as it might affect West Floridians, had ended. Two effects remained. Along with other filibustering, the Burr conspiracy contributed to an aura of general instability in the borderlands. At the same time, the preponderance of filibustering schemes also muted the significance of any one effort to "liberate" West Florida. Although Spanish officials had to regard any stated attempts to overthrow the Crown with severity, residents and even royal officials could note that without serious discontent among the people living in West Florida the various raids could accomplish little more than to draw the ire of locals.

Filibustering would continue after the Spanish had lost West Florida, beginning with West Floridians themselves, who planned an attack on Spanish-held Mobile in 1810. Further east, in July 1814, Col. George Nixon would lead a series of raids into what remained of Spanish Florida between the Escambia and the Perdido rivers, threatening Pensacola.[90] In that same year Andrew Jackson invaded Spanish Florida, this time capturing Pensacola. In Spanish East Florida in 1817, Gregor MacGregor, a student of Simón Bolívar and a veteran of South American battles, led a raid near Saint Augustine to emancipate slaves and establish a "Republic of Florida." When the United States did not give him official support, he began selling captured slaves to support his expedition and eventually left the province. Within months "Commodore" Luis Aury, a French pirate, again attempted to capture the Saint Augustine area for the "Republic of Mexico." He stated that he would bring liberty and free institutions to East Florida and planned to reward service with land grants. Nonetheless, Aury also engaged in privateering, smuggling, and slave sales. In fact, Aury's base on Amelia Island, near Saint Augustine, served as an illegal entry point for slaves brought to the United States from Africa.[91]

If one measure of the efficiency of a government lies in its reaction to crisis, the Spaniards in Baton Rouge and Feliciana certainly demonstrated both efficiency and a keen understanding of social relations. Furthermore, if one measure of the residents' contentment with the government lies in their response to a crisis, Anglo-Americans in the Feliciana area certainly demonstrated a loyalty that subsequent secondary literature has not recognized. Rather than groups of "Anglo-Americans who resented the fact that they were not included in the transfer at New Orleans, and who showed their dissatisfaction . . . by open disobedience," residents of Feliciana responded by not only ignoring the call to arms presented by the Kemper gang and various other threats but indeed by working to capture the Kempers and support the local government in other ways.[92] Rather than lump the Kempers and their motives in with "many of their neighbors," we instead must look on their actions as an aberration not shared by other Baton Rouge residents during this period, though they certainly represent a common borderlands archetype.[93] During the Kemper raid, rather than an "uncertain militia . . . force of only fifty-six" reluctant to participate in the capture of fellow Anglo-Americans working to overthrow an oppressive government, we instead find Alexander Stirling, whose call for a single patrol on June 23 immediately brought sixty men, exceeding his expectations.[94] In fact, at no time did any Spanish official complain of an inability to muster the local militia to track down members of the Kemper gang, nor did anyone complain of the inability of the militia to meet the threat. If anything, the militia seemed eager to partake in the almost warlike quality of the affair. Stirling's letter spoke of a force ready to storm the Kempers' hideaway and "take [Kempers' men prisoner] or put them to death."[95] The militia force appeared more than willing to join in what must have appeared to them a war writ small.

The various revolutions, criminal activity, and filibustering efforts that plagued the southern tier can and should be viewed as part of a larger pattern of raids that dotted this area from Florida through Texas from 1778 through 1819. Some of the raiders clearly wanted nothing more than a chance to loot, seek revenge against former neighbors, and gain a sort of glory in making unofficial war against Spain. However, others appear to have had a genuine interest in bringing the Floridas and Texas under U.S. control. Still others, like Father Hidalgo in Mexico, worked for independence by revolution.[96] The actions of filibusters lend themselves to two different—but not necessarily contradictory—interpretations. Gwendolyn Hall and others have clearly demonstrated the ways in which the rhetoric of liberty infecting the New World from the 1780s onward made its way into slave consciousness—an argument could be made that this rhetoric also found an outlet in the filibustering raids of 1778 and 1804. In this sense nationalism served as a convenient vehicle for opportunism. Or perhaps the filibusters themselves simply found a convenient cover in the rhetoric for their criminal activities. Witness the "proclamation of independence" brought by the Kempers to West Florida. Clearly intended to induce the residents to revolution, the declaration fell on deaf ears and indeed served mostly to further the Kempers' activities as cattle and slave stealers. The most likely explanation is some combination of the two motives.

However, the seeming disconnect between the Kempers'—and for that matter, James Willing's—rhetoric of independence and their subsequent actions, such as cattle raiding, might help us understand why these raids, for the most part, ended in failure. Residents understood implicitly that whatever the stated intentions of the filibusters, stealing slaves and livestock, burning plantations, and making off with the silver and table linen was an indication of the raiders' true mission. The reaction in West Florida was indicative of how little the American nationalistic sentiment resonated with residents in 1804 and 1805 and how much their loyalty remained with the Spanish government.

Residents may not have identified with the filibustering forces sufficiently to join the raiders' cause and begin an overthrow of Spain's West Florida government. Moreover, the various filibustering activities did not represent a personal threat to their livelihood or their means of profit. It had no effect on land prices, nor did any of the raiders make threats toward the system of slavery by trying to enlist slaves to the cause of rebellion. In this the events in the West Florida borderlands followed the same patterns as elsewhere in the North American borderlands, where studies of Virginia and Georgia have demonstrated the ways in which credit and access to land served as a greater indicator of loyalty than did oppositional military activity. However, during the American Revolution the British government pushed colonists to rebellion in Virginia and the Carolinas not through conquest but instead by offering freedom to slaves who joined the fight against the rebels or through ham-handed attempts to induce Native Americans to support the British cause. In West Florida, despite more than a decade of circum-Caribbean slave revolts, no serious challenge to Anglo-American control over slaves had yet manifested itself. That would soon change.

CHAPTER FIVE

Strains on the System II

Slavery and the Law

By 1806 no serious extension of the slave rebellions that rocked the Caribbean and Virginia had landed on the shores of Spanish West Florida, though rumors frequently circulated in New Orleans. It must have been with no small sense of dread, then, that George de Passau, acting in his role as alcalde, began an investigation into an attempted poisoning. That he was the victim and that some of his slaves stood among the accused could only have heightened his fear. For slave owners poisoning represented one of the most fearful of all forms of slave resistance; unlike armed insurrection, poison was an invisible killer that usually came from the most trusted of house slaves. At the same time, poison bespoke the possibility of a horrible death at the hands of an invisible invader. Two slaves named Nancy and Bill, who belonged to Passau, and another slave named Edmond, belonging to planter Joseph Sharp, immediately confessed to the crime. Those three slaves also implicated another slave, Caesar, who also belonged to Sharp; a slave named Abraham, belonging to planter Elias Beauregard; and a free Negro named Glascoe. Their capture, confessions, and subsequent indictment began a seventeen-month trial that ended in a manner not foreseen by the white man who may or may not have ingested some kind of poison. That a governor of French heritage administered Spanish law in an area peopled mostly with Anglo-Americans makes this particular trial an excellent case study of the application of that law, as well as of the legal culture in a place theoretically administered by what historians have called "lax" Spanish government. Finally, this case represents an ideal test of the proposition in chapter 3 that the law could in some situations apply equally to masters and slaves in the borderlands.

To American, British, and French residents living under Spanish rule, the idea that slaves would receive such a lengthy trial in a capital case in which the accused had confessed might have seemed strange. That Spanish law allowed slaves to testify against and in defense of one another, as well as against Passau, must have been appalling. It is easy to imagine that Americans and Frenchmen in the area were stunned when the Spanish judge eventually acquitted the slaves of attempted murder. The final blow came when the judge assessed Passau, in absentia, court costs for a trial in which his own slaves had been accused of—and actually confessed to—trying to kill him. The trial, like the area surrounding it, existed within the context of a mélange of American, Spanish, and French notions of law and social relations and helps us to understand the dynamics of slavery in a frontier area that was slowly becoming more Americanized. This case also suggests, however obliquely, that historical complaints about lax Spanish rule had less to do with the actual administration than with the enforcement of rules distasteful to the sensibilities of early American writers. This case also highlights the complexities of maintaining two disparate slave systems in two empires sharing a borderland, with one empire expanding, the other contracting.[1]

In fact, from 1805 through 1807 the Baton Rouge area experienced a series of slave trials that could have tested the residents' ability to work within the existing system of slavery. More specifically, a trial in which slaves stood accused of poisoning and possibly fomenting a small rebellion could reveal the ways in which residents had or had not accepted the particular exigencies of the Spanish system. The trial of Joseph Sharp and George de Passau's slaves demonstrated that the legal system could apply to both slaves and masters but also that whites in the area were willing to work within the system as much as possible and to a large degree had accepted the Spanish application of the Siete Partidas in West Florida. The trial also showed the ways in which slaves could manipulate Spanish law to their advantage—even under charges as serious as poisoning. Finally, this trial highlights both master-slave and intraslave relationships in the Spanish frontier-borderlands.

Not much is known about Passau other than he owned land in the Baton Rouge district and served in a variety of official capacities. He came from Pointe Coupee, making him neighbors with the former Indian-slave-owning land magnate Marie Decoux.[2] The attempt on Passau's life was apparently a long time coming. In late October 1806, the day he returned to his Montezuma plantation from militia service—possibly on the Sabine River—George de Passau drank a cup of coffee and retired for the night. Several hours later he awoke with "a swimming head." In response he took a purgative and attempted to go back to sleep, but the sensation continued. A few days later the still-sick Passau left Montezuma for Bayou Fourche to conduct some business and socialize. Passau apparently left without speaking to his slaves and without them speaking to him or giving him any indication that they knew why he was ill. During the course of the next week—after "passing a quantity of Blood downwards"—he felt well again. At the beginning of November, Passau returned to Montezuma from his trip, then left immediately the next morning for the Baton Rouge Society, a social club. He returned that night to tales of an attempted poisoning. Over the course of the next several days, Passau heard rumors from his housekeeper Susan, a free mulatto, that two of his slaves, Nancy and Bill, had been working for two years to try to poison him and had finally succeeded in slipping some "truck" into his coffee the past Saturday evening.[3]

On the sixth of November, Passau, with the help of several other local landowners, arrested Nancy and Bill and a slave named Edmond, owned by local planter Joseph Sharp. Bill and Nancy implicated another local slave named Abraham, and Passau arrested him as well on November 11. And so began one of the most convoluted and telling slave trials in the history of Spanish West Florida. The eighteen-month trial can be broken down into four separate phases and the acquittal. Phase 1 encompasses the *sumaria*—the fact-finding stage of a trial—at Passau's residence; phase 2 involves a *sumaria* by Governor Carlos de Grand-Pré to confirm the testimony of those involved in phase 1; phase 3 consists of an investigation into the conditions at the jail where the court had confined several of the slaves since the end of November 1806; and phase 4 includes more slave testimony, the depositions of several doctors, and a cross-examination of two slaves.[4] In each phase residents were careful, within the boundaries of their particular cultural backgrounds, to extend the fullest rights to the slaves that the law required. Although Spanish law ultimately brought the trial to a conclusion diametrically opposite from that which would likely have occurred on American soil, the process also uncovered a strange tale of adultery and revealed the ways in which both slaves and masters used Spanish law to exact legal revenge for social ills.[5]

Phase 1

In Spanish West Florida, the peculiar American/Spanish understanding and application of the Siete Partidas could work against slaves, as we have seen in chapter 2. For example, in 1807 a South Carolina man on his way through the district with seven of his slaves killed one of them during a whipping. The Spaniards arrested him and put him on trial for murder. He used as his defense that the slave had died in the midst of "routine correction" and that he had not intended to kill the slave. During the course of the trial, as allowed by Spanish law, all of his slaves testified against him, arguing that he was an unduly cruel master well known for beating his slaves excessively. As permitted under Spanish law, the slaves asked the court to take them away from their master, but the judge in the case decided that the slaves would stay with their master and found that the master was not guilty of murder. For an American court this decision would not have been unusual, though the slaves' testimony would have been. Ameri-

Table 4. Timeline up to Poisoning

Date	Event
Up to 1804	Slaves Eve and Bill married
1804–6	Bill takes up with slave Nancy
1804–6	Eve marries slave Ned
1804–6	Eve bears child with white overseer, McCoy
1804–6	Slaves supposedly plot to kill Passau
October 26, 1806	Passau returns to his plantation
Early morning, October 27, 1806	Passau awakens with "swimming head," is sick for next three days
By Saturday, November 6, 1806	Slaves Bill, Nancy, Eve, Edmond arrested

can and British colonial courts frequently used the term "moderate correction" as well as provocation to justify acquittal of masters and to justify abuse as a means of maintaining racial control. This case, however, produced an unusual rationale for the verdict. The judge did not believe the slaves' testimony, he said, because if it were true, then the slaves "surely would have petitioned to leave the man" prior to this incident. The judge, an Anglo-American who had lived under Spanish rule for several decades, might have assumed from his experience with local slaves and Spanish law that the South Carolina slaves would been familiar with Spanish law and have tried to leave their master as soon as they arrived in Spanish territory.[6]

Spanish legal process allowed local alcaldes to conduct the *sumaria* phase of a judicial procedure, although Grand-Pré would also have to conduct the later inquiries and the sentencing. Not only did Passau work within the Spanish legal system when he began his investigation, he was also conducting its most important stage—a phase that "placed the accused at a distinct disadvantage" and that "loomed large in criminal procedure because of the weight accorded to it in subsequent portions of the trial."[7] He gathered four Anglos and one Frenchman to help sort out the events by serving as "witnesses of assistance" in taking the depositions of both the accused slaves and various witnesses. No Spaniards were present for the *sumaria*—as an alcalde, Passau acted within his rights to begin a judicial proceeding. The depositions of Susan, Fanny, and Eve provide us with key information about the attempted murder.

SUSAN

The first witness was the mulatto housekeeper, Susan, and her story furnishes us with the most comprehensive picture of the days leading up to, and the week

Table 5. Timeline of Initial Poisoning

Date	Event
November 6, 1806	George de Passau begins *sumaria*
November 6, 1806	Depositions from Passau, George Crouse, Rachel, George, Fanny, Amos, Nelly
November 7, 1806	Depositions from Eve, Harry, Nicholas; confession from Nancy
November 8, 1806	Nancy recalled; confession from Bill
November 9, 1806	Bill recalled; Edmond confesses after whipping and threat of more
November 11, 1806	Abraham arrested
November 12, 1806	Depositions sent to Grand-Pré
December 23, 1806	Passau gives deposition to Grand-Pré

after, the poisoning.[8] Her story began with a fight among several slaves in a cotton field prior to the poisoning. According to Susan, she and Mr. McCoy, the overseer, were "at Supper together" when she heard "a riot at the negroe cabins." McCoy went to the cabins but "could not make head or tail of the matter, as [the slaves] contradicted one another so much." What the slaves would not tell the white McCoy they confided in Susan the next day. Bill, eventually one of the accused poisoners, had caught his wife, the slave Eve, "with Mr. McCoy." Eve asked Susan to mention the incident only to Passau, but Susan rebuked her for "having been caught with Mr. McCoy," whereupon Eve ran crying to the slave cabins, and a great deal of fighting again commenced. According to hearsay testimony, Eve said, "[Y]ou know not Bill as I do Nelly, he is a d——d Rascal & has been trying in conjugation with Mr. Sharp's negroe Edmond to poison *master* [sic] these two Summers." The next morning, the day before the poisoning, Susan herself heard Eve say to Bill that he was "fond of running to Susan to tell of his catching her with McCoy, he was not so ready to run & inform of his having rec'd [sic] truck from Edmond to poison his Master." Susan noted that Bill made no effort to deny the charge; instead he silently left the house and walked off the plantation grounds. The "truck" was what had caused Passau's illness over the course of the weeklong trip, according to Eve.[9] "Crying with Rage," Eve continued her tirade against Bill, accusing him of attempting to poison Passau in an effort to obtain his freedom and "get back to the States & travel where [Bill] please[d]." The entire incident occurred two days before the poisoning.[10]

A small note in the margin gives us what might have been the genesis of this conflict. Eve and Bill had once been married, but Bill had "discarded" Eve and "taken up with Nancy who had been a sweetheart of Edmond." In the meantime Eve had remarried, this time to a slave of Passau's named Ned. Yet she also was

Table 6. The Major Players: Slaves

Name	Master	Job	Relations with	Implicated in plot?
Nancy	George de Passau	Field hand	Formerly with Edmond, now "taken up with" Bill	Yes
Bill	George de Passau	Field hand	Formerly married to Eve, now "taken up with" Nancy	Yes
Eve	George de Passau	Field hand	Formerly married to Bill, now married to another slave named Ned; also mistress of McCoy, at least one child from union	No
Edmond	Joseph Sharp	Unknown	Formerly with Nancy	Yes
Caesar	Joseph Sharp	Unknown	None known; records suggest he was a competitor for Nancy's affection	Yes
Abraham	Elias Beauregard	Unknown	None known	Yes

"being kept," in the slaves' words, by the overseer, and the two had produced a child. Nancy and some of the other slaves ridiculed Eve for her affair with McCoy, and Bill had gone so far as to "rebuke Eve for having had a white child," but to the other slaves Eve defended their ongoing union as consensual. Yet she still seemed to harbor anger toward her former husband, Bill, possibly for his leaving her and for his later condemnations. The antagonism between Bill, Eve, and Nancy came to a head in late October while Passau was away on militia duty. Eve seemed determined to tell all the slaves, and through them Passau, that Bill had been trying to poison Passau for nearly two years. The next day Passau returned home, drank the coffee, and retired to bed. As noted, he awoke ill that night, and Eve's warnings, and Bill's plans, seemed about to come true. As previously noted, Passau left the following Monday morning without speaking to his slaves and without them speaking to him or giving him any indication that they knew why he was ill.[11]

The witnesses of assistance conducting the *sumaria* rightfully asked Susan why she had told Passau of the plot later rather than earlier. She replied that she had either been engaged in work, was being "scolded" by McCoy, or scolded by her master. She also claimed that Passau had not been around when she would have been able to tell him and added that Nancy had watched her movements while Passau was readying himself to leave after having gotten sick. That none of the slaves—Susan, Eve, Fanny, or any of the others who had overheard the talk of poisoning—spoke to the overseer might at first seem suspicious. Yet the

Table 7. The Major Players: Free People of Color

Name	Location	Job	Relations with	Implicated in plot?
Susan	Passau's plantation	Housekeeper	Possibly a mistress of Passau	No
Glascoe	Road near town	Sold potions/ medicine	None known	Yes

slaves seem to have regarded McCoy as a heavy drinker who became abusive when drunk. At the same time, his liaison with Eve might have caused an even greater level of dislike for him among the slaves than was normally common for overseers. Susan described Bill's behavior during that day as suspicious and out of the ordinary. When Passau returned home from Baton Rouge, Susan told him of the whole affair and complained: "[You hadn't] give[n] me time & you [Passau] were angry all the while you staid."[12]

FANNY

Passau's actions strongly suggest that at first he did not know what to make of Susan's story. That he had been sick was of little doubt. Yet Passau claimed to be genuinely afraid of Bill and "having nobody but a drunken overseer," as he referred to McCoy, "on the plantation to assist [him] in taking Bill," Passau decided to wait until he "could secretly procure further [outside] assistance" before acting. But then the cook, Fanny, appeared in Susan's room complaining that she felt sick with a "swimming head, which affected her eyes with blindness" and was afraid that someone had poisoned her food. Fanny said that she had "seen Bill oftener than usual about the house" and, having heard of the poisoning attempt and the talk in the fields, believed that Bill's accomplice Nancy had poisoned her to have a "better chance of their secret being kept."[13]

The next day she felt better but then became sick again after eating breakfast, experiencing hallucinations, dizziness, and fainting spells. At that point Passau gave her oil and water to drink and "something else which made her puke very violently," administered an enema, and then had her alternately drinking the oil-water combination, receiving enemas, and taking the purgative. But Fanny did not believe that Nancy was capable of poisoning someone "of her own accord." She believed that Bill must have put her up to the deed. Fanny's husband, Amos, corroborated his wife's story and added that he too had become sick that evening with symptoms mirroring those of Fanny, although he had not eaten any stew. He also noted that Bill was "in the habit of going out at nights under pretense of hunting & remain[ed] longer than [was] necessary for

Table 8. The Major Players: Free Whites

Name	Part in plot	Job	Relations with	Pertinent information?
George de Passau	Possibly poisoned	Master of plantation	Possibly Susan	Once whipped Caesar
McCoy	Not directly	Passau's overseer	Produced one child with Eve	Abusive when drunk
George Crouse	Not directly	Passau's former overseer	None known	Testified
Carlos de Grand Pré	Not directly	Governor of territory, judge in trial	None known	Frenchman charged with administering Spanish legal system

that purpose." Because Bill often was not dressed for hunting and frequently returned without any game, the slaves in the area believed that Bill was using the opportunity to meet with Edmond to plot Passau's death. Another slave corroborated the stories of Fanny and Amos and added some hearsay to corroborate Susan's story.[14]

EVE

Along with other slaves, Eve claimed that Edmond had been trying to talk anyone who would listen into poisoning George de Passau, and her testimony begins more than a year before, when Bill had received "truck" from Edmond "for the purpose of sprinkling before the garden gate to poison her master." This use of the poison in a symbolic way provides us with a small glimpse into the world of slave medicine and ritual. Eve refers to Mr. Sharp's Edmond as a "Doctor." Other slaves also referred to Edmond in this way, and when asked why he was called a doctor, Eve notes that Edmond "knew how to kill everybody he had spite against"—an honorific that resulted from a combination of the ability to heal, kill, and perform magic. Nancy mentions in her confession that Edmond and Bill, using "conjuration, were continually trying to destroy" Passau. The slaves clearly believed that the poison could serve multiple purposes: they sprinkled the poison around the plantation grounds to make Passau sick. When that did not seem to work, Nancy spread it in the house to ensure that Passau would walk across it and die—though she never revealed whether she believed it would work via absorption or magic. But failing in that manner, Nancy finally placed the substance in his coffee as a direct poison. The tribunal confiscated what they believed was the substance, which consisted of some items resembling soap and a bottle containing a blue liquid. Several other slaves described the poison as either a whitish powder, ground bark, or some small items wrapped in leaves.[15]

George, a young slave who served as Passau's valet, reported to the *sumaria* that Eve had told him "that every morning before Hornblow Edmond & Bill used to put truck before the gate" to kill Passau, in essence repeating Eve's story. Yet Eve was not the only source of testimony with regard to Edmond's abilities, and Passau's slaves clearly believed that Edmond had the power of magic. While Jane Landers has argued that "no overt practice of *vodun* was recorded in Spanish Florida," this foray into "conjuration" mixed with direct poisoning was an indication of at least some syncretism of science and magic on the part of the slaves. The continuance of some form of vodun in West Florida, with its heavily African population, is consistent with Charles Joyner's argument that it would be found "in areas where slaves were concentrated in large numbers."[16]

Edmond was known to have placed "something in Mad. Henson's yard to make her horse throw" her, and that she "was very sick after." According to Eve, Edmond openly bragged that no master would whip him and no other slave would defy him because of his abilities as a "Doctor." Whether this was true is unknown; however, the slaves believed in Edmond's powers to the point that Bill confessed to having paid Edmond two dollars, a new coat, and two leather straps for the poisonous compound used against Passau—a great deal of money and goods for a slave. Eve claimed in her testimony that through Edmond, Bill tried to poison Passau and then on his own decided to poison Fanny, the cook, and Eve's present husband, Ned. The tribunal never inquired why Bill would want to poison Ned, and there is no record of his ever having been sick, but the witnesses of assistance seemed to accept on the word of the slaves that Edmond was the source of the poison, as well as of the effort to kill Passau.[17]

EDMOND

Mr. Sharp's Edmond presents an enigma. His confession in phase 1 was beaten out of him. Yet his confession was really no confession at all—instead he implicated a blind free Negro named Glascoe and two slaves named Caesar and Abraham. Edmond "confessed" to Caesar having obtained the "truck" and giving "tobacco, Chicken & money" to Glascoe in return for the "truck." Yet he never admitted to selling the poison to Bill or any other slave, although the tribunal clearly assumed such.[18]

But here Passau's tribunal made its first serious legal mistake. Although some historians argue that "torture was commonplace in civil law systems, such as Spanish Louisiana," and the image of the Inquisition certainly brings to mind torture as a means of extracting a confession, in reality the confession "of the defendant usually took the form of a denial, or at least, a declaration in which he gave his version of the story."[19] The court gave Edmond no such chance, as

Passau's tribunal took Edmond's confession for granted and only asked him to fill in some details. Of the three confessions taken during phase 1, Edmond's was the only one in which there was no direct admission of guilt, and Passau did not allow Edmond to explain the circumstances of his involvement in the crime. The four Americans and one Frenchmen instead resorted to a more American method of extracting a slave's confession. In the U.S. South whites readily used torture—the whip—to obtain a confession, especially if there existed the possibility of insurrection.[20] But if Passau and the others suspected an insurrection, however unlikely, why whip only Edmond? Because he was the property of someone else? Were Bill and Nancy spared the whip by their ready confessions? Perhaps.

There does seem to have been a greater impulse behind Passau's resort to the lash. The proceeds of the trial vaguely hint at some past trouble between Passau and Edmond's owner, Joseph Sharp. In Passau's deposition he notes that he saw Sharp on the road back from Baton Rouge after his day at the Baton Rouge Society Club. Sharp invited Passau "to remain & sup at his house: a conduct that appeared very extraordinary because for some time before [Sharp] had behaved toward [Passau] with the greatest coolness," and residents of the area claimed "that Passau was not on friendly terms with . . . Joseph Sharp."[21] They evidently did not like each other and may have had an unknown quarrel. There is also the possibility, suggested in some of the documentary evidence, that Passau had been a competitor for the hand of Sharp's eventual wife. Also, according to most of the slave testimony (which Passau could have gotten prior to convening the *sumaria*), Sharp's Edmond was the source of all the discontent among the slaves, had been offering Passau's slaves a way to obtain their freedom, had apparently spoken openly of killing Passau, and had prompted Bill and Nancy to seek revenge against Passau for whippings they had received. Edmond's actions threatened, at the very least, to disrupt the slave routine on the plantation. At the most Edmond seemed to be trying to incite Passau's slaves to rebellion. Whatever the case, the whipping of Edmond to extract a confession would have its consequences during phase 4 of the trial.

Passau's motivation was unclear. However, his status as an outsider—new to the district from Pointe Coupee and possibly new to the territory as a whole and unaware of either the Spanish system of slave treatment or of the slave mores in Spanish Florida—could be the root of this problem. The involvement of the slave Caesar was suggestive in this regard. Initially the other slaves only implicated Bill, Nancy, and Edmond. But during the course of phase 1, other slaves testified that Caesar had also incited Passau's slaves to murder, and Caesar's motivation for wanting Passau dead is much clearer. According to his later testimony, Caesar encountered Passau at the head of a group of men on a road near Baton Rouge about two months prior to the attempted poisoning. Passau demanded the slave's passport. Caesar, on his way to visit his mother, who had fallen sick at another plantation, replied that "he had been in this country for fourteen years and ha[d] always traveled without it."[22] Nevertheless, Passau and the other men took Caesar "to the plantation of Mr. Duplantier to have him whipped." Duplantier, another Frenchman and longtime resident, was not at home, so the group took Caesar to William Hicky's plantation, where "they gave him twenty-nine lashes" and turned him loose.[23] When he got to the gate of the plantation, Passau and the group grabbed Caesar again and "administered him ten more lashes, [Caesar] not having asked Mr. Hicky for a passport."[24]

Caesar's desire for revenge, then, stemmed from his twofold humiliation. In the first place, he was clearly accustomed to moving around the Baton Rouge area without a passport. He also "had the use of a horse on which he could ride to Baton Rouge two nights in the week." But while the Spanish system of slavery allowed a far greater flexibility in this area than did the French or the American system, this was still a matter of privilege. To have this status for fourteen years implied that Caesar was well trusted not only by Sharp but also by the other planters and the community in general. To then have this privilege called into question and receive a whipping for exercising it would have been a blow to his ego, as well as a violation of customary Spanish law with which Passau might not have been familiar. In the second place, to have the men set him free after the first whipping, only to chase him down and whip him a second time seemed an intentional effort on Passau's part to torture and humiliate the slave. Caesar blamed Passau for his treatment at the hands of the men, and Edmond would have represented a kindred spirit and possible collaborator in a common cause.

Was Passau's mistake due to his unfamiliarity with the social codes of the area? Passau had been a resident for at least two years, so it is unlikely that he either did not know who Caesar was or did not know that some slaves traveled without passes. Edmond traveled extensively at night, and although the records make no mention of a system of passes, he was "in the habit of visiting [Passau's slaves'] cabins til he was once driven off" by Passau.[25] Yet Passau's own slave Bill enjoyed the privilege of nighttime hunting. If the status of these three slaves is any indication, slaves in Spanish Florida enjoyed some measure of freedom to travel, whether with a passport or without. Passau and the men, however, decided that Caesar did not warrant such privilege. Was it because Caesar also belonged to Sharp—and was merely a handy outlet for Passau's dislike—that he suffered the two whippings? Or was the cause of the whipping less complicated—local planters out on the road encountered a slave and decided to have some fun? Did the whippings prompt Caesar to help incite

Passau's slaves to murder? Caesar denied the charge, although Edmond implicated him. In his confession Edmond stated that Caesar "did not use to come
to [Passau's] plantation with malicious designs till he had received the flogging
by [Passau]."[26]

NANCY

The slave Nancy's confession sheds some light on the problem. She told the
tribunal that "after the arrival of the negroes on this plantation & before her
Master had come" to Montezuma from another plantation in Pointe Coupee,
"Edmond had made acquaintance with herself, Bill, and Eve—and that Edmond
mentioned to them that it would good [*sic*] to stop their master from coming."[27]
Nancy further stated that all the accused had at times "sprinkl[ed] certain poi-
sons in the places [Passau] frequented most," and that Nelly had also "obtained
some Truck to put into [Passau's] coffee."[28] Nancy then blamed Edmond for the
entire idea of poisoning Passau. She confessed to spreading a powdered "poison" around the house where Passau walked during the two weeks prior to his
actual sickness. In her most incriminating testimony and most direct evidence
so far of the poisoning, she stated that she herself had sprinkled the powdered
poison into Passau's coffee the night he became sick. She also told the tribunal
that Bill had put additional poison in Passau's coffee the day that Susan told him
about the plot—coffee Passau did not drink because of the warning. She noted,
too, that Caesar only began to attend the meetings between Bill and Edmond
after Caesar had received the whipping at Passau's hands, and that she had also
tried to poison both Fanny, who became ill, and Susan. Finally, Nancy "confess[ed] that Caesar & Edmond were to have waylaid [Passau] as he returned
from the Baton Rouge [Social Club]."[29] They had planned then to leave for U.S.
territory. As evidence of the poisoning, Nancy gave the tribunal "some liquid
in a bottle, some large saline particles . . . & a rag containing a small flat piece
of soap."[30]

Nancy's testimony is instructive for several reasons. She confirmed the statements of several other slaves to the effect that Edmond, Bill, and Caesar were
at the heart of the plot. Nancy also corroborated the notion that Caesar sought
revenge for Passau's whipping. Her confession, unlike Edmond's, did not come
at the prompting of a whip; rather, she talked as freely as a slave could under
those circumstances. She readily admitted her role in the affair and produced
the "murder weapon": a bottle of the poison used against Passau and Fanny and
intended for Susan in order to silence her. However, she accused Eve of trying to
poison Susan, "in order that Eve might succeed to her place" as housekeeper.[31]
This raises the possibility that Eve, to avoid punishment and afraid that her

part in the plot might come to light, decided to inform Passau of the impending attempt on his life. Yet none of the other slaves indicted Eve, and Nancy might have had ulterior motives for accusing Eve—Nancy was, after all, now living with Eve's former husband, Bill. Nevertheless, Nancy's testimony seemed enough to doom her, Bill, Edmond, and Caesar to death for attempted murder of the master. It remained only for the *sumaria* to hear Bill's confession, but Bill did not shed any more light on the case.

The only white man to testify in phase 1, aside from Passau, was George Crouse, former overseer for Passau. He swore that over the course of two years' service he did not have "reason to believe it was through harsh treatment on [Passau's] part to his slaves that occasioned their desire to destroy him."[32] In his deposition Crouse also testified that "with regard to food and clothing [in comparison to] the common run of negroes in the Country," Passau's slaves "were better off" and "had always as much corn as they chose without any stint; and meat twice a week, till they were detected in killing their master's Hogs after which, they had no regular allowance of salt meat given."[33] This hardship represents a violation of Spanish customary law in that depriving slaves of food was not a normal way of punishing them. The remainder of Crouse's testimony dealt with some stolen items from Passau's plantation. Crouse claimed that the slaves used one item, a hoe, to pay Edmond for the poison, and he also believed that Edmond had stolen some leather straps.

It is not clear how, aside from hearsay, Crouse could have known what was used to pay for the poison, but his testimony established two things both for the tribunal and for subsequent Spanish authorities who would review the initial *sumaria*. First, it established that Passau was not an overly cruel master within the bounds of the slave system. The Siete Partidas specifically outlined that a master could not "abuse [a slave] against reason, nor starve him to death."[34] Failure in this regard meant that a slave could lodge a complaint, and if the judge found the master guilty, the court could sell the slave to another master. For Spaniards the purpose of a confession during a *sumaria*, as manifested in northern New Spain, was to allow the accused a chance to proffer "a denial of guilt or an explanation to mitigating circumstances."[35] The circumstances would have to be dire indeed to mitigate attempted murder. George de Passau stood not only to lose Nancy and Bill to the death penalty if the court found them guilty, he might also lose the remainder of his slaves if he were found to have been unduly cruel to them. Crouse's testimony would head off any such talk by protecting Passau from accusations of abuse. However, on a separate level, in his testimony George Crouse sought to establish that Passau's slaves had no reason to want him dead, which would put the blame for initiating the entire affair squarely in the lap of Joseph Sharp's slaves Edmond and Caesar. In a twist on the normal racial basis for testimony, Passau had, in effect, used the testimony of a white man, George Crouse, to enhance and corroborate that of his slaves. And what of the benefit to Crouse? As an overseer he occupied one of the lowest rungs of white society. Testimony to protect Passau would, at a minimum, enhance his job prospects with Passau and other local planters in the coming years.

As a whole, the phase 1 testimony provides us with a unique glimpse into several facets of slave life, social relations, and the legal culture of Spanish Louisiana during the transition period of 1800–1810. At its most basic the initial *sumaria* established the rule of law in the territory and showed that in phase 1, at least, Passau and the other witnesses followed the forms of Spanish legal procedure to a great extent. The depositions established that both Passau and Fanny had been sickened by a substance that Bill and Edmond admitted to having obtained to poison Passau. According to the testimony of every slave, Edmond had procured the poison for Bill and encouraged him to use it. According to both Bill and Nancy, Bill had given the poison to Nancy. Nancy admitted placing the substance in the coffee of Passau and Fanny. Passau and Fanny did indeed become sick, Fanny violently ill over the course of the night, Passau for more than a week. Nancy and Bill, both of whom belonged to Passau, confessed to the crime without enduring any known whipping, although the threat must certainly have been there. Nancy turned over the remainder of the "poison." Edmond confessed only after receiving a dozen lashes. If Passau had whipped Nancy and Bill, Passau would have said so in the records—he noted the whipping of Edmond as a matter of course.

The *sumaria* also shows us an intricate social system among the slaves. Two of the accused, Bill and Nancy, were married, and Nancy and Edmond had at one time been married. Bill and Eve had also been married, and Eve apparently still harbored a great deal of anger toward Bill for his having left her. Although she was married to another slave, Ned, who never appears in the trial records, Eve was "being kept" by the overseer, voluntarily, and the two had produced a child. Coincidentally, Nancy had also been the object of Caesar's affection prior to her marriage to Bill. The reason for Eve's anger toward Bill, and perhaps her shame, then, is very clear. The other slaves' taunting of Eve seems to have led her to reveal—or perhaps manufacture?—Bill's plot to kill Passau and in turn helped implicate Edmond and Caesar.

Yet the testimony of the slaves also reveals a third level: the unstated conflict, yet "well-known" dislike, between Passau and Sharp that may have found an outlet in Passau's dealings with Edmond and Caesar. Indeed, this conflict may have provoked Passau's initial treatment of Caesar that day on the road. Edmond and Caesar, according to the other slaves, were at the heart of the effort to poison Passau and had for some time been stirring up trouble on the plantation. Caesar's motivation is obvious; Edmond's less so. Caesar's whipping by Passau and the questioning of Caesar's status drove his hatred of Passau. The court records mention no direct conflict between Edmond and Passau, but Nancy testified that when the slaves initially moved to Montezuma with Passau, Edmond warned the slaves "that it would be good to stop [Passau] from coming [to Montezuma], and [Edmond] wanted to persuade them to get the other negroes to assist him in the business."[36] The only hint of any prior conflict is a curious statement in Eve's testimony. She notes that "Edmond asked Bill if [Passau] had not flogged [Bill] twice since he had belonged to him. To which [Bill] answered 'yes.' Edmond replied 'He is a good Doctor for that.' "[37] Perhaps Passau had subjected Edmond to the same sort of treatment that Caesar had received. The possibility also exists that among the slaves Passau and his overseers relied heavily on the whip, hence Crouse's testimony. Several of the slaves also testified that Edmond had offered them a way to obtain their freedom, and that Bill and Edmond had talked openly of ways of doing so.[38]

The overall manner in which Passau conducted the *sumaria* hewed fairly close to the formal requirements of a Spanish trial. Passau claimed that at first he searched for another alcalde to serve as chief magistrate and then acted as such himself when nobody else "was then to be found at less than a day's journey."[39] In reality Passau should have brought in another alcalde; presiding as chief magistrate at a trial involving his own slaves would obviously influence the working of the court. Yet he cited the need for urgency as the basis for his decision. Passau called witnesses, and the accused then made their confessions, although Edmond did not make his confession within the strict guidelines of a *sumaria*. Usually the confession occurred during the final stage of a *sumaria*, and that Crouse and Passau gave their depositions after the tribunal took the final confession does not comport with the normal mechanics of a *sumaria*.[40] The tribunal took all the testimony in phase 1, including Passau's account of the events subsequent to the poisoning, packaged the transcript along with the suspected poison, and sent it to Carlos de Grand-Pré. Phase 1 of the trial, the portion of the *sumaria* conducted at George de Passau's plantation, was at an end. Phase 2, to be conducted by the governor in Baton Rouge, was about to begin.

Phase 2

On July 20, 1807, the trial reconvened in Baton Rouge after a delay of nearly eight months, during which time the accused slaves remained in the prison at Fort San Carlos in Baton Rouge. Several factors beyond the control of any of the principal actors contributed to this pause in the trial. In early 1807 U.S. troops from Mississippi marched from Natchez toward the Sabine River, which forms part of the border between Louisiana and Texas.[41] This move required the Baton Rouge militia to mobilize and meet the very real threat that the Americans might turn toward Baton Rouge and attack. The threat was serious. George de Passau, as captain of the militia, along with Vicente Pintado, Grand-Pré, and several resident Americans, would have moved out with the troops. Illness of an unknown type suffered by the governor caused additional delay, from April to June. Finally, the multilingual backgrounds of the participants required the presence of official interpreters, all of whom were either ill, tending crops, or unwilling to travel to Baton Rouge for the trial.[42] More seriously and more ominously, the records list Passau and some of the slave witnesses as absent and give no explanation as to why, or what exactly, "absent" meant.[43] Further, when the governor asked Passau to produce a number of witnesses, he failed to do so.[44]

Nonetheless, the testimony that did occur in phase 2—characterized by a simple confirmation of the statements given during the initial *sumaria*—began and ended within the space of three days. Grand-Pré's tribunal read the previous testimony, which the slaves all confirmed, added a few details, and signed with an "X."[45] Each slave, when asked, confirmed (although untruthfully) that the previous confessions had been given freely and "of [their] own free will[s]," and all agreed that Susan's testimony was an accurate portrayal of the events as they each understood them.[46] The slaves then signed their testimony, which they had not done in phase 1. This phase was an attempt by the governor to resolve some of the problems with Passau's questioning and to ensure that phase 1 had been conducted properly. Other differences in the nature of the questioning stand out from the earlier phase of the trial. Here Grand-Pré required the slaves to state their religion. Among the five slaves, only a slave named George listed himself as Protestant, while the others all professed Catholicism.[47] More importantly, none of those questioned during this phase was among the accused. Passau failed to produce Nancy, Bill, and Abraham as directed, and Grand-Pré never asked to speak with Caesar or Edmond during this phase.

The trial suffered a further interruption when in a letter Passau complained of the "damages which he [would] suffer in case he should be compelled to bring those witnesses at the present time."[48] In September Passau clarified his problems by explaining that if Grand-Pré required Passau to produce his slaves for testimony, their absence would cause him to lose a great portion of his crop, and "as he . . . [had] had the hard luck of losing his last three crops," he asked the court to delay the trial until he could bring in his harvest, and until he "no longer need[ed] their services on his plantation."[49] This delay seems plausible on the face of it, and as Passau himself was not on trial, the Spaniards and Grand-

Pré could not compel him to bring his slaves at a risk to his livelihood. Two months would pass before phase 3 could begin.

Phase 3

The next portion of the trial marked a turning point for Passau and the accused. What before had been a simple effort to gain information with regard to the crime became in November a bureaucratic inquisition into the trial itself. Phase 3 and phase 4 after it simultaneously combine the elements of what U.S. historians have traditionally labeled Spanish inefficiency and what Latin American historians cite as evidence of Spanish attention to the formality of law. As usual the truth is somewhat closer to the center. Phase 3 involved no actual testimony by the slaves, and no component of this portion of the trial brought the defendants closer to a verdict. It began in November 1807, when Elias Beauregard wrote to Carlos de Grand-Pré with a petition for Abraham's release. The petition follows three main lines of reasoning for the release of Abraham.

With regard to the personal well-being of his slave, Beauregard argued that Abraham had remained in prison with the rest of the accused for a total of thirteen months. He then went on to argue that Abraham had "been a prisoner in an unhealthy calaboose . . . in a deplorable state of health, his body swollen and half crazy."[50] With regard to the accusations and the trial itself, Beauregard next cited the lack of a formal accusation against Abraham, the lack of witnesses, and Passau's apparent reluctance to produce the witnesses. He then noted that "at the beginning [Beauregard had] not want[ed] to intervene because [Beauregard] thought that if [Abraham] was guilty he should be punished," but noted, without mentioning his name, that because of Passau's actions Beauregard could see "the way in which the final decision [was] being sidetracked." He also noted that the whole trial and incarceration rested on "a ridiculous pretext of a conspiracy, which as it appear[ed had] no foundation."[51] Finally, Abraham's master made an eloquent plea for Abraham's return on a personal level, arguing that the slave "had always deported himself as [Beauregard's] faithful servant" and had taken care of most work around the plantation, including husbandry, housework, and fieldwork. In Abraham's absence Beauregard had suffered the loss of "much livestock" and had been "compelled to hire another [slave] in [Abraham's] place at the rate of fifteen pesos a month"—a slave "who was not worth one-tenth of [his] negro's services." For all these reasons Beauregard felt compelled to seek Abraham's release and to set the amount of recompense at three thousand pesos.[52]

Some of the problems raised by Beauregard—the lack of formal accusations, the lack of witnesses, and the lack of convictions, as well as the losses suffered by

Table 9. Timeline of Phase 3

Date	Event
September 9, 1807	George de Passau given time to bring in his crops
November 14, 1807	Beauregard petitions Grand-Pré for release of Abraham; Grand-Pré begins investigation into conditions at Baton Rouge jail; Tirado, Garcia, Miraval, Steel, and Mahier testify
November 23, 1807	Abraham testifies
November 30, 1807	Beauregard's petition denied; Glascoe dies; Grand-Pré begins investigation into Glascoe's death

Beauregard as a result of his slave's jailing—simply could not merit an answer by Grand-Pré. Those inconveniences occurred as a normal part of the trial process. However, the conditions at the Baton Rouge jail and Abraham's alleged illness required immediate action. The governor placed Lt. Thomas Estevan, a local landowner of some wealth and a member of the militia, in charge of an investigation into jail conditions with an eye toward examining the sanitary environment of the jail, the quality of the food, and "what ha[d] been the torments . . . to which the said negro ha[d] been subjected." After a great deal of examination and testimony, Estevan concluded that the conditions under which the slaves lived in the Fort San Carlos jail were no better or worse than what the soldiers of the garrison endured and that the other slaves in jail seemed healthy. All received bread, fresh meat, and vegetables, and the manner of imprisonment seemed little more than house arrest.[53]

What then was the source of Abraham's illness? Two doctors testified that Abraham had either a fever common to the Baton Rouge area in late fall—the description and the environment of Baton Rouge suggest malaria—or simple constipation.[54] The variation in diagnosis points to the nature of early nineteenth-century frontier medicine. Nonetheless, Abraham seemed near death, so Grand-Pré took his statement for the court in November 1807, six days after the doctors finished their testimony. Abraham's role in all of this remains unclear. Although Nancy implicated him, she nonetheless failed to define exactly what crime he had committed other than possibly supplying some of the poison. However, Nancy was the only slave to name Abraham as a suspect, although Passau clearly suspected a more-than-trivial role for Beauregard's slave. Abraham, unlike his fellow slaves who had confessed during Passau's *sumaria*, denied any role whatsoever in the attempted poisoning. Although he admitted that he had met Caesar two years previously "while hunting and passing by the plantation of Joseph Sharp," Abraham steadfastly denied supplying any of the slaves with poison.[55] Was Abraham telling the truth? We will never know for sure. He lied during some of the testimony: when asked if he knew why Grand-Pré had imprisoned Edmond and Caesar, Abraham said no.[56] After the three slaves had spent thirteen months in the same small fort, the likelihood that they failed to discuss the nature of their incarceration is low. Also unlikely is the possibility that Abraham could not deduce the reason for the arrest of Caesar and Edmond on his own. Does all of this undermine the remainder of Abraham's statement? Certainly not. However, given the tenuous nature of the evidence so far, Abraham's statement certainly casts further doubt on both the charges and the ability of the court to ever get to the bottom of the case.

By the end of November Grand-Pré had finished his investigation into the jail conditions by denying Beauregard's petition and by concluding that the accusations of unsanitary conditions in the jail were "entirely imaginary."[57] The governor again ordered George de Passau to produce the witnesses, but Passau was in New Orleans.[58] The final component of phase 3 came when Grand-Pré learned that Glascoe, the free Negro also implicated in the conspiracy, had died in the Royal Hospital, requiring another investigation into why Glascoe had died before the court could take his testimony. Testimony from a surgeon claimed simply that Glascoe died because he was an old man.[59] The alleged source of the poison, therefore, died without telling his side of the story.

The investigation into the jail conditions is the sort of bureaucratic exercise for which the Spaniards are usually condemned. Yet for the Spaniards the rule of law was of utmost importance. A problem with the jail conditions required immediate investigation, especially if the conditions threatened the life of one planter's property. Glascoe's death was another interruption that both vexed the governor and caused further investigation into the workings of the trial as well as of how the court could allow Glascoe to die without first taking his testimony. In the end this phase of the trial, then, was less about testimony and establishing guilt or innocence for the slaves and more about maintaining proper legal procedures.

Phase 4

Phase 4 began in February 1808 and involved a two-pronged investigation into the charges. The first part included testimony by three doctors. At the request of the court, Drs. Michael Mahier and Daniel Sayre examined the bottle of alleged poison and the contents of the wrapped leaf earlier surrendered by Nancy. After several experiments, both concluded that the nonliquid poison was nothing more than soap and "common salt," as several of the slaves had argued.[60] The bottle contained a "blue liquid which smelled like camphor" and contained some medicinal mixture of camphor and rum.[61] Both doctors concluded that whatever the bottle contained was not poisonous.

Table 10. Timeline of Phase 4

Date	Event
February 15, 1808	Testimony from Sayre
February 16, 1808	Testimony from Mahier, Goudeau, and Sayre
February 18, 1808	Nancy recants earlier testimony; Susan reaffirms earlier testimony
February 21, 1808	Edmond recants earlier testimony; testimony of Caesar
February 23, 1808	Bill recants earlier testimony
February 26, 1808	Bill and Edmond reinterrogated
March 3, 1808	Court receives notice that Passau has left territory with his slaves
March 7, 1808	Testimony of Sharp; proceedings end
March 8, 1808	Grand-Pré issues judgment; Edmond, Caesar, Abraham, Bill freed, expelled from territory

Grand-Pré and the court next retook the testimony of Nancy, Susan (with no explanation of her sudden appearance in the court), Edmond, Caesar, and Bill. Here the trial finally turned against the still-absent Passau and in favor of the slaves. Nancy recanted her testimony first. The alleged poisoner—having earlier confessed to putting the poison in Passau's coffee—Nancy now retracted her statements in the *sumaria*, saying that she had only admitted to poisoning Passau "on account of jealousy towards her husband Bill."[62] Bill, who in the eyes of the Spaniards was no longer married to Nancy, had caught his current wife, Eve, with the overseer McCoy, perhaps setting in motion this whole chain of events. Nancy also confessed that she had given false testimony to "win the good will of her master," "that all this testimony was the product of her imagination," that she had not placed anything in Passau's coffee, and that none of the other slaves had been involved in any scheme to poison Passau.

Those claims strain credibility. On the one hand, it seems highly likely that no slave would feel safe or would court the "good will of her master" by admitting to attempted murder. Rather than pleasing him, such a confession would likely result in execution. Spanish, French, British, and American slave law all specified the death penalty for attempted murder, and the extent of the plot alleged by Passau, Susan, and Nancy in the *sumaria* bordered on insurrection. Further, jealousy toward her husband might be a good reason to implicate him in the plot and even to pin the attempted murder on him or his wife, Eve. However, Nancy confessed in the *sumaria* to delivering the poison herself—certainly not the way to punish a wayward husband. This would seem to bear consequences completely out of proportion to the possible benefits.

What, then, to make of Nancy's two conflicting depositions? By themselves, perhaps not much. But placed in the context of Edmond, Caesar, and Bill's testimony, Nancy's retraction becomes a bit more understandable. Edmond began by stating that his previous confession had been taken under threat of the whip, and that he had been "warned before hand that he should confess to the charges made against him."[63] In his final deposition Edmond admitted to knowing Bill and that he was married to Nancy, but he denied almost everything else. He had never met with Caesar to exchange poison for goods, never known Glascoe, and never known of any attempted poisoning. The only link between himself, Bill, and Caesar to which Edmond confessed involved the three of them trying to win the affections of Nancy.[64] Rather than involve himself in a plot to kill Passau, Edmond argued, "his conduct toward George de Passau [had] always been proof that he ha[d] never wanted to injure him in the least." Bill noted that he had at times arrested several of Passau's runaway slaves.

The board then recalled Caesar, who recanted all his previous testimony with the excuse of a threatened whipping. Bill did the same and further stated that Passau had forced him—on threat of being whipped to death—to accuse Edmond and Caesar of supplying the poison.[65] Bill had agreed to make such statements, he asserted, because no oath by God would be required—a perceptive claim with regard to the nature of the Spanish legal system's reliance on the unity of God and law. The version of events he related to Grand-Pré was true "by virtue of the oath he ha[d] just taken."[66] Taken together, the testimony of the three slaves represented a complete reversal of their testimony of a year earlier. The depositions so radically contradicted their earlier testimony that the blame for the whole conspiracy shifted from the slaves to Passau himself.

Grand-Pré had several difficult questions before him. Was the conspiracy real, but had Edmond, Bill, and Caesar, possibly knowing the course of the trial via grapevine rumors that had made way their way into the jail, decided to change their stories at an opportune moment by shifting the blame to the one person who had never come to the trial—George de Passau? Was it false, and had Passau invented the whole incident in order to extract revenge for some wrong perpetrated against him by Joseph Sharp? Was the conspiracy false and the result of Nancy's imagination and desire for revenge against her husband? Or was it real, but had come to light because of Eve's desire to exact revenge on her tormentors? The questions would remain unanswered, because in March 1808 the court received notice from Passau's slave Eve that Passau had left the territory with his slaves and belongings, without leaving anyone with power of attorney or selling Montezuma.[67] A few days later Joseph Sharp testified that he did not know Passau's whereabouts, other than that Passau had moved to Mississippi.[68] The legal proceedings came to an end, and the governor set Edmond, Caesar, Abraham, and Bill free, per Spanish law in a case of this sort, but expelled them from the territory—also in accordance with the tradition of Spanish law.[69] Grand-Pré acquitted the remainder of the slaves.

THE VERDICT in this case must have come as a blow to George de Passau, wherever he was. Finding the slaves guilty and executing all of them would have been the prudent course of action, and Passau could normally have counted on just that. Although the drop in sugar production due to the 1803 revolution in Saint Domingue brought commercial expansion and prosperity to Louisiana, the influx of slaves, however illegal, from that island also bespoke a "moral contagion" that might incite other slaves to rebellion.[70] A conspiracy among five slaves and a free man of color seeking to poison a white man should have roused fears of a rebellion and no doubt reminded residents of the 1795 Pointe Coupee rebellion. Executing the slaves and placing their heads on poles in the road, the normal Spanish method of dealing with unrepentant rebels, would have been a sound and justified course of action by a government seeking to maintain control of the slave population. At the same time, American filibustering in the area presented the Spaniards with another problem of control—less than a year separated the attempted poisoning and the Kemper raids. In short, the Spaniards could ill afford trouble of any sort in the Baton Rouge district. But Carlos de Grand-Pré instead acquitted the slaves of all charges. His ruling reflects the dynamic of each level uncovered in phase 1 of the trial.

The method of inquiry during the initial *sumaria* was the governor's primary target, and because the *sumaria* was the most crucial phase of the trial, weakness there would spell disaster for the outcome. Grand-Pré dismissed the declarations of George on another slave—whose testimony the court did not record—as hearsay from Eve. Henry's and Nicolas's testimonies were similarly dismissed as "very weak."[71] In strong language the court condemned Passau for taking such weak confessions based on hearsay.[72] Grand-Pré noted, with some suspicion, that he thought Passau knew of the weakness of the testimony, and for that reason had not "want[ed] anybody else to take them before the tribunal but he himself."[73] Further, Grand Pré stated that Passau's *sumaria* took the first confessions illegally, especially those gained through whipping, stating that "declarations and confessions of slaves given to their own masters should never be true, due to the natural fright which they naturally labor under when in front of their master."[74] He also condemned Passau for "the irregularity of his procedure adopted against the laws, by which he tortured by whipping and threatening those who were supposed to be the guilty parties with more violent whippings so as to obtain from them their declarations and confessions," and that the proceedings were "entirely illegal" because Passau owned many of the slaves under suspicion.[75]

Also, the court noted that instead of bringing Eve to confirm her testimony along with several other slaves, Passau had sold her somewhere in Mississippi—an action the court regarded as "very strange" considering her role as the key witness. Passau had also resisted attempts to allow Susan to confirm her testimony, telling the court that "being free, she had transferred her domicile" to Mississippi, the same state to which Passau eventually fled.[76] This highly irregular action led the court to believe that Passau was trying to avoid giving certain information to the court. Grand-Pré's investigation, then, could not consider the initial *sumaria* as true evidence. This meant that the court would consider as evidence only the depositions agreed to in phases 2 and 4. The former consisted of testimony that Grand-Pré dismissed based on hearsay, while in the latter the accused all declared their innocence.

Grand-Pré's assessment of Eve's role in the affair speaks to the social dynamic among slaves as perceived by the Spaniards. In the governor's judgment, Eve was "the moving force behind the whole complicated conspiracy . . . to which her violent temper . . . drove her" and that the testimony of most of the slaves was based on hearsay from Eve.[77] This last charge Grand-Pré cited as "evidence [of] her determined intention to get revenge upon Bill, Nancy, and Edmond, against whom she [had] made very violent charges as a result of their lewdness."[78] By using the word "lewd," Grand-Pré acknowledged not only the abandonment of Eve by Bill and Bill's subsequent marriage to Nancy, but also Eve's affair with the overseer McCoy. Grand-Pré also noted that Edmond, "the principal [*sic*] in this intrigue, he being smarter and more intelligent than the rest," could trick the other slaves, who had "their superstitions of which those among them who [were] more cunning take advantage as to get some benefit."[79] In short, Edmond's role in the affair was as an instigator who used his intelligence to trick the slaves into paying him for services of which the less gullible would be more skeptical. His designs happened to coincide with Eve's in a manner that neither would have intended.[80]

Finally, as to the poisoning and the poison itself, Grand-Pré accepted that the alleged poison was not harmful and concluded that if Passau's slaves had wanted to poison him, they could have done so at any time during the previous two years—a startling but unsurprising admission that owners lived at the mercy of their slaves. In the end Grand-Pré set the slaves free and expelled them from the territory lest they cause any more trouble. Banishment, a normal part of sentencing, brought with it some implication of guilt on the part of the slaves, but only inasmuch as they disturbed the order of the community. In colonial Latin America banishment served as a common punishment for those who transgressed the moral order of the community, and adultery often resulted in banishment from an area.[81] Such punishment relieved the community of the burden of paying for incarceration as well as of the burden of troubled souls. In this case neither Passau nor Grand-Pré entered any formal charge of adultery, but Grand-Pré expelled Bill, Edmond, Caesar, and Abraham from the

Baton Rouge jurisdiction for what the court perceived as the problem of "too smart slaves not being convenient to have around, they always being the cause of trouble, and especially the Negros Edmond and Bill."[82] As with slave conjurers in South Carolina, Edmond had some power over his fellow slaves due to a combination of his intelligence and their belief in his powers.[83]

Grand-Pré then fined Passau a considerable sum for court costs to cover the expense of the trial and all the expenses incurred during the eighteen-month affair. The various charges included the cost of rations provided to the slaves while in jail, as well as food consumed by Passau during the course of the trial. Also, Passau paid for the sixty-one days of hospitalization for Abraham, the fees for the interpreters and court witnesses, and for various meticulously itemized administrative charges. Perhaps most insultingly the court ordered Passau to remit to all the accused slaves, including Glascoe, posthumously, either 1 peso or 1 real each. Slaves Nelly, Harry, Nicholas, and Eve, as well as George Crouse, the former overseer, also received either a peso or a real for the inconvenience of the trial. An additional group of slaves received 4 pesos or 4 reales each. After reaching a total for all the court costs, Grand-Pré then tacked on an extra 2 pesos for the labor involved in "fastening the chains to the feet of the negroes."[84] The total charges came to 223 pesos, or about the cost of an unskilled teenage slave during this period. Many of the charges seem designed more to punish and humiliate Passau than to recover actual costs.

Scholars have argued that the "fee system" of assessing court costs worked well in the borderlands of New Spain and obviated the need for full-time officials in an area that might see only a few such cases every few years.[85] Although the Baton Rouge district in general did not hold very many trials during this period, Baton Rouge did serve as the administrative center of the region, and in general alcaldes such as Grand-Pré used the fee system as a supplement to their meager government salaries.[86] So on the one hand, somebody had to pay for the trial, and Passau had lost. On the other hand, court costs seem to have served as a reprimand as much as an attempt to recover the cost of the trial. In his acquittal message, Grand-Pré clearly exonerates Sharp and Beauregard and places a great deal of blame for the incident on the several slaves as well as Passau's gullibility.[87] Court costs would serve as punishment to Passau, as well as a warning to other residents not to bring frivolous suits to the court. Put simply, the court costs were a reminder that the rule of Spanish law served the community, while beatings and extracted confessions did not.

The trial itself underscores the importance of the rule of law in Spanish territory. It also indicates the hegemonic sense of the law among Americans, Spanish, and French in the Baton Rouge district. Regardless of what he thought of the merits of the case—or whether he even believed himself to have been poisoned—Passau tried, at least to some extent, to follow the basic limits of the Spanish legal system. The Americans sitting on his tribunal similarly acted within the confines of a system that seemed comfortable to them.

The trial brought out the best and the worst of the Spanish legal system for Americans accustomed to a much speedier system of slave "justice" back in the United States. The governor's tribunal went to great lengths in their effort to gather information and painstakingly assemble the witnesses, interpreters, and principles involved in the case as part of an effort to ensure a fair and just trial. The repeated testing of the poison and the testimony of three doctors as to the nature of the substance attest to this. Likewise the bureaucratic delays, highlighted by an investigation into jail conditions and the nature and reason why a one-hundred-year-old free Negro could have died before the court heard his testimony revealed and continue to symbolize all the frustrations with the Spanish government about which Americans complained. Yet far from the inefficiency of the Spanish system that historians have claimed, the lengthy trial also points to an overbearing need for "super-efficiency" and the strict requirement to satisfy the forms of the law. Although the Spanish legal system, as applied to slavery, could move slowly, it also appeared to apply equally to masters and slaves in Spanish West Florida.

More importantly, however, a white man—and a master, no less—lost a trial against his own and others' slaves. A bizarre occurrence under normal circumstances, the fact that a white man lost a trial of attempted murder by a group of slaves, including his own, sent a clear message to other white residents of Spanish Florida. For the Spanish government the trial was nothing more than another instance of the rule of law working to the benefit of everyone concerned, both blacks and whites. For recently arrived Americans and British expatriates, the trial contradicted everything in their colonial experiences. The trial, in which Spanish law allowed slaves to testify against their own master, not only told resident whites that the Spaniards held the rule of law above all other considerations but also that the racial status of those on trial did not necessarily preclude a fair trial. Yet even here, within the context of slave uprisings, revolts, rebellions, and rumors of such flooding the Caribbean, Baton Rouge residents did not express dissatisfaction with the outcome of this trial or of any similar trials in the area. They left no records of protest either at the time of the verdict or later, at the beginning of the revolution in 1810, when they began to catalog their major grievances with the Spanish system. The system of slave law, even with its predilection for giving slaves the opportunity to appear before the bar with a status almost approaching that of a free person, did not cause significant ideological problems for residents during the Spanish tenure.

CHAPTER SIX

Testing the Bounds of Loyalty

Property and Crime

The period up through 1807 presented West Floridians with a se-
ries of concrete events that could have tested their loyalty to the Spanish Empire.
Filibustering and the potential for slave revolt linked them to the broader U.S.
South and the circum-Caribbean in ways that might not seem either positive
or profitable. Their loyalty weathered those trials in large part because those
tests did not fundamentally challenge the stability of their system. Spain continued to distribute land to immigrants, and residents could expect to profit
from their landholdings and the produce of that land. Yet, despite the residents'
seeming adherence to the forms of Spanish legal culture, after the Louisiana
Purchase and the Kemper raids life began to change in ways that they could
not have foreseen—and in ways that seemed counter to their interests. While
the Kempers had not brought about the revolution that they had hoped for in
1804, they nonetheless set in motion a series of events that would end with the
independence of West Florida in 1810. Records from the period between 1806
and 1810 speak of a growing dissatisfaction among some residents, and a few
of the more recent, although anonymous, arrivals from the United States be
gan to talk of revolution. Yet prominent planters and most residents did not
share this feeling; the revolutionary sentiment expressed in West Florida before
1810 took the form of the occasional anonymous broadside quickly torn down,
replaced by petitions of loyalty. Further, the dissatisfaction did not mirror emigration patterns to any discernible extent.[1] But dissatisfaction there was. For
the most part, residents usually expressed their unhappiness within the context
of solving the district's problems under the aegis of the Spanish governmental
system. Therefore, when several leading West Floridians met first in Feliciana
and then east of Baton Rouge in 1810, it was with the purpose of asserting some
local control over their government while addressing existing grievances and
quieting the seemingly rebellious sentiments among some residents.

The 1810 convention that met on July 26 and 27 did not declare West Florida's
independence from Spain. Nor did it—in the minutes and declarations—have
any stated intention of doing so. Instead the group, consisting of four men from

Feliciana, five men from the Baton Rouge area, four men from Saint Helena to the east, and one man from Tanchipaho and Chifuncté still further east, hoped only to reform the local Spanish administration. Of these fourteen men sent to the 1810 convention by their neighbors, only one bore a Spanish surname, Manuel Lopez, who had probably been sent by the government to keep an eye on the proceedings. The remainder of the men were Anglo-American settlers, including William Barrow, a North Carolinian who had been pro-American since his arrival in 1801.[2] The first act of the convention, after establishing parliamentary rules of procedure, declared its intent to "promote the safety, honor, & happiness of his Majesty's province of West Florida."[3]

Next the delegates listed their grievances, which bear close examination in that they relate directly to many of the problems experienced by residents over the previous five years. The first of the five items dealt with what were actually two problems. The committee complained: "[T]he country is a place of refuge for deserters and fugitives from Justice of the neighboring States & Territories," and at the same time "men of character are prohibited from settling among us."[4] This seemingly simple complaint strikes to the heart of nearly every major social and economic problem in the district between 1805 and 1810. The next day the committee elaborated on the issue of settlement, complaining of residents' inability to obtain titles for new land, indicating that the Spanish government had ceased survey work. Finally, the group reassured the Crown that residents of West Florida had a duty "to lessen as much as possible the burthens of the mother Country, engaged as she [was] at present in a dubious Contest for her own preservation."[5]

The committee members seemed to understand the possible revolutionary implications of their actions. Their resolutions contained not simply their grievances but also statements of loyalty, reminders to the new governor that the meeting had been sanctioned by the Crown, and reassurances that the aim of the meetings was to "promote the safety, honor, and happiness of [that] part of the Dominions of [their] beloved King Ferdinand the seventh."[6] Their professions of loyalty were so profuse and their apparent concern for the fate of the province and the mother country so evident that it is difficult to believe that any but a small minority in this earliest incarnation of the convention had an unstated or hidden inclination toward overthrowing the Crown—especially given that the subsequent revolution would offer the participants ample opportunity to alter the record to make themselves appear to have been pro-American all along. Nonetheless, a specifically anti-Spanish, pro-American group did exist within the convention, mostly sent by Felicianans. The larger group, perhaps understanding that the meetings could be used by disaffected residents as a means of seizing broader power, passed several resolutions calling for militia patrols to help round up suspected disloyal members of the community. Indeed, residents had elected to the convention men who seemed only to desire, as they put it, "some few changes in the system" by at least initially establishing local control under the aegis of the Spanish Crown.[7]

Crime and the West Florida District

Their first complaint—that deserters and fugitives from the United States had taken up residence in Baton Rouge—related directly to the problem of increasing crime and instability in the district.[8] Murders, burglaries, assaults, and arson increased in number and seriousness between 1803 and 1810, destabilizing the region and contributing to a sense that the local government could not offer protections to the residents. Many of the crimes could be traced directly to American fugitives, and some of these fugitives had even induced local slaves to commit crimes—a threat to the social order.

Although few historians have taken up the revealing problem of crime along the northern Spanish borderlands, Derek N. Kerr provides the beginnings of a framework of analysis for discussing crime in the Spanish borderlands by dividing criminal activity into three categories. "Crimes against persons" included mainly assault and murder; "crimes against property" encompassed robbery and arson; "crimes against the public order," a graver activity, could involve anything from rioting to treason to open rebellion.[9] While Kerr has placed both pre- and post-Purchase crime firmly within the context of crime in greater Spanish Louisiana, crime in Spanish West Florida points to the need for a more complex model to accommodate the idea of a surrounded borderlands.[10] In large part this is true because of the porous nature of a border situated on a far-flung periphery.

To understand crime in a borderland community, all three categories should be interpreted within the context of an international border by distinguishing between crimes committed by residents and those crimes that involved either nonresident outsiders or people who had turned themselves into outsiders by fleeing across a border into foreign-occupied territory. In West Florida this meant criminals in the Baton Rouge district moving north into Mississippi or west or south into American-held Louisiana. Crimes involving people moving into foreign territory were a more serious problem in that these fugitives could and usually did escape into an area beyond the reach of Spanish authorities—as had the Kempers. Sometimes this involved Americans either from the Mississippi territory above the thirty-first-degree line or from the Louisiana Territory after 1803. Local residents, too, used the borders as a convenient means of escape, while officials in the United States were understandably unwilling to simply hand over American citizens for trial in Spanish territory. At the same time, Anglo-American West Floridians could complicate the picture by fleeing to American territory and then claiming the protection of the American government *as Americans*. For all these reasons borderland crime created a special type of tension within the surrounded borderlands—much different from that of a port town like New Orleans or the interior lands of Louisiana, but not unlike that of the later Texas and California frontiers.[11]

When the introduction of a surrounded borderland after the Louisiana Purchase created safe havens for criminals, crime in Baton Rouge increased in both scope and severity. This is not to suggest that no crime occurred in West Florida prior to 1803. But the crimes that did occur seemed to be of a less threatening nature than those that came later. In March 1799 local authorities captured David Silvester after what seemed to be an almost comical attempt to rob Fort San Carlos, the main fort in Baton Rouge. Silvester, a farm laborer, broke into the fort in order to steal whatever valuables he could find and was caught almost immediately. His property inventory showed that he owned almost nothing of real worth, and the Spanish government did not even bother trying to attach a monetary value to the buttons, clothing, boots, knives, chalk, and wax that comprised his possessions.[12] Instead, the governor ordered Silvester locked up in the jail pending an investigation.

Similar petty crime typified that which occurred prior to 1803. For example, in October 1802 four inhabitants of Baton Rouge gathered at a local home for a day of drinking grog. Some time after the men had begun drinking, Dr. Matthias Williamson joined them. According to witnesses, a man named Luther Smith began quarreling with Williamson, "calling him dirty puppy, trifling fellow, and in fact a great deal more of such language."[13] After a tense standoff between the two men, Smith took a mug of grog and smashed it into Williamson's face, blackening Williamson's eye and severely cutting his head. After Smith's arrest, the court gathered witnesses to the event, all of whom agreed that while Williamson had entered the house and was "rec'd with friendship," Smith had both instigated the quarrel and had refused to let the matter drop after numerous pleas from other guests.[14] Unfortunately, as with most criminal records in West Florida, these documents contain no record of the outcome.

Other crimes in the pre-1803 period point to the sometimes-violent and perhaps transitory nature of the frontier. The month after Silvester tried to rob the fort, a body washed up on the banks of the Mississippi, on the western side a bit south of the fort. The landowner on whose plantation it had come to rest discovered the body, and the governor sent Dr. Mahier to perform an autopsy. What must have been a short examination revealed that the man had a bullet wound in his chest, and his throat had been slit. The doctor attributed the cause

Table 11. Reported Crimes in West Florida, 1799–1810, by Suspect

	Incidents involving *deserters/"the line"*	Incidents not involving *deserters/"the line"*
Arson	2	0
Assault	1	4
Fighting	1	1
Attempted murder	1	0
Murder	3	0
Robbery	4	2
Total	12	7

of death to the bullet, which had passed through the man's lungs.[15] With more than one thousand miles of frontier river to the north, Baton Rouge would have seen more than its share of detritus washing up on the banks of the rivers, and the trespasser elicited no other official comment or action, other than an order to inter the body on the plantation where it had been discovered. That Spanish officials accorded this murder little attention is unsurprising.

Over the span of the eleven years from 1799 to 1810—the period for which there are reported crimes in West Florida—twelve of the nineteen incidents involved either American deserters or criminals who had fled into American territory to avoid capture.[16] (See table 11.) More problematic for understanding how the purchase would affect the borderlands, only three of the nineteen cases occurred prior to the Louisiana Purchase, which virtually surrounded West Florida with American territory. (See table 12.) Although nineteen crimes may not seem like a large number, the nature of crime and criminal justice in the Spanish borderlands was such that many petty crimes such as fighting and drunkenness went unreported. The crimes that appear in the surviving records are those that tend to threaten the community in some way. Therefore, rising crime in West Florida represents two things: increased criminal activity, and an increased need to turn to Spanish authorities to address the problem. Tables 11 through 13 present a picture of an area where reported crimes increased dramatically after the Louisiana Purchase, with slightly more of them having been committed either by U.S. Army deserters or by people who then fled into American territory. These two groups are an important category because they represent, in different ways, a type of outsider who disturbed the peace of the province.

Occasionally, the outcome of a case appears in the records and, when known, conforms to standard Spanish methods of handling crime in the community. In April 1805 David Stuart accused three local men of breaking into and robbing his house. Employing some detective work, Stuart matched footprints outside

Table 12. Reported Crimes in West Florida by Time Period

	1799–1802	1805–10
Arson	0	2
Assault	0	5
Fighting	2	0
Attempted murder	0	1
Murder	0	3
Robbery	1	5
Total	3	16

his house to those of another man and filed a complaint.[17] After a confession, Grand-Pré sentenced the three accomplices to forty days in the Baton Rouge prison and then expelled them from the territory. This is a significant case, because one of the men owned land in Feliciana—the origination point for the Kemper raids and other local unrest after 1806. As Charles Cutter has noted, the purpose of the law and justice in Spanish America, including the borderland areas, was to maintain harmony and provide for conflict resolution.[18] Thus expulsion of a landowner occurred only rarely in West Florida and usually indicated a history of crime or disruptive behavior in the community that could not be controlled or assuaged through the usual methods of land grants. Spanish officials usually reserved expulsion for transients, the landless, and those without high social standing in the community. It also usually came after one or several witnesses testified to the bad character of the individual. However, during the investigation nobody entered testimony against the man's character, leaving unanswered questions regarding his history in West Florida.[19]

Other crime in West Florida involving only residents and occurring after 1805 sometimes suggests traditional societal roles in flux. In 1809 Andreas Gil, a doctor, beat up Pierre Goudeau, another doctor. Later, Susanne Vaucherez, Gil's wife, appeared at Goudeau's house in tears, begging for mercy for her family. She claimed that criminal action against her husband would ruin her family of seven children, "who would finally be the victims of the bad conduct of their father." Further, the incident had only happened because of her husband's frequent drunkenness and bad behavior.[20] Goudeau immediately sent a note to the governor, withdrawing the charges, but qualified his request by asking that the government fine Gil to reimburse him for income lost while he recovered from his wounds. While it was not uncommon for women in the Latin American world to plead for mercy on their husband's behalf within the courts and to use the safety and security of the family as an excuse for leniency, it was unusual for

Table 13. Crime in West Florida by Suspect and Year

	Deserters/"the line," 1799–1802	Nondeserters, 1799 1802	Deserters/"the line," 1805 10	Nondeserters, 1805–10
Arson	0	0	2	0
Assault	1	1	1	4
Fighting	0	0	0	0
Attempted murder	0	0	0	1
Murder	0	0	3	0
Robbery	0	1	3	2
Total	1	2	9	7

Vaucherez to take the issue up with the accuser rather than the governor. Because of what Jane Landers has called "the intimate nature of [a Spanish legal] tribunal," a personal plea to the governor or the alcalde in charge of investigating the crime would usually have been a more profitable route.[21] At the same time, as a doctor's wife, Vaucherez would normally have enjoyed high status in the Baton Rouge community. Her plea, then, did not reflect what was perceived as the normal actions of upper-class women.[22]

The actions of Gil's wife may have indicated a prior relationship between the two doctors. Or her direct appeal to Goudeau instead of the governor could signal the near-universal distaste with which West Floridians had come to regard the new governor, Carlos De Lassus.[23] Another likely but unprovable possibility lies in the description of Gil's drinking as frequent and his behavior as "notoriously bad."[24] The further allusion to his bad behavior as something known to the community (this latest incident meant that the family would "finally be the victims of the bad conduct of their father") could mean that his previous conduct had already reduced the social status of the family to such an extent that having his wife get involved in the legal process could not possibly lower their standing any further. Whatever the motivation, Susanne Vaucherez's plea represents a reversal from the usual role of middling-class women in Spanish society, where the man was responsible for his wife's actions. On the periphery of empire, with its mix of racial and sociocultural attitudes, such an intervention would not have carried the same social stigma that it might have in the center of empire, but it nonetheless signaled trouble for the Gil family.

Crime and Petit Politics

Other intracommunity disputes found an outlet in criminal activity that generated—and then reflected—long-standing grievances. Of all reported crime between 1785 and 1810, the Mink-Burris case most tellingly brought together many of the features of life in the West Florida borderlands and continued to surface in seemingly unrelated crimes long after the initial dispute had been resolved. The affair began in June 1800, when Alexander Bookter, an alcalde in Saint Helena, held a logrolling at his plantation. Following tradition, he invited his neighbors and served food and alcohol. According to Bookter's testimony, a man named Gabriel Burris showed up, apparently uninvited and in the company of six U.S. Army deserters who lived nearby. A drunken Burris then proceeded to assault several men at the house, including Bookter's cousin, John Mink, and then ranged around the yard drunk. Badly injured but able to escape with the help of some slaves, Mink took refuge in Bookter's house. The motivation for the attack was that Burris believed "himself the best man to fight that God Almighty had yet created and it was his wish to succeed in that business of fighting."[25] In this, Burris followed a backcountry-Virginia tradition of using the brawl to either save face or increase his social status.[26] Bookter arrested Burris, who in the morning apologized profusely for his conduct and blamed the entire incident, unsurprisingly, on rum.[27]

The aftermath of the fight proved more of a flashpoint than the fight itself and symbolizes how some frontier "criminals" represented a more serious threat to the social order of the communities in which they lived. The alcalde Bookter, who portrayed Burris as "a master among black guards" and alleged that the latter had been "brought up amongst Choctaw indians, and will ever act as such," assembled a group of men as character witnesses against Burris.[28] Most described the assailant in unflattering terms and testified to his past misconduct—one man alleged that Burris had lured his thirteen-year-old daughter into the woods for an unspecified liaison. However, one person described Burris as a "good and peaceable man," while another said that he knew "nothing of him good or evil."[29] Burris remained in jail for two years until fifteen neighbors petitioned for his release, arguing that he and his family had suffered enough for his disorderly conduct. That the government did not expel Burris is a sign of his standing among his neighbors.

In the face of the overwhelming evidence that Burris drank too much and fought with his neighbors, the earlier statements in support of his good character seem out of place or even suspect. But when placed in the context of a later incident, this crime and the positive character witnesses shed light on an emerging division among several political factions within the frontier community. In 1805 several residents of Saint Helena petitioned Grand-Pré to remove Bookter from his position as alcalde—the only recorded instance of such a petition in West Florida.[30] The complaint charged that Bookter was a drunkard, had falsely accused the residents in his district of harboring disloyal sentiments toward the government, and, most seriously, of having conspired with the Kemper brothers to overthrow the Spanish government. Fifty-one signatures appeared on a petition from the Saint Helena district forwarded to Grand-Pré, whose investigation revealed that at least some of the signatures had been forged in an effort to depose Bookter as alcalde.[31] Additionally, several of the signatories had not read the petition but had asked other men to sign their names at the request of friends and relatives.

In a rambling reply that included not only a defense of his own character but also complaints about local Indians supplying him with rum, Bookter professed his loyalty to the government and expressed his surprise that anybody in the district would want to see him lose his position. Bookter should not have been surprised at the complaint, however. Several of the men involved with the anti-Bookter petition had also signed the earlier petition to get Burris out of jail, and another had signed both petitions and then testified on behalf of Burris in the earlier case. Still another had signed the petition because he believed that the alcalde Bookter was collecting fees not due an alcalde.[32] In this case the petition served as a convenient and safe vehicle for many personal grievances against the office of the alcalde, as well as against the person himself.

Another alcalde, William Bell, testified that he had not signed the petition against Bookter but had asked another to do so for him. He was also aware of the charges and alleged that a friend of Bookter, captain of the militia and alcalde Michael Jones, had also spread false rumors of residents' disloyalty during the Kemper affair.[33] Two year later, in 1807, Bell called on Grand-Pré to mediate yet another related dispute in which Jones ordered a small company of militia to break into Bell's home to retrieve a runaway slave who had turned himself in to the Spanish. The master, living in New Orleans, had not come to claim his property over the span of several weeks. Jones's motivation for the raid seems to have been revenge for a long-simmering dispute involving the various factions in the Saint Helena district.[34] The petition to remove Bookter, then, was less about Alexander Bookter and his accusations of disloyalty than it was about interpersonal frontier politics that happened to involve the man. Grand-Pré, perhaps sensing the potential for conflict, removed Alexander Bookter from his position as alcalde, a serious loss of honor.[35]

Nonetheless, in 1809 Bookter remained in the district and ran a tavern where neighbors gathered to drink and eat and that also served as an inn for travelers. According to one witness, in November of that year Jacob Byers entered Bookter's house. The two exchanged "a few offensive words," after which Bookter called Byers "a liar and a thief." Bookter also claimed that Byers owed him money, asked him to leave the house, and then struck him in the face. Byers did leave, but with Bookter in pursuit and carrying a chair. Outside in the yard

Alexander Bookter began to hit Byers with the chair, causing Byers to flee. When Bookter threw the chair at Byers, Byers retrieved it and advanced on the former alcalde, who went into his house, "got a rifle and threatened to shoot him." Byers dropped the chair and ran off to file a report with the governor. That and other reports contained a litany of complaints against Bookter, including several past incidents of fighting and unpaid fines stemming from assaults on residents, and residents complained of being afraid of the man.[36]

In a sense Bookter symbolizes in West Florida what Bertram Wyatt-Brown discusses in terms of upholding the Southern sense of *communitas* through the use of violence. Both Wyatt-Brown's U.S. southerners and West Florida borderlands residents acted in many of the same ways to maintain "the balance wheel of race, order, and rank."[37] However, the Spanish system of justice, of course, diverged from the model put forth by Wyatt-Brown. As noted, Spaniards tended to deal with serious troublemakers—such as filibusters and the potentially treasonous—by issuing pardons and land grants. Alexander Bookter and many other Americans in the district seem to present a foreshadowing of Wyatt-Brown's Old South. However, nothing in the application of violence as a way of recovering honor in West Florida speaks to the issue of class or education. Instead, serious violence in the West Florida borderlands was either brought about by outsiders from the United States and its territories, or involved people who used the U.S.-Spanish border as a means of evading justice. At the same time, a growing number of people—including Alexander Bookter—who had migrated into West Florida had begun to take the law into their own hands in their attempts to solve personal disputes, supporting the idea that the growing problem of crime in the area and the Spanish government's inability to handle that problem had begun to contribute to a growing uneasiness over Spain's ability to govern its empire.

Deserters

If local officials recognized that Alexander Bookter had been involved in previous fights and that he seemed to be a locus of disturbance in West Florida, then the crimes committed on the West Florida frontier that involved deserters from the U.S. Army and Navy, as well as those who fled over "the line," caused even more concern among residents. Unfortunately these deserters provide few records regarding their background, leaving the question open as to whether their crimes reflected their status as fugitives from the U.S. military, or whether their status as fugitives reflected some criminal background. Demographically most deserters in this area came from the U.S. military, and much of the U.S. military stationed in Louisiana and Mississippi had been recruited in Georgia, Tennessee, and especially Virginia.[38] However, another pool of potential deserters also presents itself: naval deserters. For example, while trying to dock at the port of New Orleans with prize ships in tow, the pirate Jean Lafitte reported that eighteen or nineteen men had deserted ship. Several of the deserters were people of color from Saint Domingue, which points to the Spanish borderlands as a haven for criminals of varying types and to the diversity in the makeup of deserters in West Florida.[39] Thus while many in West Florida were fugitives from the U.S. Army—and therefore of a familiar national background and perhaps common state to many residents—others such as those from Lafitte's ship *La Seur Cherie* came from more alien and threatening environments. For West Floridians deserters embodied some of the tensions in the borderlands, and residents approached the problem of how to treat these refugees with uncertainty.

On the one hand, many deserters lived as a kind of "resident alien," serving as hired hands on local farms or working as laborers in the trades. This group lived in the district with the written permission of the governor and hired themselves out to residents either by the task, by the day, or by the month.[40] Day labor and task labor (for example, chopping a cord of wood) were fairly common. Monthly labor occurred less frequently, although it did exist. Unable to own land and subject to recapture at any time, U.S. deserters were a kind of necessary evil in that they allowed those who could not, or did not, own slaves to hire farmhands. In fact, U.S. attempts to recapture deserters by sending armed parties into West Florida met with a strong rebuke from Grand-Pré, who resented both the armed incursion as well as the kidnapping of men on Spanish soil with the governor's permission.[41] If U.S. forces captured deserters, or if they turned themselves in or were turned in for a reward, prisoners could expect to receive up to five sets of fifty lashes "with wired cats," hard labor shackled to a ball and chain for up to a year, an extension of their enlistment for the time away from post, and to "reimburse the U.S. all expenses incurred by the desertion."[42]

This meant that, on the other hand, a great number of deserters lived in the district without the permission of the Spanish government, trying at all costs to avoid return to U.S. territory. These men took up residence on farms and plantations, sometimes with the permission of the owners—sometimes not—and worked many of the same types of jobs as the "resident alien" deserters. The only thing that separated the two groups was their status with regard to the Crown. However, a third category of deserter existed. This group might be called the "transitory deserters," or those who did not live in Spanish West Florida. Because this group lived in the Spanish- and American-held territories in and around West Florida but came into Spanish West Florida to trade and work, their numbers are also impossible to gauge.

These groups placed Spanish Florida in a unique position with regard to the New World borderland–frontier areas. This was the only settled European borderland surrounded by another major power, the United States. For the two countries and their inhabitants, this presented a unique situation. Unlike the western borderlands of the United States or the northwestern borderlands of New Spain with its steadily weakening Indian tribes, Florida gave the citizens and subjects of both powers an "escape valve" into the territory of another European nation. Criminals from the Spanish borderlands could escape into U.S. territory, while criminals from the United States could move into Spanish territory. Each would enjoy the unstated but unassailable protections of governments more interested in asserting control over their borders than in catching criminals. Simply by its location and the fact of its existence, the borderland-frontier area contributed to the instability of both countries' border areas.

The reported crimes committed by these men followed several patterns, and in many cases it is difficult to determine the true nature of those crimes. For example, many of the reports contained an antigovernment element. In one case Joash Miller had knowingly hired John Herbert as a monthly laborer, despite knowing that Herbert was a deserter and in the country illegally.[43] According to two witnesses, Herbert was eating supper on Miller's plantation when the foreman "ordered the wench to clear of[f] the empty dishes and plates." Herbert began arguing with the foreman and threatened to kill the woman if she cleared the table. He then flew into a rage, broke a bowl, several dishes, and a table, "broke open the store Room containing all the Groceries," including the liquor, beat up the foreman, tore down a wall, and then wandered off to a back room to drink.[44] When Miller returned and ordered Herbert off the property, the latter refused to go. After another exchange of insults, Herbert tried to attack Miller, who responded with a pistol shot that missed. The two fought until several men dragged Herbert from the plantation.

In his testimony Miller claimed that Herbert refused to leave when ordered off the plantation and said "he would go when it suited him, and not before, [Herbert then] damn'd [Miller], Government, Governor, the officers."[45] If true, damning the government and the governor would possibly bring additional charges. However, the likelihood also exists that Miller simply wanted to focus the governor's attention by playing on fears of rebellion and so padded his testimony with a false, but believable, accusation. After all, residents alleged that other deserters had made antigovernment speeches and declarations, and other witnesses called Herbert a "quarrelsome, rangling, riotness [sic] man, and abusive & cruel."[46] The uncertain loyalties of American deserters, especially those in the country illegally, fueled suspicion on the part of residents and lent credence to accusations that deserters and fugitives lay at the heart of the region's instability.

In 1808 John Collins, a deserter, helped three slaves burn and rob a plantation and then cover up the crime.[47] Further complicating the affair, one of the slaves had been trying for some time to buy a shotgun from another slave so that he could escape and take up life as a sort of highwayman, living in "the hills . . . wait[ing] for those traveling around there and kill them." The slave planned to use the money to go to Cincinnati and freedom.[48] All the slaves placed the deserter Collins at the scene of the crime and said that he had been paid to keep quiet. Collins may have actually been involved in the crime, or he might have been a convenient scapegoat for the slaves. In either case, the idea that slaves would pay a white man to keep quiet about a crime as great as arson (with the possibility of murder as well) speaks to the place of deserters and lower-class whites in a society where race—as noted earlier—was already so fluid. Aside from the spectacle of slaves selling guns to one another, that slaves on the borderlands by 1808 already associated the northern portions of the United States with freedom should cause scholars to rethink the relationship between slavery in the borderlands and slavery in the United States. Amazingly, Cupid, according to his own testimony, also owned two millstones. That slaves in the Spanish Empire owned guns was not unusual.

More importantly, though, the connection between John Ellis and the American deserter was what made this crime so serious for Spanish officials. Ellis had for some time been under suspicion of disloyalty, and during the depositions several witnesses declared that Ellis had bragged that he was going to overthrow the government, go to Baton Rouge, "sword in hand, thrust it through the body of the governor and send him to hell, together with all his officials."[49] Another witness added that Ellis had had discussions with an American, through George de Passau, "concerning the indefensible state of the fort and the means of overtaking it."[50] Officials included in the testimony a letter of now-unknown content from Reuben Kemper to Ellis. What had begun as a simple case of arson and robbery involving several slaves and an American deserter had suddenly become the seeds of an insurrectionary plot. But several residents testified that Ellis had neither the ability nor the local support to begin a revolution, and so in the interest of maintaining peace in the community Spanish officials accepted his pleas of innocence. Ellis's threats, however, further contributed to a growing atmosphere of instability in a region that was unstable anyway, and in a place where criminals of all types could regularly flee "above the line" to Mississippi. The threat and rumor of such was enough to help destabilize the region.

"The Line"

That thirty-first-degree mark served as both an unfortunate barrier to the Spaniards' ability to maintain order in the borderlands and a convenient means of escape for frontier criminals. The Kempers had repeatedly used "the line," as residents called it, to evade capture. Other criminals moved across the border with ease—as had Daniel Waltman when he stole some pigs in 1803—and the territorial governors of Mississippi and American Louisiana assisted them by refusing to extradite a single criminal back to West Florida between 1795 and 1810, rendering thirty-one degrees north latitude a marker for criminals and a wall for officials.[51] From time to time, officials on both sides stole into foreign territory and removed criminals. However, U.S. officials reacted swiftly when their own men did this, as when the secretary of the navy ordered Commander David Porter to return a man forcibly taken from Spanish territory by a U.S. naval officer.[52] A lack of official sanction, though necessary, forced people on both sides to resort to extralegal means of recovering criminals through petit invasions by armed parties.

For example, in June 1808 Spaniard José Bernardo de Revie landed his pirogue and several sailors on the banks of Spanish-held Bayou Manchac to get supper at a local inn run by George Mars. Unable to get food, the group nonetheless found that William Blount, a criminal, was hiding in the house.[53] Blount left the house, crossed over to the American side, and alerted his brother to the possibility of trouble. The brothers and several other men—now armed—watched Spanish officials from the other side of the Bayou, firing insults for half an hour before Revie's men went to Pintado's plantation to report the encounter.[54] Blount's men then spent the evening and next morning moving back and forth between U.S. and Spanish territory in an attempt to locate Revie and his party, who themselves were moving between territories looking for the fugitives. In this way Blount's group was able to evade capture and enjoy the implicit protection of U.S. law. At the same time, however, Revie, an official of the Spanish government, was leading armed men into the territory of a foreign power.

Blount's crime was the attempted murder of John Ross, a prominent resident of Baton Rouge. As noted in tables 11 through 13, the records contain no reports of murder until the 1805–10 period, and deserters and transients account for the three that then did occur. This highlights a greater problem for the social order of the Spanish community when criminals used "the line" to evade capture for crimes against prominent citizens. In a spectacular episode in 1805, for example, William Flanegan murdered Joseph Sharp, a local schoolteacher, while the latter was eating breakfast in the home of a man named Peter Lawrence.[55] Flanegan, who had shared the meal, rose suddenly, grabbed his gun, and accused Sharp of spreading rumors about Flanegan's brother.[56] At the same moment Flanegan fired, Lawrence's wife and young son grabbed the gun, causing the ball to miss. Sharp ran out of the house, followed by Flanegan, who by this time had reloaded his rifle and was carrying an axe. A struggle ensued between the wife and Flanegan, who eventually chased Sharp around the house and shot the schoolteacher in the back, then again grabbed the axe and advanced. Another scuffle ensued between Lawrence's son and Flanegan, during which Flanegan cried, "May God damn my soul if I don't split your Brains out" and then ran off.[57]

Witnesses carried Sharp back to his plantation, where a doctor examined him and pronounced the wound mortal. The ball had entered his back to the left side of his spine below the kidney, passed through his intestines, and had lodged near the navel—close enough for the doctor to feel it through the skin. Sharp related his version of the events to the doctor and then expressed his wish that "the Perpetrator be prosecuted, as he had ungratefully used against him the same powder which a few days before he had lent him." Unfortunately for the authorities, Flanegan, his brother, and his sons had already begun to sell their holdings and then had "gone above the line" into Mississippi territory, from which the U.S. government refused extradition.[58] The Spanish government responded in the only way possible—by auctioning off the remainder of their property to pay for the expense of investigating the case.

The method of Joseph Sharp's murder made it an ugly crime in the eyes of the residents, but it also represented something more. Sharp came from a prominent family and enjoyed extensive connections within the West Florida community. In testimony many witnesses described knowing the Sharps almost immediately upon entering the territory. His father, uncles, and grandfather owned large holdings in Bayou Manchac, the more established section of the district. The Sharp family was among the first European settlers in Spanish West Florida and served in the militia and in various other official capacities. Moreover, as a schoolteacher, Joseph Sharp taught not only the children of wealthy planters but in many instances had helped educate the planters themselves. As with the earlier attempted murder of John Ross, the killing of Joseph Sharp contained an element of conflict between the newer, less established families and the older, wealthier residents. Although the records admit of no explicit pattern of class conflict in an economic sense, Sharp's access to, and position within, the Spanish governmental structure would have made whatever "false reports" he had supposedly passed around far more damaging than "reports" circulated by someone of lesser standing. Moreover, if the fact of his murder was bad, the style of the murder—an axe-wielding, maniacal Flanegan chasing Sharp around the house and then shooting him in the back—was worse. Compounding the problem, Flanegan and his family had gone to Mississippi after having quickly sold most of their property in West Florida.[59]

That pattern of criminals moving with seeming impunity from one side of the line to the other, able to evade justice, had two effects. On the one hand, it contributed to the sense that the Spanish government could not uphold the law in the West Florida borderlands—not through any fault in the Spanish system but rather through the fault of its existence in a surrounded borderland-frontier occupying the space between two nations. On the other hand, this criminal activity also contributed to the impression that crime came from the outside and may have fostered a sense of isolation among residents. Here the nature of the crimes was the problem, not so much the legal system or the way that officials administered justice if they could capture the fugitives. The real problem lay in the fact that while outsiders committed many of the worst crimes, residents could also, in effect, become outsiders by simply moving fifty miles north, south, or west, rendering the Spanish government powerless to follow. This created a fluid definition of political location for West Floridians—and for U.S. citizens in the nearby borderlands. Finally, the ability of criminals to flee into the United States, leaving behind property, created a disaffected group with an interest in removing the Spanish government in order to recover property. As a result the various crimes attributed to a few of the deserters—and the violence that accompanied those crimes—caused the residents to lump all deserters together into a larger class of undesirables in their convention declaration.

The Problem of Land

Two of the other complaints levied by the 1810 convention—that "men of character [were] prohibited from settling among [them]," along with the difficulties residents had begun to encounter in obtaining new land—derived from a single problem. After 1804 the Spanish government tightened land policies with regard to foreigners, making it more difficult for immigrants from the United States to obtain land. Meanwhile, through what the records suggest was an intentional policy, officials began to delay new surveys for local residents. In this sense, ironically, the Kemper raid and rebellion achieved its goal—but not in any way the Kempers could have foreseen. Instead, the Kemper raid and subsequent rebellion brought about a shift in relations between Spanish officials and Feliciana residents because of subsequent changes in land policy.

In the early years of settlement letters between Pintado and his Anglo-American surveyors reveal a cheerful and close, even humorous interaction. One surveyor titled his letters "In the Woods" and "Somewhere in the Wild," despite living less than a day's ride from Baton Rouge.[60] Pintado procured supplies for his assistants and for settlers, lent money, settled disputes, and acted as a chief constable in his role as alcalde. In June 1803 another surveyor wrote Pintado to borrow twenty dollars and thank him for some potatoes; other planters and assistant surveyors did the same regarding money and supplies.[61] Pintado fielded requests for everything from biscuits to beef, sugar, coffee, and rum to distribute as rations.

From 1805 onward, however, as residents engaged in lawsuits over property boundaries, surveyors found themselves dragged into, and the subject of, legal proceedings. What had once been a system of fairly peaceful coexistence and harmony between residents and government officials had become an adversarial relationship. Seemingly gone were the days of interpersonal relationships between Pintado, his surveyors, and local residents. Ira Kneeland, one of Pintado's most-used surveyors, spoke of none of the moneylending and procurement of supplies that his predecessors had enjoyed. Instead, after 1805 he spoke of clashes and disagreements with settlers already in the area, as well as with those wishing to immigrate to Feliciana.

One possible explanation for this lies in the aftereffects of the Kempers' actions and the mutual distrust it might have engendered. The real issue, however, was likely a change in the enforcement of land surveying and distribution policies in Feliciana district and the residents' reaction to that change. What was before the raid a system of fairly relaxed grants and surveying became in November 1804 a policy designed to slow down the distribution of land when Governor Vicente Folch decreed that Americans could not sell their land holdings in West Florida unless they had settled and cultivated the land for ten years. This represented a six-year extension of the normal four-year waiting period imposed by Spanish law.[62] A December 19, 1804, notice of land transfer is the earliest mention in West Florida official records of a suspension of land grants for Anglo-American immigrants there.[63] And on March 5, 1805, Pintado wrote to one of his surveyors, Christopher Bolling, forbidding him from completing any surveys without Pintado's express written consent. He also prohibited Bolling from making any preliminary survey marks and from promising to undertake surveys for anyone, local or otherwise. He also rather ominously threatened to "take any steps necessary to prevent it." Six days later he reiterated his orders.[64] This represented a sharp departure from the earlier system in which established planters could make their own surveys and simply have them confirmed by one of Pintado's men.

Whether Pintado acted unilaterally is unknown but unlikely. Spanish officials of Pintado's station who took individual action in interpreting colonial orders or policies could expect harsh consequences. Someone at Pintado's level could not carry out a policy of *obedezco pero no cumplo* without severe repercussions. More likely is that Grand-Pré simply required Pintado to attempt to slow and more closely regulate but not necessarily halt Anglo-American settlement in the disputed area of West Florida. Assistant surveyor Ira Kneeland's letters to Pintado began in early 1805 and ran throughout the year. From his first note in March and continuing to August, he constantly complained of a lack of equipment and materials to properly complete surveys. The lack of equipment could have been due to the remoteness of government supplies in relation to the frontier. Yet Kneeland's tone indicates his belief that Pintado deliberately withheld survey apparatus. Some of Kneeland's suspicion and frustration stemmed from the fact that he could not complete surveys in several areas because for eight months Pintado had delayed sending him a general map listing all the properties, which would allow him to divide new lands with accuracy.[65]

The problem became so severe that by the end of August Ira Kneeland spoke of a backlog of 150 survey orders and wrote to Pintado throughout June, July, and August that "the people are in every sense of the word *land mad*" (his emphasis) and on the verge of revolt.[66] His talk does not seem to be mere hyperbole; he had been accosted by several local planters and nearly beaten.[67] Pintado, for his part, did not seem overly concerned. The policy seemed intact in 1807, when Kneeland wrote to Nicholas Highland about a man seeking to obtain land in Spanish West Florida. "As he is an American citizen," Kneeland wrote, "he cannot possibly even claim the land under our present regulations."[68] The normally permissive system that had allowed immigrants to take a loyalty oath had apparently been tightened and remained so through 1810. Contrary to the earlier belief that populating West Florida with U.S. citizens-cum-Spanish subjects would help stem U.S. expansion into the borderlands, the Spanish government had at last decided that Americans brought more trouble than they prevented.

This policy did not, however, prevent Americans either inside or outside Spanish West Florida from purchasing land through secondary sales. An examination of these sales reveals several patterns that speak to the changing nature of the West Florida borderlands. Land sale records generally included the residence of both the buyer and the seller as part of the Spanish policy of establishing community and defining its parameters. In 1800 land sales to outsiders began to increase, as individuals and land companies located outside Spanish West Florida purchased more than 10 percent of all land between 1800 and 1810.[69] The land companies no doubt hoped to profit in the same way that land companies had profited in Kentucky, Tennessee, and other parts of the U.S. frontier. At the same time, these groups may have anticipated a change in government, or perhaps they believed that, barring land grants (which the Spanish government would not give to speculators), they could still make a profit buying parcels from already-established residents.

The largest of the companies was the firm of Cochran and Rhea. Although based in New Orleans, the partners occasionally appear in the records as "residents" of Baton Rouge. Between 1803 and 1806 Cochran and Rhea purchased twenty plots of land ranging in size from 240 to 1,200 arpents, for a total of 10,140 arpents—about 7 percent of the land sold during that period.[70] On the individual level landowners could sometimes realize huge profits through petit speculation. On May 23, 1800, John Ross sold a 1,000-arpent parcel of land located on Bayou Sara to John Mink for 1,000 pesos. At 1 peso per arpent, that price was almost exactly the average price for land on the Baton Rouge frontier for that year. That same day Mink resold the land to John O'Connor for the same price, plus twenty cows. Again on that same day John O'Connor sold the land for 2,000 pesos to William Cobb and Elijah Adams, two Mississippians engaged in speculation.[71] In that sale O'Connor doubled his investment in one day. In some cases landowners broke up the land they had purchased in order to make a profit while remaining landowners. For example, in 1803 John Buck purchased 320 arpents for 930 pesos and then resold 300 arpents from that parcel for 1,200 pesos.[72] He retained 20 arpents, enough to support his family and allow him to engage in small-scale agricultural production.

However, secondary sales in West Florida represented a double-edged sword. An analysis of land prices reveals, unsurprisingly, that for the most part the price of land in West Florida grew steadily from 1785 through 1810.[73] (See figure 1.) The rise in prices reflects two things. On the one hand, West Florida had become a seller's market, especially in the years after 1805, when the Spanish government tightened its land grant policies. On the other hand, as the land became more densely settled and West Floridians improved their plots by clearing the land, planting crops, and constructing buildings and fences, the land also gained value.

When the data are broken down by region, two exceptions to the rise in prices present themselves and may go a long way toward explaining discontent among residents over the issue of land. Instability in West Florida had always been centered in the frontier areas—Feliciana (including Bayou Sara) to the north and Saint Helena to the east. Unfortunately not enough data on land sales exist regarding Saint Helena to draw any firm conclusions in that regard. In Feliciana, however, land sales account for nearly one-third of the total sales in West Florida from 1797 through 1810 and permit an analysis of the relationship between land and land sales on the frontier and the burgeoning revolutionary sentiment in West Florida. Naturally, having obtained their land later than those residing in the more established areas like Manchac, immediately south of the town of Baton Rouge, residents north in Bayou Sara and west in the less-settled districts trailed with regard to improvements. This helps explain why land prices in Feliciana lagged behind those in the areas that had been settled earlier. But for the most part prices in Feliciana rose in proportion to those in West Florida as a whole. As settlers in Feliciana improved their land, prices in their district also rose.

But as figure 2 indicates, the average price of land in Feliciana rose from 1796 through 1802 and then experienced a drop of more than 50 percent in 1803 and

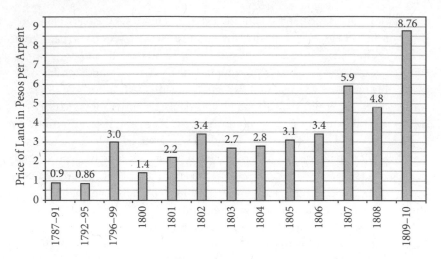

Figure 1. Average Price of Land in West Florida, 1785–1810

1804.[74] Land prices in Feliciana then rose again from 1805 through 1807. However, after 1807 land prices experienced a three-year drop that again equaled an almost 50 percent decline. Land elsewhere in West Florida rose steadily during the same period, dropped only slightly in 1803, and then continued its previous rise with little reduction through 1807. Landowners suffered a small drop in prices in 1808 and then experienced a sharp spike in 1809–10, just prior to the revolution.[75]

The pattern of land prices, then, shows two periods of decline in Feliciana, a decline that becomes even more pronounced when placed in the greater context of prices elsewhere in West Florida. While residents in most of Baton Rouge enjoyed an increase in the value of their landholdings, those in Feliciana saw their fortunes decrease. Given that the Spanish government had, from the 1790s onward, used land to buy the loyalty of immigrants, it should hardly come as a surprise that closing off access to that land at a time when land prices began to drop drastically undermined loyalty to the Spanish government. Suddenly residents' investments seemed no longer secure. This occurred at the same time that U.S. citizens were moving west in ever-greater numbers.[76] Not coincidentally, the same periods of low ebb saw the Kemper rebellion, in 1804, and then the West Florida Revolution in 1810. Separating cause and effect here can be difficult. Did the drop in prices cause the unrest or reflect worries over it? Given that land prices in Feliciana and Bayou Sara dropped prior to, and then rose during and after, the Kemper rebellion, land prices would seem to be a cause rather than an effect, as would the arc in land prices prior to the 1810 revolution.

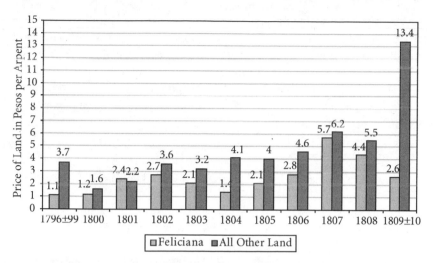

Figure 2. Average Price of Land in West Florida, 1785–1810, by Region

The problem, then, for West Floridians was that after the Kemper raids the Spanish government began to enforce an older, more restrictive policy that prohibited U.S. citizens from coming into West Florida, taking a loyalty oath, becoming subjects of the Spanish Crown, and then obtaining land. This also meant that the relatives of those Americans who had already migrated could not join their families as landholders in Spanish West Florida except by purchasing land at possibly inflated prices. Finally, Americans living in the Mississippi and Louisiana territories could not obtain land grants but instead had to buy land from already established residents. For landowners in most of the Baton Rouge district, this presented an opportunity for land speculation—and property values for the most part showed that residents could expect to double their land values every few years. Except in Feliciana—land values in that area were only slightly higher in 1810 than they had been in 1805, and less than in 1802. Residents of Feliciana seemed to be losing money while everyone around them profited by their holdings. Meanwhile, landowners in the rest of the Baton Rouge district could profit through minor speculation in the land they already owned, or through that which they might purchase from their neighbors. But access to the readily available, cheap land that could bring a true profit had been closed.

In the final analysis Spanish land policy in the Feliciana district from 1805 to 1810 and Spanish reaction to the local crisis have direct implications for understanding intracommunity relations in West Florida at the beginning of the 1810 revolution and the causes that pushed Anglo-Americans in the area to agitate for U.S. intervention. On the one hand, we are presented with a picture in 1803 of a district where residents enjoyed good rapport with Spanish officials. Land distribution worked against the creation of a large class of planter elite, although some planters clearly enjoyed greater status than others. On the whole, however, average distribution implies a relative equity of ownership. A network of lending and assistance existed between Spanish officials and local landowners. The disruption of the initial Kemper raids, rather than pitting Anglo-Americans against the Spaniards, drew most of the inhabitants together in an effort to pacify the region.

It was only after the raid and the resulting shift in Spanish land policies that discontent grew in Feliciana. What had been the normal Spanish system of allowing settlers to obtain land quickly and easily slowed for established planters and stopped altogether for immigrants. A government that had operated efficiently in completing surveys, dispensing justice, and supporting a network of assistance between Spanish officials and landowners prior to the Kemper rebellion began to change into something that no longer met the needs of the Anglo-American residents of Feliciana. When paired with the rise in crime and the general instability created by the proximity to "the line," which criminals could cross at will, the issues raised at the convention come into sharper relief. The two problems represented the tangible nature of residents' growing dissatisfaction with the administration of the Spanish government from 1805 through 1810. Beginning in 1807 other, less tangible, but equally critical problems would arise that would spell the end of Spanish authority in West Florida.

CHAPTER SEVEN

Breaking the Bonds

The End of Spanish Rule in West Florida

Internal events in the Baton Rouge district, including crime, a restriction in land distribution policies, and fluctuating land prices, contributed to growing instability from 1805 to 1810. At the same time, political, social, and economic ties kept West Florida bound to the United States (from which many migrants had come), to the various colonies in the circum-Caribbean (to which much of its trade went), and to Europe and Spain (from which its government flowed). Residents, therefore, could not help but feel the influence of events outside West Florida that would play a large role in changing the course of its history. Three incidents, initially separate but bound to connect, stirred up the residents of the Baton Rouge district. The alliance and later war between France and Spain, the American embargo against Great Britain, and the recall to Havana and ultimate death of Carlos de Grand-Pré formed a tangle of affairs that would explode from the center to the peripheries of the Spanish Empire and profoundly affect West Florida.

The demise of Grand-Pré was a severe blow for West Floridians and came, indirectly, as a result of other incidents. Barring the embargo and the war, Grand-Pré might have remained in West Florida, governing the Baton Rouge district with little change in the foreseeable future. Grand-Pré's recall in turn initiated a chain reaction of incidents that thoroughly disrupted the social and political fabric of the area, bringing to West Florida its second American revolution in three decades. All these events relate to the residents' complaints, cataloged in their 1810 convention, of French families migrating to West Florida and becoming a potential threat to the stability of the area. However, just as West Florida did not exist in isolation from the Caribbean, Latin America, or the United States and its frontiers, neither did it exist in isolation from its mother country. While district residents wrestled with issues of land and crime, Spain experienced a series of political trials that threatened the future of both the mother country and its colonies.

International Problems

After having been at war with Great Britain from 1779 through 1783, Spain experienced an economic rebound after the resumption of trade with Great Britain, Spain's colonies in the Caribbean, and the new United States. Yet Spain continued to suffer from fiscal mismanagement, a smallpox epidemic, and food shortages that swept the country in the mid-1780s—King Charles III himself died of a fever in December 1788. An alliance with Great Britain from 1793 through 1795 preceded an alliance with France in 1796. However, this opened up Spanish shipping to English privateering, resulting in the near annihilation of Spanish commerce in the Atlantic. It also severed ties with its colonies and necessitated permitting neutral shipping of goods from Spanish to foreign ports—something never before allowed under Spanish law. The chief beneficiary of this policy was the United States and its citizens, who rushed to take advantage of the economic opportunities presented by Spain's misfortunes.[1]

After Great Britain, France, and Spain signed a peace treaty in March 1802, Spain set about trying to modernize its military forces. Yet within a year after Napoleon Bonaparte seized power in France in 1801, France and Britain resumed hostilities, placing Spain in a position that required it to side with France and endure a six-million-livres-per-year tribute to Napoleon as the price of neutrality.[2] This, in turn, led to renewed war with Great Britain. The possibility of war between France and Portugal brought French troops to Spanish soil and furnished Napoleon an opportunity to change Spain from a client state subject to his commands to a conquered territory. He then used the 1807 Treaty of Fontainebleau as a springboard to occupy northern border towns, Figueras, and the important city of Barcelona. In March 1808 Charles IV abdicated the Spanish throne in favor of Ferdinand IV. The two royals then traveled to Bayonne, France, to meet with Napoleon and begin discussion of peace. Instead, Napoleon jailed them both and installed Joseph Bonaparte on the Spanish throne.

Spanish-speaking residents of New Orleans and West Florida received this news somewhat belatedly in an October issue of *El Misisipi*. In a single issue the newspaper reported Charles's abdication and Ferdinand's accession, French troops entering Spain, and reports of a Spanish force counterattacking at Bayonne. The report revealed that "all was not going well" and detailed a battle between French and Spanish forces. An article also reported the coronation of Joseph I as the new King of Spain.[3] In a telling indication of local sentiment, the paper called Spain's *Bayonne Gazette* "an official organ of the usurpers" and reported the "gloomy silence" with which Spanish subjects witnessed Joseph's coronation ceremony in Saint Sebastian.[4] In response the Spanish people rose up against Napoleon's army, and Spain descended into its own war of independence against France. The result, as one historian put it, "deprived [Spain's] colonies of a metropolis."[5] More problematically, as Jay Kinsbruner has noted, the Spanish colonies "did not belong to Spain but to the Crown of Castile," which no longer existed.[6] Consequently, as peninsular government fell to the towns and their juntas, Spain's colonies in the New World followed the same model.

This would have important consequences for West Floridians, for whom Charles and Ferdinand represented the center of their monarchy-based political loyalty. For West Floridians, as for other Latin Americans, the loss of their sovereign and the seeming demise of their mother country was more a psychological and political blow than an economic or social problem. West Florida had always been a mixture of many different cultures and remained tied economically to several other places, Spain being one among many. But the sovereign king had always been a tangible object of their loyalty and one to whom they swore their fealty in document after document. After 1808 that person had disappeared, replaced by Joseph Bonaparte, himself the son of the man whom the papers in New Orleans reported as making war on nearly the entire Western world. More importantly the invasion of Spain and the subsequent jailing of Ferdinand and Charles signaled instability for West Floridians, which American officials recognized, albeit two years later.[7] In the meantime, as long as Spain at least appeared to maintain some colonial strength, it could counter the precarious position of West Florida with regard to the United States, France, circum-Caribbean slave rebellions, and regional filibustering. Napoleon removed that support.

The Embargo and Continental Problems

Further complicating matters for West Floridians and the European powers, the U.S. Congress in December 1807 had passed the Embargo Act, directed against Great Britain. The near destruction of the frigate *Chesapeake* by the British frigate *Leopard* in June of that same year signaled the immediate antecedent for the embargo.[8] The Embargo Act prohibited American ships from entering foreign ports and foreign ships from entering American ports. In West Florida, however, the embargo was a political and economic disaster of potentially epic proportions, as the embargo officially closed West Florida and Baton Rouge to American trade. West Floridians obtained many foodstuffs from American territory and traded their produce in New Orleans, but the embargo left them cut off from the United States and restricted in their trade with the rest of the world. The Spanish government inquired about an exception to the embargo, only to be denied by Secretary of State James Madison. Jefferson here missed an opportunity to assert U.S. sovereignty over West Florida: had Jefferson exempted West Florida from the embargo, it would have meant that the U.S. government was treating the area as de facto American territory.[9] Instead, American officials would only allow Spanish ships on authorized government business to transit the Mississippi. Further, the U.S. Navy stationed ships on Lake Ponchartrain and along the Mississippi, effectively blockading West Florida.[10] It seemed to Spanish officials that the United States intended to effect the withdrawal of Spain from West Florida. For residents of Baton Rouge, the embargo signaled the closure of their primary port of trade and the beginning of large-scale smuggling operations overland to New Orleans. West Floridians also began to revive discussions concerning the possibility of building a canal linking Baton Rouge with Mobile, eliminating the need to transit the Mississippi for trade.[11]

Even though Jefferson intended the embargo as the first step toward war with Britain, the United States was neither ready for war in 1807, nor would it become ready in 1808. Under Jefferson's administration the navy never grew to more than eight ships, of which only two could be considered true warships. And with no tangible threat to the nation's security, the volunteer army never realized its recruiting goals. When war failed to materialize, Jefferson turned to the embargo as an instrument of peace. Because the act also prohibited "reexport" ships from entering U.S. ports—that is, ships bringing goods from, say, Caribbean islands to American ports and then carrying those same goods out of the American ports to European ports—the embargo would also make trade more expensive because of increased shipping costs. However, islands in the British Caribbean depended heavily on American produce and so would surely face economic chaos and ruin under the embargo. All of this, Jefferson reasoned, would force Great Britain to capitulate to U.S. demands without a shot fired. Jefferson also hoped that although the embargo would prevent all foreign goods from reaching U.S. shores, it would also further the Jeffersonian-republican dream of making the United States a self-sufficient nation. Through the embargo, Jefferson reasoned, the United States could decrease its dependency on foreign goods. After a time, Congress could lift the embargo, and American ports would once again receive foreign manufactures. By this time American self-sufficiency would ensure that the only goods imported would be luxury items purchased by the wealthy, which Congress could then tax.

In reality the embargo brought economic disaster for the United States. Unfortunately, options in the United States, much as in West Florida, included only smuggling or economic ruin. Because Jefferson knew that any U.S. schooner plying its trade from port to port could easily slip off for the Caribbean or Europe, the United States restricted its own ships to docks. And because most inter-American trade relied on shipping rather than roads, American commerce ground to a near standstill. New Englanders, many of them recently unemployed because of the embargo, rioted. Southerners felt the embargo more keenly. The plantation South relied heavily on both incoming foreign produce to feed its population and outgoing staple exports to fuel its economy. The embargo cut off both of these. So the U.S. South suffered along with West Florida and worked out solutions in much the same way. By December 1808 the strong outcry against the Embargo Act forced Congress to repeal it in favor of a nonintercourse law that barred trade with Britain and France. The act did not prohibit trade with Spain or any of its colonies, thus reopening New Orleans to West Floridians.

By early 1809 a more complex dynamic existed between France, Spain, Great Britain, the United States, and the West Florida periphery. War between the three European powers brought both opportunity and danger to West Floridians. The opportunity came, as always, from the increased trade that all wars bring. However, the dangers involved in a conflict between Spain and France, on the one hand, and Britain, on the other, presented a problem for West Floridians. The people of Baton Rouge, as with many living in non-French possessions in the New World, believed that France had sent agents to the New World to cause unrest and foment rebellion. This belief was not without foundation. Napoleon had encouraged Spain's New World possessions to rebel, and the ideology of the French Revolution had spread to the nearby island of Saint Domingue, whose slaves had risen up and overthrown the colonial government in 1791. In that same decade Edmond Charles Genet, minister to the United States for France, arrived in the United States on a mission from the French government. Genet's mission included negotiating a new treaty with the United States that would more closely tie the two countries together commercially. At the same time, Genet would secure the payment of the U.S. Revolutionary War debt to France—about $5.6 million. Finally, but perhaps most ominously for Spanish America, the Genet mission included provoking the people of Canada, Florida, and Louisiana (then still a Spanish possession) into rebellion, based on the principles of the French Revolution. Specifically for West Florida, Genet tried to enlist Americans living in Georgia to his cause, asking them to prepare an invasion of Spanish Florida—an effort that failed.[12] To accomplish the third part of his mission, Genet employed propaganda, agents provocateurs, and Kemperesque borderland types.[13] Genet, of course, overstayed his welcome in the United States. However, the threat of French agents with regard to West

Florida continued long after his departure, in part because Genet had already sponsored a filibustering raid into East Florida in 1795.[14]

Both the French revolutionary regime and later Napoleon employed spies and secret agents to further their New World aims. One such person, Gen. Octaviano Davilmar, came to West Florida in 1808. An agent of Napoleon, Davilmar was thus an agent of Spain's ally, although the Spaniards distrusted him. Spanish vice-consul José Vidal voiced unkind words about Davilmar and further cautioned that the general could manipulate the unsuspecting. But perhaps for reasons relating to cultural affection, Grand-Pré received the French agent in July 1808. Davilmar rested at Grand-Pré's house, and the latter provided the French agent with a boat for his journey up the Red River toward Mexico.[15]

Local Problems

The timing of this event was unfortunate for Carlos de Grand-Pré, who had served as the governor of the Baton Rouge district for nearly two decades. Word of the French invasion of Spain had just reached his district, and in August came news of Davilmar's arrest in northern Mexico. Spanish officials had again raised the specter of expelling the French from Louisiana, as they had throughout the 1790s.[16] Governor Someruelos in Havana had also begun to exile French citizens—including those from Saint Domingue—from Havana as a precaution against Napoleonic intrigues in that city.[17] Vicente Folch, commander of the Spanish fort at Pensacola and governor of West Florida, reported Davilmar's presence in Baton Rouge to his superiors in Havana in a manner that suggested collaboration and guilt on the part of Grand-Pré. As a result, officials in Havana recalled Grand-Pré to Cuba.

West Floridians reacted by circulating a petition declaring their loyalty to Grand-Pré and the Crown and further proclaiming their opposition to Grand-Pré's removal. However, the possibility of French-inspired revolt and the threat of French intrigue ran too deep for Grand-Pré to avoid, and he returned to Havana in late 1808. Prior to his departure, Grand-Pré had already entertained a petition from the residents to meet and discuss what historians and some contemporaries have called "unrest."[18] The troubles to which they refer are unclear in the records, but the wording indicates that they relate to filibustering, a nascent independence movement in Mexico, and the crisis in Spain. When a group of Spanish subjects from West Florida met in December 1808, they proposed that Cuban officials postpone Grand-Pré's recall and allow him to remain in West Florida to train his successor.

In their deliberations, the group also discussed the duties paid when trading in New Orleans and suggested the levying of similar taxes in the Baton

Rouge district. Historians in the past have seen this proposal as the first step toward either representative government or revolution, depending on whether the Spaniards would accept the proposal.[19] Yet some form of limited elected government had always existed in the various Spanish colonies, so this action was not unusual. Witness, for instance, the election of alcaldes and constables in West Florida. However, nothing in the documents or in the actions of West Floridians up to this point suggests that they saw their proposals as anything more than a means of standardizing the system of taxation to distribute the burden more equitably while at the same time raising funds that the armies back in Spain could use in their struggle against Napoleon. The other proposals similarly tried to quell the filibustering and crime in the area and address the problem of restricted land distribution.

As a means of further establishing its autonomy—and perhaps to secure his future loyalty—the assembly also offered Grand-Pré a salary paid by locals in recognition of his service to the community and then called for a second meeting that would follow up on the proposals from the first. Unfortunately, by offering Grand-Pré a salary and protesting his removal to Havana, the assembly likely placed the now-former governor in an awkward position. He could either sanction that meeting and any that came afterward and thus appear to be party to what might be an extralegal gathering, or he could disavow the proposals and risk that the citizens would meet again anyway and thereby invite a possible military response by Governor Someruelos in Havana. Perhaps he thought that his connections within the community would help mitigate any serious problems in West Florida. However, in April 1809 Grand-Pré died.

The impact of Charles Louis Boucher de Grand-Pré's death on West Florida cannot be overestimated. His family was intimately connected to Baton Rouge society, and as governor he had moved among the upper class of West Florida. He was by no means the wealthiest man in Baton Rouge, although his position brought with it a grant of land from the Crown. But as governor he collected a percentage of the fees paid for new land grants. Although his will and the announcement of his death does not contain a succession that includes an accounting and valuation of his possessions, clues to his wealth can be found in the gilt sword that he bequeathed to one of his sons, the collection of books divided among his youngest children, and an assortment of firearms given to his children. He also left slaves and some cash to each child. However, the best clues to his status and his connections to the community come from the marriage of Charlotte Sophie de Grand-Pré, his daughter.

With his written permission—required by Spanish law—she entered into a marriage contract with New Orleans merchant Antoine Cavalier in March 1809, while Grand-Pré was still in Havana but before he died.[20] In some ways the

timing of Sophie's marriage was fortuitous, because the death of someone of
her father's stature would certainly have thrown his estate into a lengthy probate
process and possibly delayed her marriage indefinitely. Moreover, her dowry
represented "the first legal acknowledgement of [her] personality" and "assured
her right to share in the inheritance" from her father's estate.[21] Sophie's dowry
included 500 arpents of land, apparently her third of 1,500 arpents divided between three daughters. Assessors valued the land at 1,500 pesos. Sophie also
brought to the union a slave valued at 800 pesos, 560 pesos in "furniture and
jewels," and 2,860 pesos in cash. Altogether the dowry totaled a stunning 5,720
pesos, making Sophie a very eligible frontier bride and her husband, Antonio,
a wealthy man, if he was not already. Sophie brought only movable property to
the marriage—not the norm for Spanish dowries—and could use this wealth
to help control future marital property.[22]

For his part Antonio brought an uncertain fortune to the marriage; the contract listed his assets as "cash which [was] employed in trade, for which reason
it [was] not possible for the said future husband to state the sum to which it
amount[ed]."[23] The assets a partner brought to the marriage union helped establish the person's social standing, and a marriage contract would be an opportunity to, in essence, "show off" one's wealth. Marriage in colonial Latin America served as a means of uniting elite families.[24] Antonio's witnesses, however,
remained vague about his true wealth, which might have been tied up in debt
or in lucrative shipping ventures. Nonetheless, Sophie de Grand-Pré's assets remained safe. Because the two had married in a Spanish court, the wife's dowry,
along with any increase gained from its investment, would be hers again in the
event the two separated or the husband died.[25] One of Grand-Pré's daughters,
Hélène, had already married and had likely taken a dowry into her marriage—
one that was at least as much as, if not more than, Sophie's. That Sophie could
bring more than six thousand pesos to a marriage indicates the wealth of the
Grand-Pré family.

In the long term Grand-Pré's death removed one of the final pieces of the
support structure in Spanish West Florida society. Without Grand-Pré the government apparatus and, perhaps more importantly, the people's relationship
to it began to collapse. His death added immediacy to the weight of the local
failure of the Spanish government, compounded the difficulties regarding the
political economy of the United States and Spain, and left the ongoing disputes
over land policies without a trusted mediator. In short, after having lost their
metropolis, and at a time when the rest of their world was crumbling around
them, residents of Spanish West Florida then lost the personification of their
loyalty to the Spanish Crown.

The Collapse of Spanish Authority in West Florida

Up to this point, the burgeoning West Florida revolution had followed a pattern typical of the revolutions that had begun to spread across the rest of Latin America. That is, local elites moved to gain greater autonomy between 1808 and 1810 to offset the loss of Spain as a political and psychological center.[26] However, the wealth generated in West Florida for the Spanish Crown, like that of Chile but unlike that in the Rio de Plata area of South America, did not amount to a significant portion of Spain's New World revenue. As a consequence of low revenue, administration in the poorer areas of the New World had always been in the hands of the local elite—a local elite that had included Carlos de Grand-Pré. His death virtually guaranteed that colonial authorities in Havana, eager to both reassert and extend their power during Spain's troubles in Europe, would replace Grand-Pré with someone from outside Baton Rouge. In Grand-Pré's place came the new governor, Carlos Dehault De Lassus, a man about whom not much is known other than that West Floridians despised both him and his secretary, Raphael Crocker, from the outset. Basically a placeman, De Lassus came from Havana—though he had been the governor of Upper Louisiana some years earlier—and had contacts in Baton Rouge prior to his arrival. In large part De Lassus suffered from the fact that he was not Grand-Pré. His tenure, however, also brought with it complaints of bribery, increased taxes and fees, and open corruption.[27]

Historians have wrestled with the role of Governor David Holmes—a Virginian appointed to his office in 1809—of Mississippi in the West Florida rebellion.[28] Although no letters survive linking Holmes directly to the events in West Florida in 1810, circumstantial evidence nonetheless points to his support and encouragement of the rebels. A series of letters to President Madison and Secretary of State Robert Smith described Spanish authority as "relaxed," and from Smith's point of view the inhabitants had a "sense of danger.[29] Despite Holmes's ulterior motives—his constituency clearly favored the annexation of West Florida, where many residents felt that they would profit handsomely by such action due to the increase in land prices—his letter does provide insight into the nature of dissatisfaction in West Florida. Holmes claimed that the residents had become divided into national factions, the majority of whom favored American intervention; he divided these factions into an "American Party," a "British Party," a "Spanish party," and what had been a "French party," though he did not indicate which of the four were the most numerous. He did note that the Spanish and the British had found common cause in a kind of monarchophilia, but clearly used the factional elements to raise the possibility of French or even British intervention. Playing on the vague specter of outside intervention, he told Smith that the United States could obtain West Florida with little or no expense but that these circumstances could change if another powerful country invaded. In a clear attempt to prod the Madison government into action, Holmes constantly emphasized in his writings what he called a "determination" among the elites to bring about U.S. rule in West Florida. He also repeated that inhabitants from Bayou Sara wanted to ask for the protection of the United States but cautioned that West Floridians would not act without some indication of U.S. support.[30]

The motivation behind Holmes's support of rebellion in general and of U.S. intervention in particular is evident in his statement that slaves comprised a large portion of West Florida's population. For Holmes this group, along with the more amorphous "persons without character" mentioned in the letter, threatened the stability of Mississippi's slave population.[31] Historian Isaac Cox suspects the body of Holmes's letters of being "not merely coincident but collusive," although he does not state his reasons for such assumptions.[32] It seems clear, moreover, that Holmes's probable motivation calls into question the veracity of his notes. Ascertaining the extent of rebellious sentiment in the Baton Rouge district is quite difficult. In January 1809 John Adair—a conspirator in Aaron Burr's scheme then exiled to Mobile—wrote to James Madison stating that nine out of ten residents in West Florida had come from the United States or the British colonies during the revolution. Most of those, he claimed, favored U.S. rule over that of Spain, and he described them as "ripe fruit awaiting the hand that dare[d] to pluck them." Adair conversely noted that in New Orleans and Louisiana "the gov't of the U.S. ha[d] many enemys [sic]; and few warm friends," and that the French in the region, despite the ongoing war between France and Spain, would rather see the Louisiana Territory rejoin Spain than remain in the hands of the United States. In this opinion he echoed the earlier assessments of Wilkinson with regard to the province.

To some degree this letter told Madison many of the things that the president wished to hear concerning the weakness of Spain—though Holmes's assessment of U.S. weakness south and across the river would have been less welcome. However, Adair also admitted that he had a personal stake—regaining the trust of the U.S. government—in writing his letter and did mention pro-British and pro-Spanish factions in and around Baton Rouge.[33] In this case, Adair's letter mirrors a trend among those evaluating West Florida's loyalty in 1809–10, especially when compared with similar attitudes in Louisiana. Virtually everyone describing pro-U.S. sentiment in West Florida—from Adair to Governor Holmes to Claiborne to Wilkinson to the pro-American revolutionaries themselves— had a great deal to gain by convincing others of widespread pro-U.S. sentiment in the region. At the same time, many of those very people tended to describe anti-U.S. sentiment elsewhere, something U.S. government officials clearly did not want to hear. The most logical conclusion is that anti-Spanish sentiment existed in sections of the Baton Rouge district, fueled by a number of causes. The extent of that sentiment had become significant by 1810 and helped precipitate the immediate events that brought about the revolution.

Beginning in 1810, both under and as a reaction to the rule of Governor De Lassus as well as to transatlantic factors, West Floridians began to openly express their dissatisfaction with the local government, and De Lassus seemed to serve as the touchstone for their unhappiness. Not surprisingly, most of the early revolutionary sentiment centered in and around Bayou Sara. That region had experienced the greatest fluctuations in land value, was the center of the Kempers' filibustering raids, and seemed to be the locus of a great deal of other criminal activity by U.S. Army and Navy deserters and other vagabonds. In May and June 1810, a few wealthy residents in Bayou Sara began a series of then-secret meetings, partially in response to rumors that several French citizens had gathered in New Orleans with the purpose of raising an army and attacking the fort at Baton Rouge.

Then, on July 6 several prominent residents asked De Lassus for permission to hold a convention for the purpose of securing the peace and continued existence of the Spanish Crown in West Florida. In this the residents followed the tradition of the 1810 *cortés* in Spain, as well as some of the early *cortés* governments in Central and South America.[34] Each district in West Florida sent delegates to the meeting. Some delegates wished to bring in the U.S. government, some to invite in the British, and a large faction to continue under Spanish rule. For the British and the Spanish factions, the issue was not so much what to do about the Spanish monarchy but how to handle the twin problems of the growing pro-U.S. faction and De Lassus. Initially, the promonarchists retained the upper hand because of fear by the American party that the entire movement might fail, leaving them open to retaliation by loyal residents.[35]

De Lassus, as aware of the situation as anyone, believed that most residents still preferred Spanish rule to the uncertainty of independence—or the possibility of French invasion. He had granted the inhabitants the right to send delegates to a meeting designed to help keep order in the province. However, the rebellious sentiments in Bayou Sara did not represent the opinion of most people in West Florida. Farther to the east in the Saint Helena district (still a part of West Florida), Shepherd Brown, commandant of that district, became alarmed at the news of such a meeting. Brown could not believe that De Lassus would permit such a gathering given the instability in Bayou Sara and the rumors of both French and British conspiracies in West Florida. Accordingly, the commandant sent a representative to Baton Rouge to determine if De Lassus had agreed to the meeting of his own free will and whether he might somehow be involved with conspirators planning to overthrow the Crown. Brown also pledged five hundred militiamen for the defense of the lands of Ferdinand VII. After obtaining assurances that the new governor had not betrayed the Crown and that the assembly had only the best motives, Brown set about organizing an election of delegates from his district for a convention that would begin on July 25, 1810.[36]

In the meantime, however, De Lassus had made yet another mistake in his governance of Baton Rouge. In response to rumors of a possible French invasion of Baton Rouge through New Orleans, De Lassus had expelled from West Florida several residents of French descent. Those families, who only had three days to sell their belongings, crossed over into American territory to Iberville, southwest of Baton Rouge.[37] De Lassus disingenuously claimed that the initial meetings of residents in Bayou Sara had actually been uprisings themselves and used that as his basis for action.[38] Unfortunately for the Spanish government, many of the exiled families had been residents of West Florida for more than a generation, had business and social contacts within the community, had served in the militia, had taken oaths of allegiance to Spain, and retained connections in that community. Expulsion only served to cultivate or harden whatever anti-Spanish sentiments they might already have had, and the exiles immediately threatened to start an uprising designed to overthrow the government that had expelled them from their own lands. De Lassus, in a sincere but misguided attempt to return stability to West Florida, fed into the hands of the already-discontented and created a self-fulfilling prophecy.[39]

Convention and Independence

By the time the initial thirty-six-day West Florida convention met from late July through August 1810, Peru, Venezuela, Columbia, Chile, and Mexico had all begun their revolts against the Spanish Crown. Some of the most prominent members of Baton Rouge society attended West Florida's convention. The group of fourteen included four men from the Feliciana district, five from the Baton Rouge district, four from the Saint Helena district to the east, and one from the district of Tanchipaho and Chifuncté still further east. Aside from listing their complaints, the members also went out of their way to establish that the committee was not an extralegal meeting, that the 1810 convention had been sanctioned by De Lassus himself, and that the group had only the best interests of the Spanish Crown at heart. The governor, more concerned with the possibility of French revolutionaries than anything else, trusted the convention in its initial stages, though he clearly mistrusted the people living in Feliciana and Bayou Sara. More to the point, George Mather and Philip Hickey, two delegates to the convention, firmly supported the Spanish Crown and agreed to keep watch on the gathering for the governor.[40] These men reported to De Lassus on the attitude expressed in the various gatherings, and had there existed any revolutionary intent up through the end of August, De Lassus would have been informed.

The governor reciprocated the convention delegates' initial overtures with an acknowledgment of their loyalty and patriotism and an expression of his firm belief that the convention truly supported the interests of West Florida and the Spanish Crown. However, two Spanish documents from late August attest to a growing sense of helplessness and isolation on the part of De Lassus and his fellow government officials. In his "Report of the Events on August 14, 1810," De Lassus discussed the appearance of an anonymous broadside on one of the public roads in Bayou Sara. The broadside, nailed to a tree and signed "A Friend of the People," apparently contained "very war-like" language exhorting the inhabitants to revolution.[41] A surveyor quickly removed the document.[42]

Coincidentally on that same day John Johnson, a resident of Bayou Sara, wrote to Mississippi governor Holmes about the situation in West Florida. Johnson, prevented by illness from attending the convention but nonetheless a member, thanked the governor for his support in the current situation—one of the only accounts indicating that the government of Mississippi somehow had a hand in the events surrounding the convention. Johnson, in rather flowery language, decried the "old Tories & their descendants [and] the villainous court sycophants, who ha[d] for a long time fattened on the spoils of the land."[43] He then went on to ask by what means the West Floridians might be incorporated into the United States. Tellingly with regard to the residents' attitudes toward the Spanish and Spanish land policy, he noted that among other things West Floridians would want a continuance of the policy that "actual settlers be entitled to as much land as the Spanish government ha[d] been in the habit of granting to Families (in proportion)."[44] Here, then, is the crux of the residents' relationship with the Spanish government—loyalty based on security and a liberal land policy. That neither of those conditions remained boded ill for the continued presence of the Spanish government in West Florida.

The governor clearly felt pressure. In response to the broadside, De Lassus inspected the artillery at the fort, ensured that the cannons remained primed, and put the guard on alert. Meanwhile, he also requested more powder and reinforcements from Governor Folch in Pensacola. De Lassus also invited the president of the Baton Rouge convention, John Rhea (of the land-speculation partnership Cochran and Rhea), and his deputies to dinner. After the requisite flag raising, Rhea again made sure that the convention had met, and could continue to meet, with the permission of the Spanish government. De Lassus assented. Rhea also asked for a pardon "for those blamed in the uprising"— most likely the Frenchmen De Lassus had expelled in June, who had grumbled after their expulsion that they would work for the overthrow of the Spanish West Florida government.[45] The governor expressed the fear that such a pardon might appear to have been issued from a position of weakness. In response, Thomas Lilley, a deputy to the convention, suggested that De Lassus add to the pardon the statement: "Whoever be suspected of treason . . . after this date, will be arrested and punished according to the fullest extent of the law."[46] Previous historians have interpreted this decree as a sign of weakness. However, a pardon followed by decrees of enforcement was the standard method by which the Spanish Crown handled dissension, and this had worked well in the past both throughout the empire in general and in Feliciana in particular.

De Lassus met for dinner with representatives of the convention several more times, events always accompanied by toasts to Ferdinand VII, prayers for his release, and patriotic songs. Alcohol helped lubricate the meetings, and at one toast everyone agreed, somewhat ironically, that the arrest of Ferdinand VII "should stand as an example to the monarchs of other nations who should not trust usurpers."[47] Nevertheless, the anonymous broadside had changed the character of the debate for De Lassus in that he believed he could no longer trust any of the residents of Bayou Sara, and the pressure was clearly such that he felt the need to act independently and against the West Florida convention.[48]

Other than futile requests for troops, however, the most the governor could do was attempt to protect his reputation, and possibly his life, by making his "conduct . . . known to the public [i.e., his superiors], so as to avoid calumny as far as possible, which might taint [his] reputation and sincere patriotism." He therefore called together several army officers and close associates. His intention, he further stated, was "to avoid subjecting [his] honor to doubt."[49] To accomplish this, De Lassus outlined all the ways in which he had warned his superiors of the incipient rebellion in advance. He noted that in February and April 1809, he had asked for "veteran troops to back the militia" when dealing with the residents of Bayou Sara, that he had allowed the assemblies because of their good faith toward Ferdinand VII, and that despite warnings to his superiors in Pensacola, West Florida was continuously threatened "by perverse intrigues of the French."[50] De Lassus, perhaps anticipating what he considered inevitable, was trying to cover his personal retreat, though tellingly his note mentioned the French but not the Anglo-American residents as the main threat.

The 1810 convention met fourteen times without attempting to subvert the laws of Spain or to overthrow the local administration—most likely because of the balance between Spanish loyalists and the pro-independence faction from the Felicianas. Nor did De Lassus's representatives report any revolutionary sentiment among the representatives. Nonetheless, the residents mostly tried to separate themselves from Carlos De Lassus, and a culture of deep and mutual suspicion emerged over the course of the convention. For the most part this development was less revolutionary than practical, as the convention delegates attempted to circumvent what they saw as De Lassus's corruption. Thus the committee asked De Lassus to allow the convention to appoint local residents to the office of sheriff and to nominate officers of the militia—actions that would remove the potential for De Lassus to demand bribes—but would also draw more power to the leaders of the convention. The committee also asked permission to form local physicians into a medical society with the power to grant licenses and requested the establishment of a newspaper "subject to such regulations as the Governor of [that] Jurisdiction [might] prescribe."[51] De Lassus accepted all of the delegates' proposals, save an instance in which one proposed alcalde had not lived in the area for the required two years and another in which the unknown (in the Spanish Army) title of brigadier general of the militia would instead be called by its Spanish equivalent of colonel commandant.[52] In all likelihood he was either bowing to the reality of the situation—he had very little control over events by this period—or he was stalling for time, hoping that troops under the command of Folch would arrive and give him greater bargaining power, or both.

During the later period of the meetings, the convention also began sending its correspondence to the Spanish governor Someruelos in Havana, hoping to bypass De Lassus altogether and reassure Havana of its loyal intentions. In Pensacola Governor Folch had received fairly regular reports from De Lassus and suspected the entire convention of treasonous motives, but placed a great deal of the blame on De Lassus. To quell the situation in Bayou Sara, Folch decided to lead a party of 150 men to Saint Helena, where he could restore what he believed to be the natural tranquility of the province.[53] In late September the Baton Rouge convention intercepted a letter in which De Lassus claimed that "he did not consider himself bound" by any of his previous agreements with the assembly and claimed that Governor Folch was on his way to Baton Rouge at the head of an uncertain number of troops.[54]

Those troops never arrived, and it is unclear whether they ever set out for Baton Rouge at that time. Although no firm evidence exists, it seems likely that the report and De Lassus's declaration prompted more drastic action by the committee. After the rumors of troops marching from Pensacola began to circulate among the residents of Baton Rouge, the final stages of the revolution proceeded quickly. Again the main push for open revolution and independence centered around Bayou Sara and Feliciana, the site of the greatest instability in Spanish West Florida. De Lassus and Crocker received numerous warnings of a possible rebellion, and as late as September 20 De Lassus had written to Governor Folch asking for troops to reinforce the decaying fort at Baton Rouge. On the twenty-second De Lassus received a warning from Bayou Sara that residents had begun to gather a militia to attack the fort the following morning.

Independence

Indeed, on the same day the West Florida convention met, they issued what they termed a "preliminary Declaration of Independence" resolving that De Lassus "be divested of all authority as Governor of [that] Jurisdiction." The declaration, inasmuch as is possible, only called for quasi independence. That is, the group ordered the commandant of the militia, a resident of Bayou Sara, to enforce the laws of Spain, capture the fort at Baton Rouge, and secure the governmental archives to make safe the land records.[55] At this point more than half the delegates (perhaps smelling a rat), including three of the five from Baton Rouge and all the delegates from the eastern districts, resigned their seats in protest. This allowed the remaining delegates to pass the declaration. Because the people of the districts elected their delegates, the defection of these men points to the still-powerful pro-Spanish sentiment in West Florida, as well as the countervailing power of the Bayou Sara delegates to shape the debates and actions of the province.

Nonetheless, the convention had taken the final step toward separation from the mother country. An hour after midnight on September 23, Spanish troops in the fort received yet another warning that an attack was imminent and went to awaken De Lassus. Although all signs pointed to a final, military culmination of the past year's meetings, conventions, and discussions, De Lassus did little in the way of preparing a defense of the fort. Not until one half-hour after the latest warning did he walk the two hundred yards from his residence to the fort.[56]

Not that it would have mattered much. Despite a contingent of twenty-eight troops in the fort, the structure itself, according to contemporary testimony, could hardly be considered defensible in 1810. The stockade of the fort contained gaps, such perimeter defenses as existed did not include a ditch to slow or repel invaders, and the gate served as a guard post rather than a defensive structure. Further, the government had no funds with which to repair, much less enhance, the defenses in and around the fort. De Lassus could hardly feed his troops. In August, De Lassus had written that the "treasury owe[d] its employees, as well as a great amount of money to the party who ha[d] contracted to furnish the meat."[57] The hungry troops who served the fort lived in the town of Baton Rouge and only stayed in the structure while serving on guard duty. In addition to this, while the fort may have been well equipped with cannon and arms, there was by late 1810 little powder with which to fire the weapons.[58]

At four o'clock on the morning of the twenty-third about eighty armed cavalrymen under the command of three local residents, including George de Passau, attacked the fort at Baton Rouge.[59] The attackers had received instructions to order the defenders to lay down their arms—but to only issue those orders in French and English, which may have reflected either the unwillingness or the inability of the rebels to communicate in Spanish, or may have simply meant that George de Passau issued the commands rather that one of the other leaders of the rebel cavalry.[60] That they chose French as a means of communication probably reflects the makeup of the group and the fact that Carlos de Grand-Pré's son commanded the garrison, given the anti-French sentiment that pervaded West Florida during this period.[61] The fort fell to the attackers within minutes, whereupon the militia found De Lassus at his house and arrested him. By arresting De Lassus, taking control of the fort, and seizing the government archives, the convention virtually guaranteed that the governor of Havana would be forced into military action.

Two officials in service of the Spanish government died in the defense of Baton Rouge. Ironically, one of the casualties was twenty-three-year-old Louis de Grand Pré, son of the former governor, who had led a countercharge against the attacking forces. Louisianans reacted with genuine sorrow to his death.[62] The elder Grand-Pré had been a beloved member of the community, and his family, as noted, had become thoroughly integrated into West Florida society. The *Louisiana Courier* in New Orleans printed a eulogy to Louis in the obituary column of its October 29 edition that points to the still-warm sentiments felt by residents toward the family of the former governor. Submitted by an anonymous, but nonetheless one of the "most respectable inhabitants of this country," the writer dedicated the panegyric to "his late magnanimous friend Louis de Grand Pré." The first part of the column described the calm and heroism with which Louis faced death several days after receiving his wounds and called him "generous at heart" for "the remembrance of the atrocious persecution which his respectable father endured in the Spanish service." In one sentence, then, the anonymous writer managed to condemn the now-deposed Spanish West Florida government and separate the former governor and his family from any complicity in its corrupt practices.[63] The eulogy finished with a poem, in French, that began, "Un seul trépas ternit votre victoire"—only one mistake tarnishes your victory.[64] The writer left unstated whether the mistake was in leading the final charge or in supporting the Spanish regime past the end of its useful life.

On September 26, a newly reconvened convention, composed of the delegates who had initiated the militia action against the fort, formally declared "the several districts composing the Territory of West Florida to be a free and independent state." The Declaration-of-Independence-style document sought to make "known to the world with how much fidelity the good people of this Territory ha[d] professed and maintained their allegiance to their legitimate sovereign, while any hope remained of receiving from him protection for their property and lives." The convention noted that residents had tried to work within the system, out of preference for a government that had protected their rights. They did not reject the idea of monarchy, and indeed, the West Florida declaration argued that many of the regions' troubles stemmed from the absence of a strong king. As opposed to its American counterpart, the West Florida declaration of independence contained none of the bold determination found in Thomas Jefferson's Declaration of Independence. For example, while Jefferson's declaration talked about the duty of a people to overthrow an oppressive government, West Floridians expressed near regret at the necessity of breaking the "attachment to the government which had heretofore protected" them and never argued for the right or the duty to revolution.[65]

But the document also shows the legacy of a political ideology borne of British-American-European notions of government nurtured far from the West Florida borderlands-frontier. With regard to their relations with the Spanish government and the negotiations to assuage the residents' grievances, the convention claimed that in relation to their duties to King Ferdinand VII, "this compact which was entered into with good faith on [their] part [would] forever remain an honorable testimony of [their] upright intentions, and inviolable fidelity to [their] king and parent country."[66] Certainly, the signers of the declaration, non-Spaniards all, must have known that their relationship with the Spanish Crown was not regarded as a compact by officials in Havana, much less by the royalty on the other side of the Atlantic. After all, West Floridians were subjects, not citizens, of the Spanish Empire. Nonetheless, by the contemporary understanding of Spanish (in the form of the *cortés*), British, and perhaps most importantly, American political traditions, the term "compact" defined all political relationships and carried with it certain weighty assumptions. As the Spanish Crown, by its absence, had lost the ability to protect the residents' lives, liberty, and pursuit of happiness, the contract, according to the tradition of Locke, Rousseau, and emerging Spanish legal tradition, had been broken.[67]

Had the Crown really lost its ability to protect and further the residents' well-being? In many senses yes—and clearly Bayou Sarans and Felicianans thought so. But the only complaint not related to De Lassus listed in the declaration of independence crafted by the convention was the absence of a strong monarch.

The West Florida declaration contained grievances not with the king, whose capture citizens sincerely lamented. Instead, the remainder of the document railed against the application of that government by De Lassus, who, the residents complained, took "those measures which were intended for [their] protection" and "pervert[ed] them into an engine of destruction, by encouraging in the most perfidious manner, the violation of the ordinances sanctioned and established by himself as the law of the land." Revolution became necessary when, "left without any hope of protection from the mother country," West Floridians had been "betrayed by a magistrate [De Lassus]."[68] Had the king and Grand-Pré remained in power, the dissatisfaction present in West Florida would most likely still have been there, but Grand-Pré might have worked to dampen it, as he had other interpersonal and community conflicts during his tenure. Certainly Grand-Pré would not have made the same errors of corruption that his successor had. Moreover, residents of West Florida might have found it much more difficult to rebel against a beloved governor and neighbor than a corrupt and hated placeman and his lieutenant. Not surprisingly, upon De Lassus's release and repatriation to Havana, officials there arrested him and put him on trial for his role in the loss of the colony of West Florida. The Baton Rouge convention, in a sign that their cultural allegiance had not yet been settled, restored the functions of Spanish law in the days after the revolution and even proceeded to set a date for the election of an alcalde, all according to Spanish tradition.

The victory of the local militia over Spanish forces was clearly a military triumph, though certainly not a representation of every resident's desires. Governor Holmes recognized this when he wrote to Secretary of State Smith on October 3, noting that the inhabitants of the lower portion of the Baton Rouge province were "inimical to the new order of things." In what would seem to be a blatant attempt to bring U.S. forces to the region, Holmes argued—incorrectly as it turned out—that pro-Spanish loyalists had set about arming Indians and slaves in an attempt to foment rebellion. Playing on a theme common to many of Holmes's letters, the governor claimed that all these events threatened the stability of both Mississippi and U.S. interests in the area.[69] However, he also noted that the attack on the fort made local possession and control a fait accompli, raising the question of whether the attack itself, led by George de Passau among others, was an expression of the residents' wishes to overthrow Spain's government in West Florida or merely an attempt by a smaller group of disaffected Bayou Sarans to effect by force something they might not have achieved through negotiation with fellow residents.[70] By mid-October word had filtered back to Governor Holmes in Mississippi that a pro-Spanish group of residents had assembled in the southern part of Baton Rouge, intending to attack and retake the fort. By unknown means Holmes managed to exert his influence, while at the same time conventioneers moved to co-opt the opposition.[71] Despite American fears that Spain might retake West Florida, by October and November 1810 the Spanish government in Havana had lost the power to reassert their control. Despite two and a half decades of loyalty and support for the Spanish monarchy, the local population seemed resigned to either independence or American assimilation. Spanish rule in Florida west of Mobile was at an end.

EPILOGUE

Though a full treatment of the events that ultimately brought the Baton Rouge district and the whole of the Florida peninsula under the control of the United States is beyond the scope of this work, these events do require some attention. After independence members of the convention and militias loyal to that body set out to disarm Spanish loyalists and members of the pro-British and pro-French factions. Some predation on the plantations of old Tories occurred as well. On October 10, 1810, the West Florida convention, through its elected leader, John Rhea, appealed to the United States for annexation. For the United States transatlantic politics once again favored its interests in West Florida. Having never recognized the Spanish junta claiming to govern in the absence of a legitimate monarch, the United States could argue that by extension the government of West Florida was similarly not legitimate. Moreover, events on the peninsula, in the rest of Europe, and in Latin America meant that Napoleon did not have the resources to interfere with American designs on the province—even if he had possessed the will.

Having taken the Baton Rouge district from Spain, the West Florida convention next turned its eye on Mobile—the closest port not affected by the American embargo. The Mobile River, fed by the Alabama and the Tombigbee rivers, served as an important waterway, bringing goods and settlers from the interior as far away as Virginia. Moreover, the country that controlled the Mobile, the Alabama, and the Tombigbee rivers also controlled access to the powerful Creek Confederation. Therefore, on the same day the convention appealed for annexation, the group also appointed Reuben Kemper and a man named Joseph White to raise a body of men to capture Mobile and Pensacola.[1] Confirming the suspicions of some West Floridians opposed to Kemper's appointment, his group immediately set about plundering farms and plantations along the route to Mobile Bay. Kemper might have expected some help in taking Mobile from a group of disaffected residents who had formed themselves into the Mobile Society in early 1810. Centered around Fort Stoddart in American territory just north on the Mobile River, these men promised to raise an army to capture Mobile.

For the United States ownership of this valuable highway was too important to leave to Spain, much less to West Florida rebels. The United States, however, preferred not to stir up tensions with Spain any more than necessary and empowered the commander of Fort Stoddart, Col. Richard Sparks, to arrest any locals involved in the plot. In this respect the reappearance of Nathan Kemper in the Florida borderlands was a serious problem for both Spanish and American officials. In November 1810 the state department received a letter from Fort Stoddart complaining that Nathan Kemper had come through the area at the behest of the West Florida conventioneers trying to drum up support for an invasion. Worried American officials believed that Reuben Kemper might stir into action those American citizens who had previously been "friends and not enemies to the people of Mobile" and had him and some leaders of his newly formed group arrested.[2]

Although the Spanish government in Havana and Mexico might have felt that it could possibly retake the West Florida province militarily, the need to defend Mobile presented it with a defensive problem it could not ignore. Having Mobile in the hands of an independent and—if the alliance with Reuben Kemper served as an indicator—chaotic West Florida raised the very real possibility that the city would serve as a base from which to attack Spain's holdings. Accordingly, while American officials set out to arrest Kemper and the leaders of the Mobile Society, Spain bolstered its defenses in and around the port. Taking Mobile would have to wait until 1813, when a resurgent James Wilkinson, now a general at the head of American forces in the War of 1812, led a successful American attack on the city.

Meanwhile, the end of October saw two momentous events. On the twenty-fourth the West Florida convention adopted a constitution modeled on that of the United States. On the twenty-seventh Madison reiterated the U.S. position that the Louisiana Purchase included West Florida through an official proclamation. This was hardly surprising—it had long been the policy of the United States and such an assertion represented the easiest means by which the United States could take control of the territory. Consequently, at the end of October the United States empowered William C. C. Claiborne, governor of the Orleans Territory, to "take possession, in the name of the United States, of the Territory south and East of the Mississippi River as far as the Perdida River."[3] For the United States, an independent West Florida represented perhaps even greater instability than a Spanish-held West Florida. Militarily weak and isolated, the new West Florida Republic might come under further attack by filibusters from Mississippi and Alabama, straining negotiations between Spain and a U.S. government aimed at placing East and West Florida in U.S. hands. Likewise, the new territory might fall prey to British or French occupation, which if combined with a similar occupation of Mobile could force the United States to abandon New Orleans. On December 7, after negotiations with local elites, Governor Claiborne moved American troops into Bayou Sara, formally incorporating that territory into the United States. Three days later American troops entered

Baton Rouge, and, after some negotiation, the flag of the West Florida Republic came down, replaced by the Stars and Stripes.

An article that appeared five months later in a local paper reflected the reluctance with which many, if not most, West Floridians declared independence in the first place and showed that the victory over Spanish forces was as yet only a military triumph. Only six issues old in May 1811, the new *St. Francisville (La.) Timepiece*, the first newspaper published in the largest town in Feliciana, had earlier advertised an upcoming demonstration of combat between a tiger and a bull. The tiger was part of a traveling display making its way across the southern United States that had stopped in Baton Rouge. In May the *Timepiece* reported that the tiger and the bull, chained in a thirty-foot-square pit—the bull with its horns sawed off—engaged in a one-minute combat. The bull apparently got the best of the tiger before men separated the two animals to prevent damage to either. However, the editor of the paper decided to use the combat as a warning to any residents who might still harbor pro-Spanish sentiment. "This battle may be considered as ominous," he began. "When the Spanish tiger fretted the West Florida bull he met the same fate; and those who know his powers, would do well to treat him *kindly*—for although when well treated, he is the most docile and tractable of animals on earth, yet he will not bear *too much goading & once enraged*, he becomes the *terror of his assailants*."[4] It was a not-so-subtle warning to those in West Florida who continued to harbor pro-Spanish sentiment.

Perhaps unsurprisingly, the *Timepiece* spent a great deal of ink on pro-American sentiment, celebrating the Fourth of July with a reprint of the Declaration of Independence and publishing long tracts on the value of independence and liberty. At the same time, the editor penned a series of one-sided debates with himself on the need for unity among the now-citizens of West Florida. In short, the *Timepiece* had become the unofficial organ of the elite for shaping the internal and external views of West Florida's revolution. It was a source of what Benedict Anderson has called "imagined linkage" and furnished elite members of the community a means of establishing a new sense of national identity among Felicianans and all West Floridians.[5] In West Florida, much of which was still a frontier area, the newspaper could take the place of, or at least supplement, face-to-face communication and interaction among residents. Thus people living in Saint Helena, for example, could be drawn into the same community as those living on the river coast of Feliciana.

Not that the newspaper-as-mouthpiece was a new phenomenon for anyone, least of all the residents of West Florida. And in the sense that West Florida had always been a nexus of trade and social relations, it is fitting that other cities around the New World took notice of the revolution. News of the various assemblies and the September 23 revolution in West Florida spread across the United States in the months after the assault on the Baton Rouge fort and the declaration of independence. The timeline of the story's progress across the country is instructive. Few papers except the *Charleston (S.C.) Gazette* ran any stories regarding the initial assemblies and conventions. Referring to the 1810 convention, the *Gazette* noted that on August 26 De Lassus had accepted the proposals of the Baton Rouge assembly and "thus ha[d] terminated the Revolution in West Florida." The *Gazette* further noted that the convention would meet again on November 2. Ironically this story ran on September 29, by which point West Florida was beginning its fourth day of independence from the Spanish government.[6] However, the Charleston paper received its news from a New Orleans paper rather than either the *Washington (D.C.) Intelligencer* or the *Natchez (Miss.) Weekly Chronicle*, the main sources of news for most other papers that reported the revolution. This connection perhaps highlights to some extent the nature of the ties between the two port cities. This is especially relevant, because the various papers for the most part picked up news of the revolution and the convention from those two main sources. Outside of the lower Louisiana Territory, the *Tennessee Gazette* (Nashville) first picked up the story on October 9, repeating the story from the *Natchez Weekly Chronicle*, which in itself was merely a communiqué from John Rhea on behalf of the convention. The story told of the initial attack on the fort, the death of Louis de Grand Pré, and the West Florida declaration of independence. The headline of the article proclaimed "West Florida Free."[7]

On October 17 the *Louisiana Gazette of St. Louis* reprinted a letter of unknown origin noting that a militia had taken the Baton Rouge fort.[8] Eleven days later, Charlestonians finally received word of the revolution.[9] The papers in both cities went on to report that Governor Folch had planned to arrest members of the convention and was in the eastern districts of West Florida trying to raise an army against the West Floridians. Both gazettes received the exact same letter and reprinted, word-for-word, the header of the letter explaining the cause of events. The headlines constituted the only differences in the two stories, meaning that the *Natchez Weekly Chronicle* composed a series of identical letters picked up by papers in cities with which the residents of Mississippi and West Florida had regular contact. This tactic allowed Mississippians to help the Baton Rouge revolutionaries "spin" the story of the West Florida Rebellion through papers across the United States. The articles began:

> At a late hour last night we received the subjoined extract of a letter, which we lose no time in laying before our readers. From this it will be seen that the Florida Convention have been compelled to have recourse to military force, and that the fort

of Baton Rouge and Gov. Delassus is in the power of the Patriots. We are informed that a few days since the Convention received intelligence that they were betrayed, and that Gov. Folch had a galley at Galvestown, in which he meant to embark the Convention for Pensacola [i.e., arrest them], and that he himself was in the eastern part of the province alarming and sowing dissention among the people. In this dilemma, prompt and vigorous measures became absolutely necessary, and the result is here related.

The remainder of the text contained a byline from Pickneyville, the first town north of the Mississippi border (and, incidentally, the home of the Kemper brothers and many of the other criminals who had crossed into Spanish territory in the past seven years), and a short explanation of the events that had occurred on the morning of September 23.

News of the revolution had made its way to New England by the end of October. The *Boston Repertory*, a Federalist paper, printed the declaration of West Florida independence under the headline "Florida Affairs."[10] The Natchez papers must have believed that an event of this type, in which a supposedly democratic revolution had occurred against the Spanish Crown, should have stirred the revolutionary sentiment of any American citizen who read it—especially given the manner in which the editors or residents provided the information. No doubt they believed that by portraying the movement as a revolution akin to that of the American colonies, they would gain sympathy for West Floridians.

Some measure of the attitude of far-off New Englanders is evident in the headline from the December 7 *Repertory*, "More of the little mimick Revolution of Florida."[11] Although the body of the article duplicated others from around the nation, on the same day U.S. troops occupied Bayou Sara the *Repertory* used the headline to call into question the scope and scale of the revolution, if not the motivation behind the rebellion. Bostonians, after all, remembered their own Declaration of Independence and could now read for themselves the kind of declaration Floridians issued. The headline seemed to say that if the West Florida rebellion was in fact a revolution, it was one that the residents should not consider on par with the "real" revolution of 1776.

Was it a "real" revolution? Of course. Certainly the residents of West Florida exchanged one form of government (the Spanish monarchy) for another (independence, to be followed shortly by American occupation and political assimilation). For more than twenty-five years, West Florida residents had lived under the aegis of the Spanish Crown, with no sign of dissatisfaction. When their social, economic, and political networks began to dissolve, however, they revolted. Was it a "mimick" revolution? In some sense, yes. But not in the way that Bostonians thought. It followed a pattern similar to contemporary revolutions all across Latin America. Its main similarity, and one for which it should be given more credit, is that it did not occur as part of some "patriotic" plan to become American.

Rather, settlement and loyalty under Spain's rule had always been fueled by the promise of easy land and a stable government. When land was easy to get, immigrants came to the area and then prospered and existed under a system not all that foreign to them. While the government and the surrounding territories operated with some kind of stability, residents demonstrated a willingness to abide by Spain's government and profess loyalty to the Crown. By 1810 that stability had disappeared. The revolution began as a reaction against what the residents saw as potential for political chaos generated by the collapse of the Spanish monarchy and was propelled by overly strict land policies. Moreover, by 1810 crime was on the rise, the borderlands were surrounded by a foreign albeit familiar power, and instability was the order of the day. At its base, this was a revolution of pragmatism on the part of some locals; when the government no longer served their immediate economic needs, they shrugged it off. By 1810 West Floridians had more to risk than in 1804. Baton Rouge had changed from a small frontier post into a town with streets and small plots of land with houses for sale. Land prices had risen steeply, and even Saint Francisville on the frontier of Feliciana had evolved into a place with town lots and a general store.

More accurately, this revolution was one by "default" rather than one driven by ideology. The various declarations contained none of the rhetoric of liberty found in numerous other declarations of independence in the Western Hemisphere during this period. West Floridians, having no other recourse, chose independence and eventual incorporation into the United States over the uncertainty brought on by falling land prices, rising crime, the absence of a strong, honest governor, and the collapse of their mother country. Because of the anti-French sentiments present in West Florida, and because the British had virtually withdrawn from the North American colonies, West Floridians had little choice. The Baton Rouge district did not contain enough land and resources to make the area a viable independent political and economic unit, and its proximity to the United States meant that once the revolution began, it would inevitably end with the intervention of U.S. troops—not because residents in 1810 necessarily wanted intervention, but because West Floridians in 1811 had little choice.

The United States had claimed West Florida as American territory since 1803 and could not in good conscience return the area to Spanish rule—even had the U.S. government had the means to do so. For the British, all but removed from the southern parts of the New World save for a few Caribbean islands, the main concern was to prevent the province from becoming captive to French interests—although some Baton Rouge residents in 1809 had explored the possibility of a British invasion of Mobile and West Florida. Napoleon, who had exhorted Spanish colonies in the New World to independence, had neither the political or economic capital nor the military might to take control of the area.

The residents of Baton Rouge and West Florida, then, became American because they had nowhere else to turn. This speaks to the place of loyalty and nationalism in West Florida, the lower Mississippi Valley, and perhaps the South itself. Eric Hobsbawm describes protonationalism as "the consciousness of belonging or having belonged to a lasting political entity."[12] In some sense the French, the British, and then the Spanish Crown provided that sense of belonging up through 1810. For West Floridians the Spanish Crown received the loyalty due it as a protector of their ability to obtain land and move up the ladder of wealth by using the opportunities available to settlers in the borderlands. At the same time, many of the original West Florida settlers had moved to the province to flee either the American Revolution or religious persecution. With regard to the former, that they remained loyal to a king should come as no surprise—they had fled a movement in the 1770s and 1780s designed to replace one. Many West Floridians were *comfortable* with the idea of a sovereign, even a Catholic sovereign. However, once the stability of the region began to suffer after 1803 and particularly after the Kemper raids, and after the Spanish Crown restricted the ability of residents to prosper by amassing land, the residents became restless and uncertain.

Yet any dissent present between 1804 and 1809 clearly reflected a minority opinion. Also, with the further constraints on economic opportunity following the American embargo, the disastrous political chaos brought on by the death of Grand-Pré, and the confluence of international events, virtually every prop that might assure the loyalty of a people to the existing government had disappeared. The political loyalty shown by West Floridians, as applied in the layers of community, region, province, and country, had been reduced one by one, until only loyalty to the local community remained. West Floridians chose their community, as they had to, because it was the source of their prosperity, contentment, and independence. The revolution allowed them to replace the layers with the most convenient blanket available, the United States. In 1810 West Floridians simply underwent their third change of government (the fifth for those with property on the west side of the Mississippi) in a process familiar to anyone who had lived in the area since 1763.

NOTES

Abbreviations

AGI   Archivo General de Indias, Papeles de Cuba, Louisiana State University Libraries, Special Collections, Baton Rouge

ANC   Archivo Nacional de la República de Cuba, Havana

LOC   Library of Congress, Washington, D.C.

NARA National Archives and Record Administration, Washington, D.C.

PVP   Papers of Vicente Sebastián Pintado, Library of Congress, Washington, D.C.

SD   Slave Database, at WFP

WFP   Archives of the Spanish Government of West Florida: A Series of Eighteen Bound Volumes of Written Documents Mostly in the Spanish Language (West Florida papers), deposited in the Record Room of the Nineteenth Judicial District Court, Baton Rouge

Introduction

1. The terms "American" and "Anglo-American" can encompass a number of different meanings. Following the contemporary standard, I use "American" to mean any person from the United States. Where national origin is not clear for whites, I have used "Anglo-American" to designate any white person from either Great Britain (including Ireland and Scotland) or the United States. When possible, when the records permit, or when an explanation requires more specificity, I have been more precise in identifying nationality. However, here I am following the definitions as found in most records from the period. When it becomes necessary to identify Anglo-Americans living in West Florida, I will refer to them as "resident Anglo-Americans." The West Florida district runs from the Mississippi River in the west to the Apalachicola River to the east. The Baton Rouge district, a subset of West Florida, extended east to the Pearl River and included four divisions— Feliciana, Baton Rouge proper, Saint Helena, and Saint Tammany. The thirty-first degree of latitude defined the northern boundary, while Bayous Manchac and Iberville defined the southern land boundaries.

2. Weber, "Spanish Legacy in North America." The initial historiography on the West Florida Revolution dates back to Monette, *History of the Discovery*. The explicit anti-Catholicism of the period along with the decline of Spain's empire influenced Monette, and his book informed later works such as Cox, *West Florida Controversy*. Cox's work remains the standard reference for the period but also treats American expansion as inevitable and the monochromatic settlers' sentiments as invariably anti-Spanish and pro-American. Stanley Clisby Arthur, a journalist in Saint Francisville, Louisiana—a town in what is now West Feliciana Parish—wrote the most influential and hagiographic work on the subject in a series of newspaper articles in the *St. Francisville (La.) Democrat*; see the July 8, 1933, edition, "Pictures of the Past: The Story of the Kemper Brothers, Three Fighting Sons of a Baptist Preacher Who Fought for Freedom When Louisiana Was Young,"

p. 1, and in *Story of the West Florida Rebellion*. In recent years Ann Patton Malone, in *Sweet Chariot*, cites Arthur as the main source of information on West Florida's late colonial period, and other authors have followed suit. More recently, in *Pistols and Politics* Samuel Hyde, citing Arthur and others, argues that during this period "the Spanish government appeared weak and corrupt to the inhabitants of West Florida," and the Spaniards "failed to appoint district courts to deal with the growing criminal activity in the territory" (19). The argument over a lack of judicial review is common but stems from a misunderstanding of the Spanish system of law. Finally, Frank Lawrence Owsley and Gene Smith's recent *Filibusters and Expansionists* lists Arthur and three other contemporary authors as the main sources of information on the West Florida parishes during 1803–10 and notes that filibusters during this period "wanted an efficient, responsible local government," something "Spain's archaic administrative system could not provide" (9).

3. Other works have described the general political situation in the Floridas, most recently Paul E. Hoffman's excellent *Florida's Frontiers*. Hoffman's work passes over the 1810 West Florida Revolution entirely in favor of a discussion of the Patriot War (in 1812) and then refocuses on East Florida. However, he does note that American efforts to stir up anti-Spanish, pro-American sentiment north of Mobile in that period mostly failed. Likewise, Rembert Patrick's *Florida Fiasco* and Joseph B. Smith's *Plot to Steal Florida* brush by the 1810 revolution with a nod to the supposed anti-Spanish sentiments of the locals.

4. Holton, *Forced Founders*, and Hall, *Land and Allegiance*.

5. Perhaps the two best examinations of the events that culminated in U.S. annexation of the Floridas is Cusick, *Other War of 1812*, and Owsley and Smith, *Filibusters and Expansionists*. However, Bice, *Original Lone Star Republic*, Hoffman, *Florida's Frontiers*, and Landers, *Black Society in Spanish Florida*, also detail the process in separate chapters. For a more specific discussion of the capture of Mobile, see Gene Smith, " 'Our Flag Was Displayed.'" For a discussion of West Florida and its incorporation into the United States, see Robert Taylor, "Prelude to Manifest Destiny."

6. Starr, *Tories, Dons, and Rebels*. For a more complete discussion of West Florida during the British period, see also Fabel, *Economy of British West Florida*. On the transition from British to Spanish rule, see Haarmann, "Spanish Conquest of British West Florida."

7. Armitage and Braddick, *British Atlantic World*, 16.

8. Ibid., 23.

9. Landesman, "Nation, Migration, and the Province," 463.

Chapter 1. Settling the West Florida Frontier

1. I use the term "secondary sale" here to distinguish land transactions between private citizens or companies from land grants obtained from the government. "Marriage Contract between Carlos Bonito Grangé and Margarite Angela Dubois," WFP 1:25; Cummins, "Church Courts." All translations from Spanish and French are mine, except for WFP citations, where I have used the original Works Progress Administration translations.

2. "Inventory of the Property of Ann Michel," WFP 1:21.

3. "Sale of a House by Maria Obrien to Santiago Fuller," WFP 1:38. The Spanish system of measuring land used what they called "the arpents of the City of Paris." According to WFP 16:340, one acre equaled roughly 1.24 arpents (variously spelled arpent or arpen). One "section" under the U.S. system equaled 640 acres, or almost 800 arpents.

4. Din, "Irish Mission to West Florida."

5. Morgan's *American Slavery, American Freedom*, Isaac's *Transformation of Virginia*, Canny and Pagden's collection of essays in *Colonial Identity in the Atlantic World*, Greene's *Pursuits of Happiness*, and Richard White's *Middle Ground* all help to explain slavery and economic prosperity and the notion of a "contested frontier" and the complexity of the evolution of a frontier society. See also Usner, *Indians, Settlers, and Slaves*; Gwendolyn Midlo Hall, *Africans in Colonial Louisiana*; and Landers, *Black Society in Spanish Florida*.

6. Chaplin, *Anxious Pursuit*.

7. Gwendolyn Midlo Hall, *Africans in Colonial Louisiana*, 2–5. For a concise description of the French settlement of Louisiana, see chap. 1 of her work. See Conrad, *French Experience in Louisiana History*, and Eccles, *French in North America*, for good studies of French settlement in North America; Ingersoll also reviews early French settlement in lower Louisiana, though his appraisal is fraught with analytical problems.

8. Gwendolyn Midlo Hall, *Africans in Colonial Louisiana*, 11–13.

9. Daniel Richter's *Facing East from Indian Country* reverses the traditional perspective on European encroachment on Indian lands and provides a first-rate account of Franco-Indian political, social, and cultural relations.

10. For an excellent analysis of this attack, see Usner, *Indians, Settlers, and Slaves*, 65–76.

11. Nash, *Red, White, and Black*; Dowd, *Spirited Resistance*, 116; Dysart, "Another Road to Disappearance," 37.

12. Weber, *Spanish Frontier in North America*, 229.

13. Ibid.

14. ANC, fondo: Realengos. Though the records do not specify which group of Indians lived there, contextual evidence suggests the Choctaws.

15. "Declaration of the Negress Dane," part of the "Murder of Malcolm Walker," in WFP 14:12.

16. Usner, *Indians, Settlers, and Slaves*, 110; Gilbert Din, "Canary Islander Settlements of Spanish Louisiana."

17. Usner, *Indians, Settlers, and Slaves*, 111–12.

18. Fabel, *Economy of British West Florida*.

19. Starr, *Tories, Dons, and Rebels*, 230. Tantalizingly, three immigrants came from the Cherokee Nation, although they receive no further mention in Starr's work.

20. Usner, *Indians, Settlers, and Slaves*, 113.

21. Starr, *Tories, Dons, and Rebels*, 228.

22. These and other filibustering raids are covered in more detail in chap. 4.

23. Starr, *Tories, Dons, and Rebels*, 234–35, 237.

24. Haarmann, "Spanish Conquest of British West Florida."

25. Leslie Hall, *Land and Allegiance*, and Holton, *Forced Founders*, are among the most recent book-length treatments of the role of land as a determinant for loyalty in the British colonies.

26. NARA, record group 59, microfilm T-225, "Census of Louisiana in the Year 1785"; microfilm T260, roll 2, "Census of Louisiana in the Year 1785."

27. Ingersoll, *Mammon and Manon*, 155.

28. Cummins, "Spanish Louisiana Land Policy"; Cummins, "Enduring Community"; Din, "Proposals and Plans," 197.

29. Arthur, *Story of the West Florida Rebellion*, 16; Usner, *Indians, Settlers, and Slaves*, 110. In the records "Bayou Sara" is variously spelled "Sara" (the Spanish spelling) and "Sarah" (the English spelling). I have retained the Spanish spelling throughout the book. Although the Spaniards never formally created "parishes," many residents and officials used the term in official correspondence, probably as a holdover from the French period. I have used "parish" from time to time to help the flow of the text.

30. Arthur, *Story of the West Florida Rebellion*, 18; Hyde, *Pistols and Politics*, 3, 18, 22. Land grants in Feliciana and Bayou Sara go back to the British possession of the area. See, for instance, a land grant registration by John Ellis for land in Bayou Sara, said grant "based on British and Spanish claims," NARA, record group 49.

31. For a complete discussion of plantations in British West Florida, see Rea, "Planters and Plantations in British West Florida."

32. Fabel, *Economy of British West Florida*, 119. I have confined my discussion here to farming, and within that to land use as a path to wealth. However, by the 1790s the Archives of the Spanish Government of West Florida reveal that the area already had at least one nonslave in each of the following professions: apprentice upholsterer, carpenter, breeder, doctor, surgeon, interpreter, blacksmith.

33. Richard Devall to Vicente Pintado, June 20, 1803, in PVP, reel 2, container 2.

34. PVP, reel 6, containers 19 and 25, map 3.

35. Ibid.

36. Ibid.

37. See Din, "Irish Mission to West Florida," for a discussion of Spanish efforts to convert residents to Catholicism.

38. Brevard, *History of Florida*, 267.

39. Works Progress Administration, *Spanish Land Grants in Florida*, xxix.

40. Brevard, *History of Florida*, 269.

41. "Governor Carlos de Grand-Pré Inspects a Bridge Built by Thomas Lilley," in WFP 3:4.

42. The Archives of the Spanish Government of West Florida contain the most complete record of private sales under Spanish rule before 1810 in the Baton Rouge area. This list was culled from WFP 1, 2, 3, 4. The remainder of the transactions appear on the western shore of the Mississippi (31) or are unknown (11). I placed records in the "Unknown" category if they did not state where the plot was (e.g., "on the western shore of the river," "on the Hill of Fountains"), if the place could not be determined with any certainty (e.g., "on the south side of the river," which could indicate different locations depending on the

meander), or if no arpentage was listed. One transaction in these records came from the Natchez area, which was then still under Spanish control. I have excluded the western shore because the transactions, while technically part of the Baton Rouge district, fall under the administration of Pointe Coupee. After the Louisiana Purchase, the territory fell under the rule of the United States. For the sake of simplicity, and because other historians have discussed that area, I have excluded it from my estimates of land sales and surveys. See Gwendolyn Midlo Hall, *Africans in Colonial Louisiana,* for more on Pointe Coupee.

43. Of the twelve that were not used for studying the price of land, three had no known arpentage, one was a land exchange (both parcels in the Feliciana frontier), five contained some sort of barter transaction (e.g., 240 arpents of land for 250 pesos and a horse), and three occurred as part of an estate inventories. Two of the barters involved a slaves-for-land deal.

44. "Sale of a Habitation from Jean Paul Trahan," in WFP 2:216; "Receipt for a Habitation Sold by Esteban Peltier," in WFP 2:14; "Succession of James Stanley," in WFP 1:204; "Sale of a Habitation from Marie Nivet to Marie Ann Decoux," in WFP 2:99; "Inventory of the Goods of Jacob Nash, Deceased," in WFP 1:192–94.

45. An alcalde was the local equivalent of a magistrate; it was usually an elected position.

46. "Acceptance of Executorship by Those Named in the Testimony of William Dortch," in WFP 4:46.

47. "Auction of the Sale of Property Belonging to Nicolas Lamothe," in WFP 4:19.

48. Holmes, "Provincial Governor-General Manuel Gayoso de Lemos," 102.

49. Ironically, at least one namesake, Charles Grandpré Johnson, a member of a prominent Baton Rouge family, served in the militia that stormed Fort San Carlos during the 1810 revolution, when Grand-Pré's son was killed.

50. Some brief details of the life of Carlos de Grand-Pré can be found in WFP 16:212–12A. However, this Frenchman who came to serve the Spanish in a borderlands community is awaiting his historian.

51. "Will of Carlos de Grand-Pré" in WFP 16:218.

52. Pintado may have gone to Louisiana as part of the Canary Island, or Isleño, settlements in the 1770s. Din, "Canary Islander Settlements of Spanish Louisiana."

53. PVP, 1, biographical note.

54. Waldrep, "Opportunity on the Frontier," 155–57.

55. Aron, *How the West Was Lost,* 59; Thomas Clark, *History of Kentucky.*

56. Aron, *How the West Was Lost,* 71.

57. Friend, " 'Work and Be Rich,' " 129.

58. Ibid.

59. Aron, *How the West Was Lost,* 80.

60. For more on the transition from British to Spanish control north of West Florida, see Christopher Morris, *Becoming Southern.*

61. Rowland, *Life, Letters, and Papers,* 9.

62. Ibid., 10.

63. Ibid., 11–12. Dunbar also founded the Mississippi Society for the Acquirement and Dissemination of Useful Knowledge, a society with objectives similar to those of the American Philosophical Society. See *Mississippi Herald and Natchez Gazette*, November 19, 1804, p. 4.

64. "Report of William Dunbar to the Spanish Government at the Conclusion of His Services in Locating and Surveying the Thirty-First Degree of Latitude," in Rowland, *Life, Letters, and Papers*, 82.

65. Ibid. Dunbar initially labels the reptile a crocodile. After the first iteration, however, he uses the word "alligator."

66. Ibid., 90, 91.

67. Ibid., 83. The classic study of the ways in which colonists affected their environment is Cronon, *Changes in the Land*. Vale, *Fire, Native Peoples*, contains a series of essays examining the role of fire in Native Americans' intentional alteration of the natural landscape. Though the essays focus on the trans-Rockies west, Vale's "Pre-European Landscape of the United States" makes a good case that Indians throughout North America used fire to dramatically change the land. For more on reshaping and commodifying the environment of the Lower Mississippi Valley around Baton Rouge and New Orleans in the seventeenth and eighteenth centuries, see Christopher Morris, "Impenetrable but Easy." For the environmental problems facing East Floridians during settlement, see Miller, *Environmental History of Northeast Florida*.

68. Daniel Clark to Thomas Jefferson, November 12, 1799, in Oberg, *Papers of Thomas Jefferson*, 237–38; Silver, *New Face on the Countryside*.

69. Fabel, *Economy of British West Florida*, 120.

70. See ANC, fondo: Real Consulado y Junto de Fomentos, legajo 73, no. 2796, for a complete list of all goods exchanged between Spanish ports in the New World and the Old in 1803. The commodities traded in New Orleans do not represent the norm for Baton Rouge. In fact, no complete list of goods traded in and out of Baton Rouge could exist for any year, in part because some residents of West Florida traded through Mobile or Pensacola, while others went through New Orleans, where their produce was probably recorded. Still others smuggled their goods out past customs agents. However, Cusick, in "Across the Border," provides excellent detail for another Florida port, Saint Augustine.

71. Rowland, *Life, Letters, and Papers*. The references to women sawing while men made the staves are extensive. See, for example, pp. 31, 34, 35, 36, 38.

72. "Report of William Dunbar, " in Rowland, *Life, Letters, and Papers*, 98–99.

73. NARA, record group 107, microfilm M-222, Philip Nolan to "My Dear General (Wilkinson?)," January 6, 1796, and Philip Nolan to General Wilkinson, (probably January 4) 1796. The second letter suggests an overland trade between West Florida and northern Mexico. Daniel Clark to Thomas Jefferson, November 12, 1799, in Oberg, *Papers of Thomas Jefferson*, 236–37, describes efforts by the Spaniards to interdict what they saw as spy missions on Nolan's part.

74. Morris, *Becoming Southern*, 23. A more recent history of territorial Mississippi can be found in Robert Haynes, "Territorial Mississippi," which he is developing into a book-length treatment of Mississippi territorial history.

75. Morris, *Becoming Southern*, 25.

76. Ibid.

77. Parker, "Cattle Trade in East Florida," 153, 156. Parker also notes that Indians in East Florida were the main source of new livestock for settlers. This probably held true for West Floridians as well.

78. NARA, record group 59, microfilm, т-225, "Resumen General de Padron del Disto. De Natchez afines del Ano de 1795." In addition eighty-four men served in a militia equipped with thirty-nine guns.

79. For trading on the other side of Spanish Florida, see Cusick, "Across the Border." Cusick notes that Saint Augustine had a flourishing and economically crucial trade with various American ports, most importantly Charleston.

80. "Inventory and Public Sale of Stock Left by Louis Ricard at His Decease," in WFP 2:147–53. Bienville repaid Ricard's debts after Ricard's death.

81. Regarding the debt, see "Petition of Francois Merieult," in WFP 2:403, and "Decree of Joseph Vasquez Vahamonde," in WFP 2:331.

82. "Sale of a Habitation from Widow Jean Daigle to the Minor Justine Ramirez," in WFP 2:278. Bienville's X appears in the following documents: "Sale and Mortgage of Land and Improvements from Peter, Louis, and Basil Bienville to Charles Proffit," in WFP 2:122; as a witness to a land mortgage, in "Petition of Francois Merieult" for a loan in WFP 2:402–3; as a power of attorney in "Sale of a Habitation belonging to Joseph Michel, by Jean Baptiste Bienville, through a Power of Attorney," in WFP 2:224; as witness to a land sale in "Note," WFP 2:352; and as witness to an estate auction in "Auction Sale of Property Left under the Care of Bienville," in WFP 2:154.

83. "Inventory and Estimation of the Property of Jean Baptiste Bienville," in WFP 5:269–73, 280–81.

84. WFP 5:271–72. Under the Spanish system, a succession included an inventory and estimation of property and could be separate from the will.

85. Gwendolyn Midlo Hall, *Africans in Colonial Louisiana*, 124.

86. Chaplin, *Anxious Pursuit*, 193–96. Chaplin provides an excellent description of the entire process of indigo cultivation in South Carolina on pp. 193–98.

87. Rowland, *Life, Letters, and Papers*, 26, 30, 33, 38.

88. Chaplin, *Anxious Pursuit*, 193.

89. Robert Ory's name is spelled Ory, Uric, and Ury in three different extant copies of the contract. I have used "Ory" because that spelling of the name also appears on land records. This was not the first business other than farming in the area, of course; residents built several mills during the British and the Spanish period. But a dairy indicates a more stable settlement and a close market for the perishable products. Philips, "Flood Thy Neighbor," details the existence of no fewer than ten sawmills in British and Spanish West Florida.

90. "A Contract between John Buhler and Robert Uric [Ory]," in WFP 1:303.

91. NARA, record group 107, microfilm, м-222, Unknown to Baron de Carondelet, June 21, 1796. On indigo growth in Bayou Sara, see Daniel Clark to Manuel Gayoso de Lemos, July 24, 1794, in the same source.

92. NARA, record group 46, "Imports from Floridas & Louisiana for the years ending on 30th Sep 1799, 1800, 1801, 1802," "Value of the Exports of Foreign and Domestic Produce," and "Exports to Floridas and Louisiana for the years ending on 30th Sep 1799, 1800, 1801, 1802."

93. ANC, fondo: Real Consulado y Junto de Fomentos, legajo 73, no. 2807-A.

94. Ibid.

95. Ibid.

Chapter 2. Working the West Florida Frontier

1. Tannenbaum, *Slave and Citizen*. Historians have debated this point for decades; however, researchers working with French, Spanish, and Anglo sources have provided abundant evidence bolstering this particular claim. For the most recent discussion of this issue, see Landers, *Black Society in Spanish Florida*. Her book, like this one, draws from multiple-language sources, and it provides both context and a great deal of documentary evidence that Tannenbaum was, at least, on the right track. Ingersoll, *Mammon and Manon*, reached the opposite conclusion, though his work has been widely acknowledged as deeply flawed. Davis, in *Problem of Slavery*, and Rankin, in "Tannenbaum Thesis Reconsidered," provide two older but excellent counterarguments to the Tannenbaum thesis working through English-language sources.

2. One of the most complete explanations of the Code Noir is found in Riddell, "Le Code Noir."

3. Schafer, *Slavery, the Civil Law*, 1–2. Saving the life of a white person was considered a valid reason to manumit a slave; simple gratitude was not.

4. Tannenbaum, *Slave and Citizen*, 48.

5. Cutter, *Legal Culture*, 31; Tannenbaum, *Slave and Citizen*, 53. Harrington, in "*Res* or *Persona*," also traces nineteenth-century U.S. slave law to its Roman roots.

6. Cutter, *Legal Culture*, 31.

7. Ibid., 32.

8. Ibid., 107; "Castilian legal procedure rested on the thirteenth century *Siete Partidas* of Alfonso X . . . [that] had been elaborated by a juridical community steeped in the *ius commune* tradition, the product of both Roman and canon law. Transplanted to the New World, the procedural rules in the Indies as applied in the high tribunals conformed to those found on the peninsula" (107). See also Tannenbaum, *Slave and Citizen*, 48.

9. Tannenbaum, *Slave and Citizen*, 50.

10. Ibid., 52.

11. Ibid.; "Murder of a Slave," in WFP 10:212.

12. Landers, *Black Society in Spanish Florida*, 7–8, and especially chap. 8; Hanger, *Bounded Lives, Bounded Places*.

13. Tannenbaum, *Slave and Citizen*, 53.

14. Ibid., 49.

15. "List of Various Acts," in WFP 1:35; "Act of Liberty Coartación Case of Madame Maria Ana Decoux and Her Slave, Jacob," in WFP 1:73.

16. "List of Various Acts," in WFP 1:35.

17. Ingersoll, *Mammon and Manon*, 221.

18. Ibid., 222.

19. Cutter, *Legal Culture*, 38. The cases of slaves engaging in petty commerce and quasi free activities in the district are too numerous to list.

20. "Sale of Ten Negro Slaves from the African Gold Coast by Pedro Lartique," in WFP 1:57.

21. "Sale of Freedom to a Negress Slave by Alexandre Patin to William Dunbar," in WFP 2:409.

22. In other early-age manumissions in West Florida, several owners freed slaves on or before their days of birth, leading to speculation as to the parentage of the children. See "Emancipation of Virginia," in WFP 10:129; "Joseph Marchand Buys the Freedom of an Unborn Child for 25 Pesos," in WFP 11:179; "Emancipation of Camilla" in WFP 13:121.

23. Cope, *Limits of Racial Domination*, 76–78.

24. Ibid., 84, 68.

25. Ibid., 162.

26. Ibid.

27. "Inventory of the Estate of Pierre Avare," in WFP 1:115. This is the same Bienville discussed in chap. 1. Typical of Spanish racial culture, his race is not listed in the document until the death of his brother, Louis Ricard. My understanding of free black networks in this period and place is largely informed by Hanger's *Bounded Lives, Bounded Places*.

28. Ibid.

29. Weber, *Spanish Frontier in North America*, 329; Tannenbaum, *Slave and Citizen*, 98.

30. Din, "Irish Mission to West Florida."

31. ANC, fondo: Reales Cédulas y Ordenes Negros, legajo 20, no. 103.

32. ANC, fondo: Asuntos Políticos, legajo 8, no. 50 (September 13, 1802) contains a prohibition against slaves from Guadeloupe, where there was a rebellion.

33. ANC, fondo: Reales Cédulas y Ordenes Negros, legajo 20, no. 103.

34. For many years historians engaged in a kind of side debate as to whether the Spanish or the British-American system was crueler. This is a silly argument, as is the need for historians to reaffirm that the system was indeed cruel when discussing the ways in which slaves mitigated that system's cruelty.

35. This proposition will be tested in chap. 5.

36. Thomas D. Morris, *Southern Slavery and the Law*, 38, 56.

37. Winthrop Jordan, *White over Black*, 167.

38. Ibid. For more on this issue, see Jordan's discussion on pp. 167–78.

39. Kolchin, *American Slavery*, 95.

40. Ibid.

41. Jonathan A. Bush, "British Constitution," 405.

42. Thomas D. Morris, *Southern Slavery and the Law*, 39.

43. Genovese, *Roll, Jordan, Roll*, 49.

44. Ibid., 47.

45. Edgerton, *Gabriel's Rebellion*, 81.

46. Gross, "Pandora's Box," 291, 318–19.

47. A more complete discussion of Indian slavery under the Spaniards can be found in Webre, "Problem of Indian Slavery"; Usner, *Indians, Settlers, and Slaves*; and Holland-Braun, "Creek Indians, Blacks, and Slavery." However, although an extensive body of literature exists regarding Indian slavery on the southwestern Spanish borderlands, Indian slavery in late eighteenth- and early nineteenth-century Spanish Louisiana remains neglected.

48. Geggus, "Slavery, War and Revolution," 48–49.

49. In what remains one of the most concise and well-written short accounts of the Haitian Revolution, Geggus writes that "few revolutions in world history have had such profound consequences," "Haitian Revolution," 21. See also Sidbury, *Ploughshares into Swords*; Hickey, "America's Response"; and Matthewson, "Jefferson and Haiti."

50. Geggus, "Haitian Revolution," 47–48. See also Gwendolyn Midlo Hall, *Africans in Colonial Louisiana*, 348. The U.S. political repercussions of the revolution receive excellent coverage in Matthewson's "Jefferson and Haiti."

51. Newspapers across the United States widely reported the uprising in Saint Domingue, and escaping slaves and their owners became something of a problem for U.S. authorities. Among the large number of references to the news of the rebellion making its way to slaves on the mainland, see in particular Hanger's references to slaves at a ball in New Orleans specifically discussing the event in her *Bounded Lives, Bounded Places*. It seems highly unlikely, even impossible, that given the ability of slaves to transmit information over long distances and especially in major ports, the event could be known by slaves in New Orleans but not in Baton Rouge.

52. Gwendolyn Midlo Hall, *Africans in Colonial Louisiana*, 345.

53. Ibid., 367.

54. Edgerton, *Gabriel's Rebellion*, 68.

55. Ibid., 17.

56. This periodization, like many good breakdowns, is part convenience, part historical necessity. The best records begin in 1785 and help to give a full picture of the pre–Louisiana Purchase period. 1795 marks the Pointe Coupee slave rebellion, making it a watershed year for slavery in Louisiana. This period provides a large enough sample to make accurate points with regard to slaveholding in the Baton Rouge district.

57. A peso during the early national period was equal to one dollar. Figures taken from inventories in WFP. Individual records cover many pages per records, but totals for each are found on the following: 1:45 (212 pesos); 1:86 (1,294 pesos); 1:154 (614 pesos); 1:217 (495 pesos); 1:274 (379 pesos); 1:363 (315 pesos); 2:32 (20 pesos); 2:109 (499 pesos); 2:150 (186 pesos); 2:249 (1,102 pesos); 2:314 (653 pesos); 2:319 (19 pesos); 2:418 (137 pesos).

58. "Declaration of the Seventh Witness, Morris O'Brien," in WFP 2:42.

59. "Inventory of the Estate of Joseph Trahan," in WFP 2:109.

60. The records for these are found in WFP 1:117; 1:192; 1:204; 1:258; 1:338; 1:379; 2:198; 2:383; 2:460. I've left out four people whose estate inventories seem skewed or incomplete.

61. Wealth distribution (in pesos): 2,182, 2,705, 4,571, 4,604, 6,200, 6,661, 16,925, 23,346, 25,500. Slave distribution: 5, 6, 8, 10, 19, 20, 39, 45.

62. "Inventory of the Estate of George Proffit," in WFP 1:338.

63. "Inventory of the Property of Jane Stanley," in WFP 1:203.

64. "Inventory of the Estate of John Fitzpatrick," in WFP 2:454, 460.

65. Ibid., 2:459.

66. All the slave numbers are taken from WFP, which contain records of slave sales and other transactions. I created a database with entries for each individual that contained all known information, including race, sex, and age. The slave demography data are composed of a variety of transactions, including sales (101, or 35.8%), estate inventories (90, or 31.9%), successions (63, or 22.3%), property estimations (23, or 8.1%), rentals (3, or 1%), one mortgage, and one return of a runaway caught in the United States. The even distribution effectively negates any bias that might favor one type of transaction over another. In a few cases the exact age was not listed but could be determined by the language. For instance, the records list some slaves as "infants," "at the breast," "old," "very old," and so on. I define "adult" here to mean any slave over thirteen, the age at which slaves usually went to work full-time in the fields. The percentages that follow will not always equal 100 percent due to rounding. Numbers taken from this database are hereafter cited as SD for "Slave Database." For the development and definitions of "creole" and its relevance to the study of slavery, see Dawdy, "Understanding Cultural Change."

67. SD.

68. "National origin" is an approximate term, especially at a time when Europeans were imposing the idea of national boundaries on Africa. It seems safe to assume that residents knew when their slaves were from Africa, but Europeans themselves may very well have been guessing at the specific African origins of their slaves. I have used the term here in the same way as Spanish records from the period do but have refrained from making any definitive statements on African origins.

69. My general sense of the records is that with regard to children, no entry for a place of origin indicates that they were from Baton Rouge. However, that is purely speculation.

70. "Inventory of the Property of Samuel Steer," in WFP 2:197; SD; "Israel Dodge, a Merchant from Kentucky, Sells Eight Adult Negroes and One Infant," in WFP 1:301.

71. SD.

72. For more on the transition from slave child to adult, see Deborah Gray White, *Ar'n't I a Woman?*, 92–98.

73. The reason for the stipulation was simple: Cuba was always short of wheat, and the flour would feed not only the newly imported slaves but also other residents. Such a large number of slaves were probably destined to be traded elsewhere within the colonial empire. ANC, fondo: Real Consulado y Junto de Fomentas, legajo 73, no. 2807-A.

Chapter 3. Owning the West Florida Frontier

1. NARA, record group 59, "Census of the Districts of Posts of Louisiana and West Florida."

2. Thomas Jefferson to Archibald Stuart, January 25, 1786, in Boyd, *Papers of Thomas Jefferson*, 217.

3. Some scholars continue to attribute the closing of New Orleans to Juan Ventura Morales alone, despite evidence to the contrary. See Lyon, "Document," 280.

4. Ibid.

5. ANC, fondo: Real Consulado y Junto de Fomentos, legajo 73, no. 2807–A.

6. Ibid.

7. "Substance of the Speech Delivered by Lord Grenville," May 13, 1802, in British Library.

8. Weber, *Spanish Frontier in North America*, 291.

9. On August 30, 1803, The New Haven, Conn. *Visitor* even corrected an earlier column by stating: "*West* Florida is included in the Louisiana purchase, and not *East* Florida, as erroneously inserted in our last" (1).

10. *Washington Federalist*, September 15, 1804, p. 3.

11. Graviora Manent was the pseudonym under which Fernando Martínez de Yrujo, Spain's minister to the United States, wrote. Graviora Manent, "No. I," "No. II," "No. III," *New York American Citizen*, September 19, 1804, p. 2; September 20, 1804, p. 2; September 22, 1804, p. 2; author unknown, *New York American Citizen*, September 20, 1804, p. 2; author unknown, *New York American Citizen*, October 8, 1804, pp. 2–3.

12. For more on Clark, see Whitaker, "Reed and Forde," 251.

13. De Ville, *English Land Grants*, 14.

14. John G. Clark, "Economic Life," 281; PVP, reel 6, containers 19 and 25.

15. Clark, "Economic Life," 269; Wall, *Louisiana*, 75.

16. NARA, record group 107, microfilm M-222, Daniel Clark to General Wilkinson, March 18, 1796.

17. Clark, "Economic Life," 279.

18. NARA, record group 107, microfilm M-222, Contract between James Wilkinson and Daniel Clark, August 7, 1788. This contract also contains a list of people to whom Wilkinson sold the Kentucky goods. For a more detailed list of goods imported and exported by Wilkinson and Clark in 1801, see NARA, record group 59, microfilm T-260, roll 2.

19. Clark, "Economic Life," 279, 281.

20. Holmes, *Gayoso*.

21. NARA, record group 107, microfilm M-222, Daniel Clark to Manuel Gayoso de Lemos, October 5, 1796; March 2, 1796; October 18, 1796; October 14, 1796; quotation from Daniel Clark to James Wilkinson, March 18, 179[4].

22. James Madison to Daniel Clark, September 16, 1803, in Mattern, ed., *Papers of James Madison*, 428.

23. Cox, *West Florida Controversy*, 88.

24. See, for example, Madison's continuing requests for information in James Madison to Daniel Clark, September 16, 1803, in Mattern, ed., *Papers of James Madison*, 428; Cox, *West Florida Controversy*, 88.

25. LOC, Thomas Jefferson Papers, series 1, General Correspondence, 1651–1827, Wil-

liam C. C. Claiborne to Thomas Jefferson, August 24, 1803; also at http://memory.loc
.gov/ammem/collections/jefferson_papers/.

26. Ibid.

27. Joe Gray Taylor, *Louisiana*, 42, 47. For an analysis of Claiborne's influence on Spanish policy, see Jared Bradley, "W. C. C. Claiborne and Spain."

28. A short history of Folch's intendancy in West Florida can be found in David Hart
White, *Vicente Folch.*

29. Monette, *History of the Discovery*, 560–561.

30. Nasatir, "Anglo-Spanish Rivalry on the Upper Missouri," 526.

31. LOC, Thomas Jefferson Papers, Thomas Jefferson to William Dunbar, March 13
and April 15, 1804; also at http://memory.loc.gov/ammem/mtjhtml/mtjhome.html.

32. NARA, record group 107, microfilm M-370, [unknown] to William Dunbar.

33. A full account of this as-yet-unwritten-about expedition can be found in Rowland,
Life, Letters, and Papers, 216–320.

34. Ibid., 78–82. His survey of the West Florida frontier (82), in "Report of William
Dunbar to the Spanish Government at the Conclusion of His Services in Locating and
Surveying the Thirty-First Degree of Latitude," is an especially valuable glimpse of a land
as yet untamed by Europeans.

35. NARA, record group 59, microfilm T-260, roll 2, William Dunbar to Thomas Jefferson, September 30, 1803.

36. William Claiborne to James Madison, September 7, 1803, in Mattern, ed., *Papers
of James Madison*, 387.

37. ANC, fondo: Realengos, legajo 43, no. 20.

38. NARA, record group 59, microfilm T-260, roll 7, William Claiborne to James Madison, August 26, 1805; ibid., roll 6, William Claiborne to James Madison, April 21, 1805.

39. Ibid., roll 6, William C. C. Claiborne to James Madison, June 5, 1805. See also
Kastor, *Nation's Crucible*, and Kastor, *Louisiana Purchase.*

40. NARA, record group 59, microfilm T-260, roll 6, William C. C. Claiborne to James
Madison, June 5, 1805; ibid., William C. C. Claiborne to [unknown, probably James
Madison], January 19, 1805.

41. Ibid., William C. C. Claiborne to James Madison, June 5, 1805, parentheses in original.

42. Ibid., roll 8, William Claiborne to James Madison, April 16, 1806.

43. Ibid., William Claiborne to James Madison, January 1806.

44. Not a great deal has been written about Morales, who greatly influenced the U.S.
reasons for purchasing New Orleans. In a short biography Jack Holmes claims that over
the course of his career Morales consistently tried to "check the advancing tide of American settlers." However, the land sales, many of which went to Americans, seem to belie
that claim. Holmes, "*Dramatis Personae* in Spanish Louisiana," 159.

45. NARA, record group 59, microfilm T-260, roll 7, William C. C. Claiborne to James
Madison, August 6, 1805.

46. Ibid.

47. Ibid.

48. Ibid., roll 7, William C. C. Claiborne to James Madison, August 6, 1805; ibid., [Moneau Kelley] to William Claiborne, August 8, 1805; and ibid., William Claiborne to James Madison, August 10, 1805.

49. Ibid., William Claiborne to James Madison, May 19, 1805.

50. Ibid., William C. C. Claiborne to the Marquis de Casa Calvo, August 3, 1805, and William C. C. Claiborne to James Madison, August 5, 1805.

51. Ibid., William C. C. Claiborne to James Madison, August 5, 1805.

52. Ibid., the Marquis de Casa Calvo to William C. C. Claiborne, August 8, 1805.

53. Ibid., William Claiborne to the Marquis de Casa Calvo, August 17, 1805.

54. Ibid., roll 7, [Moneau Kelley] to William Claiborne, August 8, 1805.

55. Ibid., roll 7, William Claiborne to the Marquis de Casa Calvo, August 10, 1805, and August 17, 1805.

56. Ibid., William Claiborne to James Madison, August 6, 1805.

57. Ibid., Juan Ventura Morales to William Claiborne, August 19, 1805.

58. Ibid., William C. C. Claiborne to James Madison, August 5, 1805.

59. For a list of the amount of land sold and to whom it went, see NARA, record group 59, microfilm T-260, roll 7, enclosure in William C. C. Claiborne to James Madison, August 15, 1805.

60. ANC, fondo: Realengos, legajo 43, no. 26.

61. ANC, fondo: Realengos, legajo 43, no. 20.

62. NARA, record group 49, Bayou Sara land grant of John Ellis, registered with the United States in September 1805.

63. Excerpted in William Claiborne to James Madison, September 7, 1803, in Mattern, ed., *Papers of James Madison*, 387. Full text of letter in NARA, record group 59, microfilm T-260, roll 2.

64. Mattern, ed., *Papers of James Madison*, 387.

65. NARA, record group 59, microfilm T-260, roll 3, William C. C. Claiborne to Major H. L. Claiborne, February 7, 1804.

66. James Madison to Daniel Clark, September 16, 1803, 428; James Madison to Daniel Clark, September 30, 1803, 476; James Madison to Daniel Clark, October 12, 1803, 510; James Madison to Daniel Clark, October 31, 1803, 592, all in Mattern, *Papers of James Madison.*

67. NARA, record group 107, microfilm M-222, Manuel Gayoso de Lemos to Daniel Clark, March 2, 1796.

68. Ibid., Manuel Gayoso de Lemos to Daniel Clark, October 14, 1796.

69. Ibid., Manuel Gayoso de Lemos to Daniel Clark, Octobre [*sic*] 8, 1796.

70. Ibid., Daniel Clark to [James Wilkinson], May 30, 1799, in which Clark refers to Wilkinson as a "truly beloved General" and "my Dear General." By 1806 he was actively trying to have Wilkinson arrested as part of the Burr conspiracy (see, for instance, NARA, record group 59, microfilm T-260, roll 8, Daniel Clark to James Madison, November 23, 1806).

71. AGI, legajo 211, Gayoso to Pomingo, St. Ferdinand of the Bluffs, June 23, 1795, quoted in Din, *Gayoso*, 124.

72. NARA, record group 107, microfilm, M-222, Manuel Gayoso de Lemos to the king of Spain, December 5, 1797.

73. Ibid.

74. Sebastian, too, seems to have been working for both sides on the Spanish-American frontier. In 1806 a select committee of the Kentucky House of Representatives charged him with having received a pension (as did Wilkinson and probably Clark) from the Spanish government. "The Report of the Select Committee, to whom was referred the Information Communicated to the House of Representatives, charging Benjamin Sebastian, one of the Judges of the Court of Appeals of Kentucky, with having received a Pension from the Spanish Government," Special Collections Research Center, University of Chicago Library, as reproduced in LOC, *First American West*, http://lcweb2.loc.gov/ammem/award99/icuhtml/fawhome.html.

75. NARA, record group 107, microfilm M-222, Manuel Gayoso de Lemos to the king of Spain, December 5, 1797, parentheses in original.

76. Among the many letters outlining the transfer of power and its effects on elite loyalty, see the fifteen-page enclosure in NARA, record group 59, microfilm T-260, roll 3, John Watkins to William Claiborne, February 2, 1804; and the enclosure in William Claiborne to James Madison, March 1, 1804. See also William Claiborne to James Madison, March 1, 1804, in Hackett, *Papers of James Madison*, 524–25.

77. NARA, record group 59, microfilm T-260, roll 8, William C. C. Claiborne to James Madison, April 29, 1806.

78. Hanger, *Bounded Lives, Bounded Places.* Hanger's "Conflicting Loyalties: The French Revolution and Free People Of Color in Spanish New Orleans," *Louisiana History* 34, no. 1 (1993): 5–33, provides an excellent analysis of how Spain dealt with the problem of loyalty among free blacks.

79. This was a serious problem for U.S. officials, who suspected the Spaniards of plotting to return New Orleans and Louisiana to Spanish control. See, for example, NARA, record group 59, microfilm T-260, roll 7, William Claiborne to the Marquis de Casa Calvo, August 10, 1805, and William Claiborne to the Marquis de Casa Calvo, August 17, 1805; roll 8, William C. C. Claiborne to James Madison, January 7, 1806; William C. C. Claiborne to James Madison, January 9, 1806; and William C. C. Claiborne to Major Porter, January 12, 1806; record group 107, microfilm M-222, Manuel Gayoso de Lemos to Gen. James Wilkinson, March 30, 1798. That Spain intentionally delayed its withdrawal is generally recognized, and the Spanish ability to bureaucratically obfuscate is legendary. Specific to the issue of boundary lines, see Baron de Carondelet to Brig. Gen. James Wilkinson, May 23, 1797 (record group 107, microfilm M-222), in which Carondelet expresses the concerns of a local commander, Carlos de Hault De Lassus, that without a continuing Spanish presence in Natchez, the local Chickasaw tribes might find themselves subject to abuse by former Spanish subjects and incoming American settlers.

80. Brooks, "Spain's Farewell to Louisiana," 29.

81. NARA, record group 59, microfilm T-260, roll 8, William C. C. Claiborne to James Madison, January 7, 1806.

82. NARA, record group 59, microfilm T-260, roll 6, William C. C. Claiborne to James Madison, April 21, 1805.

83. William C. C. Claiborne to James Madison, February 4, 1804, in Hackett, *Papers of James Madison*, 428.

84. LOC, Thomas Jefferson Papers, series 1, General Correspondence, 1651–1827, William C. C. Claiborne to Thomas Jefferson, August 24, 1803; also at http://memory.loc .gov/ammem/collections/jefferson_papers/; NARA, record group 59, microfilm T-260, roll 4, "From William C. C. Claiborne" [probably to James Madison] (undated, probably mid-1804).

85. NARA, record group 59, microfilm T-260, roll 8, William C. C. Claiborne to James Madison, May 16, 1806.

86. Fabel, *Colonial Challenges*; Landers, *Black Society in Spanish Florida*, 229; Richard White, *Middle Ground*; Hoffman, *Florida's Frontiers*.

87. NARA, record group 107, microfilm M-222, Manuel Gayoso de Lemos to Gen. James Wilkinson, March 30, 1798.

88. NARA, record group 59, microfilm T-225, Winthrop Sargent to Evan Jones, November 7, 1799.

89. Ibid., Evan Jones to Timothy Pickering, November 8, 1799.

90. Ibid., Winthrop Sargent to Evan Jones, November 7, 1799.

91. Ibid., Evan Jones to Timothy Pickering, November 8, 1799, and Evan Jones to Winthrop Sargent, November 16, 1799.

92. Ibid., Daniel Clark to Evan Pickering, November 18, 1799.

93. Todd Smith, "Indian Policy in Spanish Louisiana," 293.

94. NARA, record group 59, microfilm T-225, "Extract of a letter from Capt. R. S. Blackburn to Lt. Colonel Constant Freeman," April 8, 1802. See also ibid., Winthrop Sargent to Evan Jones, November 7, 1799; Evan Jones to Timothy Pickering, November 8, 1799; Evan Jones to Winthrop Sargent, November 16, 1799; Daniel Clark to Timothy Pickering, November 18, 1799; and microfilm T-260, roll 5, William C. C. Claiborne to the Marquis de Casa Calvo, October 21, 1804.

95. NARA, record group 59, microfilm T-260, roll 5, William Claiborne to the Marquis de Casa Calvo, October 31, 1804.

96. Ibid., William Claiborne to James Madison, September 1, 1804; Derbigny to William Claiborne, September 5, 1804; William Claiborne to James Madison, September 8, 1804.

97. Ibid., roll 6, [unreadable] to William Claiborne, October 16, 1804; [unreadable] to William Claiborne, December 27, 1804.

98. Landers, *Black Society in Spanish Florida*, 24–28.

99. NARA, record group 59, microfilm T-260, roll 5, William Claiborne to Colonel Butler, November 8, 1804; William Claiborne to the Marquis de Casa Calvo, November 8, 1804; William Claiborne to "the Commandant at Nachitoches [*sic*]," November 8, 1804.

100. NARA, record group 59, microfilm M-40, roll 3, William Claiborne to James Madison, November 20, 1807; see continued correspondence between Madison and Claiborne during 1808, microfilm T-260, roll 9.

101. NARA, record group 59, microfilm T-260, roll 9, William Claiborne to Governor Salcedo, March 9, 1808.

102. Schafer, *Slavery, the Civil Law*, 4.

103. Ibid., 5. William C. C. Claiborne is an interesting and complex figure, and as the first governor of American Louisiana his feelings on slavery and the slave trade require greater study. In a letter to James Madison on January 31, 1804, he noted the arrival of a slave ship in New Orleans, remarking that he was "unwilling to permit so barbarous a traffic, if my powers authorized me to prevent it"; he nonetheless found that Spanish law had allowed the trade and authorized the ship's landing. William Claiborne to James Madison, January 31, 1804, in Hackett, *Papers of James Madison*, 415. A good biography of Claiborne can be found in Hatfield, *William Claiborne*.

104. Schafer, *Slavery, the Civil Law*, 6.

105. Webre, "Problem of Indian Slavery," 134.

106. NARA, record group 59, microfilm T-260, roll 6, William C. C. Claiborne to James Madison, April 21, 1805.

Chapter 4. Strains on the System I

1. Hyde, *Pistols and Politics*, 20.

2. Caughey, *Bernardo de Gálvez in Louisiana*, chap. 7.

3. Rowland, *Life, Letters, and Papers*, 60.

4. Ibid.; Caughey, *Bernardo de Gálvez in Louisiana*, 104; Caughey, "Willing's Expedition down the Mississippi"; Siebert, "Loyalists in West Florida."

5. Caughey, *Bernardo de Gálvez in Louisiana*, 103.

6. Rowland, *Life, Letters, and Papers*, 62.

7. Caughey, *Bernardo de Gálvez in Louisiana*, 107.

8. Ibid., 108.

9. Rowland, *Life, Letters, and Papers*, 63.

10. Caughey, *Bernardo de Gálvez in Louisiana*, 113.

11. Hints of a more organized rebellion in 1797 surfaced in a letter between unknown persons (though possibly between William Dunbar and a state department official) dated June 27, 1797, in Natchez. In 1795 Pinckney's Treaty established the thirty-first parallel as the southern border of Mississippi, transferring ownership of the Natchez/Walnut Hills area to the United States, as well as defining the Mississippi River as the western boundary of the United States. When rumors began to circulate that the Spanish might not evacuate Natchez, and they began to rebuild the forts there and at Walnut Hills, a group of pro-American residents organized in order to take the fort and establish American rule. After terse negotiations and some exchange of gunfire between Spanish forces and an already-organized militia, the pro-American group elected a committee of local elites to help with the transition from Spanish to U.S. rule. NARA, record group 59, microfilm T-260 roll 1, "Natchez, June 27, 1797."

12. Kesting, "Common Bond"; Devereaux, "Philip Nolan and His 'Wild Horses'"; Wilson and Jackson, "Philip Nolan and Texas"; LOC, Papers of Thomas Jefferson, vol.

115, William Dunbar to Thomas Jefferson, August 22, 1801. There has been some argument over whether Nolan should properly be called a true "filibuster"; after all, he always claimed that he was only in Texas to gather horses and information. On his final expedition he took twenty armed men, ostensibly for defense. For more on this question, see Glen Jordan, "Philip Nolan."

13. McAlister, "William Augustus Bowles," 318; David H. White, "Spaniards and William Augustus Bowles"; Douglass, "Adventurer Bowles"; Holmes and Wright, "Luis Bertucat and William Augustus Bowles."

14. Kinnaird and Kinnaird, "War Comes to San Marcos," esp. pp. 29–32.

15. Vicente Pintado, PVP, reel 6, containers 19 and 25. On the map the name of the fort is listed as Punta Corta. Official Spanish records call it Punta Cortada, the name I use. Punta Cortada boasted thirteen iron cannons of various calibers, four bronze cannons, hundreds of guns and bayonets, shot, and powder. See AGI, legajo 161.

16. Cox, *West Florida Controversy*, 153.

17. NARA, record group 59, microfilm T-260, roll 6, William C. C. Claiborne to James Madison, March 26, 1805.

18. Ibid., roll 7, William C. C. Claiborne to the Hon. James Madison, Secretary of State, August 27, 1805.

19. In fact, the official Spanish records list no private sales to nonresidents before 1805 that I could find. Nonetheless, according to maps at least a few nonresidents owned parcels.

20. More famous for his involvement in the Aaron Burr conspiracy, Smith, the son of a Baptist minister, was originally a Virginian who moved to Ohio, six miles above Cincinnati, in 1790, where he took up the position of pastor in a local Baptist church. Through land speculation in Ohio and ownership of two grain mills, Smith amassed a small fortune in the Columbus area. He worked diligently for the admission of Ohio as a state and was rewarded by both its admission and his election as Ohio's first senator in March 1803. See W. Wilhelmy, "Senator John Smith." At the same time as, and perhaps as part of, his involvement with the Kempers, Smith contracted with the Department of War to supply troops with rations, including bread and flour, meat, liquor, candles, vinegar, and salt in the Mississippi and Louisiana territories, up to Saint Louis, for the period from October 1804 through September 1807. The War Department stopped renewing his contracts at roughly the same time that his involvement with Aaron Burr became public. NARA, record group 107, entry 45, Subsistence Contracts, 1803–12, vol. 1.

21. PVP, maps, reel 6, containers 19 and 25.

22. "Deposition of John Smith concerning Some Merchandise," in WFP 4:170.

23. Ibid.

24. "Deposition of John Smith to Governor Grand-Pré," in WFP 4:169.

25. "Inventory of the Property of Reuben Kemper & Co., Sept. 26, 1800," in WFP 4:289.

26. "James Smith Authorizes William Kirkland to Receive and Turn Over a Tract of Land," in WFP 7:75.

27. "Sale of a Negress from Father Charles Burke to Reuben Kemper & Co.," in WFP 4:94.

28. "Petition of Reuben Kemper" in WFP 5:345.

29. Ibid.

30. Cox, *West Florida Controversy*, 152; John Moore et al. to Vicente Pintado, June 11, 1804, in *PVP*, reel 2, container 2.

31. "Declaration against Alexander Bookter," in WFP 10:160.

32. Gwendolyn Midlo Hall, *Africans in Colonial Louisiana*, 304; Landers, "African American Women"; Landers, *Black Society in Spanish Florida*; Cutter, *Legal Culture*; Barbara Bush, *Slave Women in Caribbean Society*.

33. Kerr, *Petty Felony*, 197.

34. Ibid., 198.

35. Cox, *West Florida Controversy*, 152.

36. John Mills to Vicente Pintado, June 16, 1804, in PVP, reel 2, container 2. It struck me as slightly humorous the words that Mills chose to capitalize in this sentence. The weapons and the trousers—the things that probably stuck most in his mind—received both mental and grammatical attention.

37. Ibid.

38. Ibid.

39. Alexander Stirling to Vicente Pintado, 12 midnight, June 18, 1804, in PVP, reel 2, container 2.

40. John Mills to Vicente Pintado, 10 o'clock a.m., June 23, 1804, in PVP, reel 2, container 2.

41. Ibid.

42. Ibid.

43. Ibid.

44. Cox, *West Florida Controversy*, 154.

45. John Smith to Vicente Pintado, June 18, 1804, in PVP, reel 2, container 2. The offer of amnesty was a standard policy of Spanish government officials in the New World. See Landers, *Black Society in Spanish Florida*, 87, for a discussion of East Florida.

46. Carlos de Grand-Pré to Vicente Pintado, June 25, 1804, in PVP, reel 2, container 2. It is unclear to which murders Grand-Pré was referring, since no deaths were reported in the course of any of the above encounters, nor do subsequent documents mention any murders committed by the Kempers.

47. NARA, record group 59, microfilm T-260, roll 6, William C. C. Claiborne to James Madison, April 21, 1805.

48. John O'Connor to Vicente Pintado, July 5, 1804, in PVP, reel 2, container 2.

49. Cox, *West Florida Controversy*, 154.

50. Carlos de Grand-Pré to Vicente Pintado, July 13, 1804, and Carlos de Grand-Pré to Vicente Folch, July 21, 1804; "Quadrillo de Nathan Kemper," all in AGI, legajo 185.

51. "Quadrillo de Nathan Kemper," in AGI, legajo 185.

52. Carlos de Grand-Pré to Vicente Pintado, July 17, 1804, in AGI, legajo 185.

53. Ibid.

54. Ibid.; "Quadrillo de Nathan Kemper," in AGI, legajo 185.

55. "Quadrillo de Nathan Kemper," in AGI, legajo 185.

56. Carlos de Grand-Pré to Vicente Folch, July 21, 1804, in AGI, legajo 185.

57. Ibid.

58. Ibid.

59. NARA, record group 59, microfilm T-260, roll 5, William C. C. Claiborne to the Hon. James Madison, Secy. of State, December 11, 1804.

60. Wyatt-Brown, *Southern Honor*, 369.

61. Cox, *West Florida Controversy*, 157.

62. Carlos de Grand-Pré to Vicente Folch, July 21, 1804, in AGI, legajo 185.

63. Ibid.

64. "By Jonathan Clark," September 27, 1804, in WFP 8:262–64. This is one among many depositions that can be found in WFP 8:255–74.

65. Cox, *West Florida Controversy*, 155. Some American newspapers reported that the fort had in fact been captured. Others simply reported that the Kempers had fired on a Spanish picket near the fort. At no time did the Kemper gang take possession of the fort. For examples of the reporting, see the *Washington (D.C.) Federalist*, September 15, 1804, p. 3 (fort captured); *New York American Citizen*, September 14, 1804, p. 3 (picket near fort attacked).

66. Cox, *West Florida Controversy*, 155–56, 156n. Also reprinted in the *Washington Federalist* and the *American Citizen*, cited above, as well as other contemporary U.S. newspapers.

67. Cox, *West Florida Controversy*, 157. Randolph apparently traded goods with local Indians, running advertisements in local newspapers for his products. See *Mississippi Herald and Natchez Gazette*, September 9, 1805, p. 1, and September 30, 1805, p. 2, housed at the American Antiquarian Society, Worcester, Mass. His anti-Spanish motivations become more clear in this light; removal of the Spanish would increase his ability to engage in trade with tribes in West Florida as well as open the market in Baton Rouge to his goods.

68. NARA, record group 59, microfilm T-260, roll 6, "Extract of a letter of a Gentleman of respectability in the District of Baton Rouge April 22 1805," enclosed in a letter from William C. C. Claiborne to Madison, May 10, 1805.

69. *Mississippi Herald and Natchez Gazette*, August 10, 1804, p. 3.

70. NARA, record group 107, microfilm M-370, roll 1, Henry Dearborn to William Claiborne, March 10, 1802.

71. Ibid., Henry Dearborn to William Claiborne, April 3, 1802.

72. Governor Robert Williams to Carlos de Grand-Pré, September 6, 1805; Lt. William Wilson to Governor Robert Williams, September 5, 1805; Governor Robert Williams to Lt. William Wilson, September 9, 1805; Carlos de Grand-Pré to Governor Robert Williams, September 9, 1805; Governor Robert Williams to Carlos de Grand-Pré, September 30, 1805; all letters reprinted in the *New York American Citizen*, December 16, 1805. The *Hampshire Gazette* (Northampton, N.H.), November 27, 1805, reported that the armed party marched the Kempers to the line, untied them, and forced them to march across into the hands of another group. In 1807 Nathan and Reuben Kemper sued their kidnappers. Reuben, apparently in debt at the time of the suit, won six thousand

dollars from a man named Horton, whose slaves apparently helped him kidnap the Kempers. See also John Smith to the President, February 2, 1807, in Carter, *Territorial Papers*, 5:510; Thomas Rodney to T. Gammel, October 2, 1805, *Pennsylvania Magazine of History and Biography* 44 (1920): 187–88.

73. Cox, *West Florida Controversy*, 158.

74. NARA, record group 59, microfilm T-260, roll 4, Marquis de Casa Calvo to His Exc'y the Governor & Intendant General of the Province, August 11, 1804; roll 5, Marquis de Casa Calvo to His Exc'y the Governor & Intendant General of the Province, September 13, 1804.

75. Cox, *West Florida Controversy*, 158–59.

76. NARA, record group 59, microfilm T-260, roll 6, "Extract of a letter of a Gentleman of respectability in the District of Baton Rouge April 22 1805," enclosed in a letter from William C. C. Claiborne to Madison, May 10, 1805. The Kempers' actions in New Providence are outside the scope of this work. For a more detailed account of that portion of their exploits, see Cox, *West Florida Controversy*, 158–61. A grudge against the governor, Grand-Pré, is understandable. The problems involving Kneeland are less obvious, given that he was one—although most prominent—among several surveyors employed by the Crown. Some hint comes in a letter from Kneeland published in the *Mississippi Herald and Natchez Gazette*, November 16, 1804, p. 2, in which Kneeland complains of a "malicious pamphlet in circulation containing representations derogatory to [his] character" and claims that a man named Frederick Kimball "and a few associates" had been attacking his character for two years. Kimball's name does not appear on the "Quadrillo" list, and Kimball's "associates" remain unknown.

77. NARA, record group 59, microfilm M-40, roll 12, James Madison to William C. C. Claiborne, November 10, 1804; microfilm T-260, roll 6, William C. C. Claiborne to the Hon. James Madison, Sec't of State, May 10, 1805; William C. C. Claiborne to His Excellency the Marquis of Casa Calvo, May 8, 1805; William C. C. Claiborne to His Excelly. Gov. Williams, Natchez, May 8, 1805.

78. Ibid., microfilm T-260, roll 6, William C. C. Claiborne to the Hon. James Madison, Sec't of State, May 10, 1805.

79. Ibid., roll 4, William C. C. Claiborne to His Excellency the Marquis of Casa Calvo, August 27, 1804.

80. "Extract of a Letter, Dated, 'Town of Washington, Mississippi Territory, October 20, 1804,'" in the *Virginia Argus* (Richmond), December 1, 1804, p. 3, housed at the LOC.

81. NARA, record group 59, microfilm T-260, roll 4, Marquis de Casa Calvo to His Exc'y the Governor & Intendant General of the Province, August 11, 1804; roll 5, Marquis de Casa Calvo to His Exc'y the Governor & Intendant General of the Province, September 13, 1804. A letter to the *Mississippi Herald and Natchez Gazette* speculated that part of the fault for the raids lay in a weak American military presence in the fort at Natchez, claiming that had troops been in the fort, the Kempers would never have been able to pull off their invasion "of a peaceable neighboring nation." *Mississippi Herald and Natchez Gazette*, August 10, 1804, p. 3.

82. NARA, record group 59, microfilm T-260, roll 4, William C. C. Claiborne to Cato

West, Esq., August 29, 1804; "Extract of a Letter from His Excellency the Governor to Julien Poydrass Esquire," August 29, 1804.

83. Ibid., roll 5, Marquis de Casa Calvo to His Exc'y the Governor & Intendant General of the Province, September 13, 1804.

84. Ibid., W. C. Claiborne to His Excellency the Marquis of Casa Calvo, September 13, 1804.

85. Ibid., W. C. Claiborne to the Hon. James Madison, Sec'y of State, December 11, 1804.

86. Ibid., roll 6, W. C. Claiborne to the Hon. James Madison, Sec'y of State, April 21, 1805.

87. A sense of the danger felt by Americans and quick chronology of these events can be gleaned from NARA, record group 94, microfilm M-565, vols. C–D, roll 2, Unknown to Capt. Elijah Strong, November 20, 1806; roll 1, "Extract of a Letter from Captain Bowyer to Lieutenant Colonel Freeman," October 13, 1805; "Extract of a Letter from Lieutenant Colonel Freeman to General Wilkinson"; Capt. Thomas Swain to Col. Thomas Cushing, March 4, 1806, and April 4, 1806; John Sibley to Colonel Cushing, June 24 and 28, 1806, July 14, 23, and 30, 1806, August 4, 6, 13, and 19, 1806, and September 12, 1806. Jack Holmes dissects this event in "Showdown on the Sabine." See also Owsley and Smith, *Filibusters and Expansionists*, 35–36.

88. For various raids and banditti expeditions, see Arthur P. Whitaker, "Spanish Intrigue in the Old Southwest"; Turner's "Origin of Genet's Projected Attack" reminds us that all of Genet's scheming appeals to the American people concealed "the most important feature of his mission, namely the desire of the French Republic to form connections with the frontiersmen of America and to seize Louisiana, the Floridas and Canada." For more on this aspect of Genet's mission, see Michael Morris, "Dreams of Glory"; Murdoch, "Citizen Mangourit"; and Turner, "Policy of France." This excludes uncounted "minor" expeditions by U.S. and Spanish troops toward the Sabine River in 1804 and 1806, others toward Nacogdoches, and constant rumors of plots by New Orleans groups against West Florida and Spanish Texas. In 1808 a U.S. Army captain named Glass marched toward Natchitoches, seemingly with the intent of capturing it. NARA, record group 59, microfilm T-260, roll 9, John C. Carr to William C. C. Claiborne, August 8, 1808, and August 15, 1808, and John Sibley to William C. C. Claiborne, August 15, 1808. Spain's government understandably viewed even simple exploration, such as that by Zebulon Pike and Lewis and Clark, as invasions of territory—accurate maps were a matter of national security, and exploration had always served as a precursor to territorial invasion for European colonial empires.

89. The Spaniards raised his salary to sixteen thousand dollars when Alexander Hamilton gave Wilkinson the rank of major general and placed him in command of the Southwest frontier in 1798. See Risjord, *Jefferson's America*, 261. Risjord has an excellent, concise summary of the Burr conspiracy. Abernethy's *Burr Conspiracy* remains the accepted overview. However, two older works remain relevant to the study of West Florida in particular: Abernethy, "Aaron Burr in Mississippi," and Cox, "Hispanic-American Phases."

90. Rucker, "Nixon's Raid."

91. Landers, *Black Society in Spanish Florida*, 244–46.

92. Cox, *West Florida Controversy*, 151.

93. Hyde, *Pistols and Politics*, 20.

94. Cox, *West Florida Controversy*, 153; Alexander Stirling to Vicente Pintado, June 28, 1804, in PVP, reel 2, container 2.

95. Alexander Stirling to Vicente Pintado, June 28, 1804, in PVP, reel 2, container 2.

96. The best English-language monograph on the Hidalgo movement remains Hamill's *Hidalgo Revolt*.

Chapter 5. Strains on the System II

1. Wood, *Black Majority*. Wood notes, in particular, that "poisoning was undeniably used by certain Africans as one of the most logical and lethal methods of resistance" (289). In the various records for the West Florida parishes, Joseph Sharp appears with some regularity, if not consistency. Through church records of marriages, births, and deaths, through land records and various sales, his name appears spelled variously as Sharp, Sharpe, Sarp, Chorp, Charp, Charpe, Charps, and most oddly, Cherles. George de Passau, likewise, appears as de Passau, de Passo, de Passn, Depassn, Depassau, and Depasso. The different spellings result from the difficulty in maintaining records on a frontier and well as from the compounded problem of records maintained in three languages, French, Spanish, and English. I have chosen to use the spellings Sharp and de Passau, as they appear earliest and most consistently. This is not the only trial in Feliciana during the transfer period in which the Spanish courts acquitted slaves accused of murder. The Spaniards tried a case in 1807 in which slaves were accused of arson to commit murder. Here the Spaniards also acquitted the slaves. The case discussed in this chapter simply provides the richest glimpse of slavery and the law as it existed in Feliciana during this period.

2. Although the evidence is sketchy, he may have been a competitor for the hand of Sharp's wife, who was Marie Decoux's daughter.

3. "Deposition of George de Passau," in WFP 10:214–15; "Deposition of Susan," in WFP 10:195.

4. The *sumaria* was considered the "initial stage of the judicial process" in northern New Spain. See Cutter, *Legal Culture*, 75.

5. "Deposition of George de Passau," in WFP 10:212. These phases are entirely my own creation to help the flow of the narrative; the residents made no such distinctions.

6. "Murder of the Slave of Joseph Clermont," in WFP 12:212–29; Thomas D. Morris, *Southern Slavery and the Law*, 181.

7. Cutter, *Legal Culture*, 109.

8. Ibid. Passau had granted Susan her freedom only the year before, and she remained in his employ. See "Slave Freedom by George de Passau," in WFP 9:29. In the record of her emancipation, Susan is listed as a "negress." In the documents after emancipation, she is listed as a "mulatto."

9. The word "truck" is never defined in the court records or anywhere else in the records of West Florida. It seems to have meant "a mixture of elements."

10. "Deposition of Susan," in WFP 10:195. Although the records do not admit of it, my personal sense is that Susan and Passau were involved in a relationship. McCoy and Susan were probably dining in the household while Passau was away. I get no sense that Susan and McCoy were involved, although it is possible and would add another dimension to the slaves' relationships with one another. See WFP 10:194–95. The entire incident occurred the day before Passau was to return home from the militia.

11. "Deposition of Susan," in WFP 10:195; "Testimony of Amos," in WFP 10:200; "Deposition of Susan," in WFP 10:196.

12. "Deposition of Susan," in WFP 10:196–97.

13. "Deposition of George de Passau," in WFP 10:215; "Deposition of Susan," in WFP 10:197; "Deposition of Fanny," in WFP 10:199.

14. "Deposition of Fanny," in WFP 10:199–200; "Deposition of Amos," in WFP 10:200–201; "Deposition of Nelly," in WFP 10:202.

15. "Deposition of Eve," in WFP 10:202. For a fascinating account of the role of magic and slavery as part of black culture, see Theophus H. Smith, *Conjuring Culture*. For more on this in a Latin American setting, see Voeks, *Sacred Leaves of Candomblé*. Some historians of the U.S. South have touched on the role of magic and vodun in several slave rebellions. See, for instance, Lofton, *Denmark Vesey's Revolt*. "Deposition of Eve," in WFP 10:203; "Confession of Nancy," in WFP 10:205. See also Moss, *Southern Folk Medicine*.

16. "Deposition of George," in WFP 10:198; Landers, *Black Society in Spanish Florida*, 132; Joyner, *Down by the Riverside*, 145.

17. "Confession of Nancy," in WFP 10:205. The claim that Edmond had tried to use magic on Mme. Henson is a revealing, although unpursued, note—remember that Passau originally came from Henson's plantation. "Deposition of Eve," in WFP 10:203; "Testimony of Amos," in WFP 10:201. The amount of money paid to Edmond, however, might not be out of the reach of slaves who could work in a city like Baton Rouge to earn extra cash. "Testimony of Nicolas," in WFP 10:204, 205; "Testimony of Eve," in WFP 10:203.

18. "Confession of Edmond," in WFP 10:210.

19. Christopher Morris, *Becoming Southern*, 238; Cutter, *Legal Culture*, 122.

20. Christopher Morris, *Becoming Southern*, 238.

21. "Testimony of Passau," in WFP 10:215; "Judgment of Grand-Pré," in WFP 12:268.

22. "Testimony of Caesar," in WFP 10:251.

23. Ibid.

24. Ibid.

25. "Testimony of Nicolas," in WFP 10:204.

26. "Confession of Edmond," in WFP 10:210.

27. "Confession of Nancy," in WFP 10:205.

28. Ibid.

29. Ibid., 10:207.

30. Ibid. The reference to a "Social Club" is tantalizing, but unfortunately has no further mention in the West Florida records.

31. Ibid.

32. "Testimony of George Crouse," in WFP 10:210.

33. Ibid., 210–11.

34. Tannenbaum, *Slave and Citizen*, 49.

35. Cutter, *Legal Culture*, 123.

36. "Testimony of Nancy," in WFP 10:205.

37. "Testimony of Eve," in WFP 10:202.

38. "Testimony of Nicolas," in WFP 10:204; "Confession of Bill," in WFP 10:208.

39. "Testimony of Passau," in WFP 10:216.

40. Cutter, *Legal Culture*, 123.

41. "Deposition of George Passau," in WFP 10:217.

42. Ibid.

43. Nothing in the records indicates the reason for Passau's absence. Had he been with the militia or off on some other official business, the records probably would have noted it.

44. "Deposition of George Passau," in WFP 10:219.

45. Each slave deposition was generally signed by six people: two interpreters if the deposition was taken in Spanish, two witnesses, the *X* made by the slave or free person of color, and Carlos de Grand-Pré. If no interpreter was necessary, the court might summon other witnesses. The witnesses and the interpreters received monetary compensation for their help. In phase 1 of the trial the same five people served as witnesses each time (George Kleinpeter, William Roddey, George Crouse, George Mather, and Lawrence Sticker), and the slaves did not sign their depositions (in violation of Spanish customary and organic law). In subsequent phases all deponents signed with at least an *X*.

46. "Deposition of Negress, Fanny," in WFP 10:221.

47. Profession of Christianity served as a way to establish competency for a trial in the Spanish world. See Cutter, *Legal Culture*.

48. "Deposition of Negress, Fanny," in WFP 10:225.

49. Ibid., 227.

50. "Petition of Elias Beauregard," in WFP 10:229.

51. Ibid.

52. Ibid.

53. "Grand-Pré Orders an Investigation of the Conditions in the Jail," in WFP 10:231; "Testimony of Antonio Tirado," in WFP 10:232; "Testimony of Ignace Garcia," in WFP 10:233; "Testimony of José Miraval," in WFP 10:234.

54. "Testimony of Doctor Andrew Steele," in WFP 10:234; "Testimony of Doctor Michael Mahier," in WFP 10:236.

55. "Testimony of Abraham," in WFP 10:229.

56. Ibid.

57. "Decree of Carlos de Grand-Pré," in WFP 10:237.

58. Ibid.

59. "Testimony of Doctor Pedro Goudeau," in WFP 10:239.

60. "Deposition of Doctor Daniel Sayre," in WFP 10:240.

61. Ibid.; "Depositions of Doctors Michael Mahier, Pedro Goudeau and Daniel Sayre," in WFP 10:241–42.

62. "Deposition of Nancy," in WFP 10:243.

63. "Deposition of Edmond," in WFP 10:247.

64. Ibid., 10:248.

65. "Deposition of Bill," in WFP 10:245.

66. Ibid.

67. "Deposition of Eve," in WFP 10:253.

68. Ibid.

69. "Judgment of Grand-Pré," in WFP 12:264.

70. Paquette, "Revolutionary Saint Domingue," 211, 213.

71. "Judgment of Grand-Pré," in WFP 12:263.

72. Ibid., 266.

73. Ibid.

74. "Judgment of Grand-Pré," in WFP 12:268.

75. Ibid.

76. Ibid., 12:267.

77. Ibid.

78. Ibid., 12:263.

79. Ibid., 12:266, 267.

80. Into this group Grand-Pré actually lumped Passau himself, whom he accused of being "credulous," and who was in essence used by his own slaves as an agent of revenge against one another.

81. Cutter, *Legal Culture*, 137.

82. "Judgment of Grand-Pré," in WFP 12:269.

83. Joyner, *Down by the Riverside*, 149.

84. "Judgment of Grand-Pré," in WFP 12:275.

85. Cutter, *Legal Culture*, 91.

86. Ibid.

87. "Judgment of Grand-Pré," in WFP 12:269.

Chapter 6. Testing the Bounds of Loyalty

1. The main problem with determining patterns of discontent relative to population and emigration arises from the fact that prior to the revolution of 1810, those residents who did post antigovernment broadsides did so anonymously. The identities of specific people are revealed at best through court records, where someone might testify that a person accused of a crime was known to have harbored anti-Spanish sentiments. However, those testimonials are suspect because of the forum and circumstances in which they were given and also the possibility that testimony could be motivated by revenge.

2. Padgett, *Official Records*, 5–6. The *Official Records* transcribed by Padgett are the only known writings by what would become a revolutionary council for West Florida and are used extensively in this and the next chapter.

3. Ibid., 8.

4. Ibid. The final three issues listed on the first day involved, first, the need for a standard system of weights and measures to facilitate business in the province—a problem stemming from the mixture of French, Spanish, and Anglo-American systems of measurement. Second, the group argued that officials of the government had billed residents for services without presenting official records of charges. Finally, they noted that the area had become a haven for French families exiled from Cuba and previously refugees from Saint Domingue, with both the slave owners and the slaves possibly bringing revolutionary instability to the region. In a sign of how residents saw the problem of Saint Domingue, the complaint concerned the French families, not their slaves.

5. Ibid., 10.

6. Ibid., 12.

7. Ibid., 22.

8. Here "deserters" refers to men who had deserted from the U.S. military. Most seem to have come from New Orleans.

9. Kerr, *Petty Felony*, xv.

10. TePaske, "Integral to Empire," 31–40.

11. Crime on the Texas and California borderlands during their respective Spanish colonial and early U.S. territorial periods is a field with rich potential.

12. "An Inventory of the Effects of David Silvester," in WFP 3:262.

13. "Deposition of Thomas Clayton," in "Information concerning the wounds inflicted with the fists by Luther Smith on Doctor Williamson, October twentieth, 1802," in WFP 5:386. A different witness lists the epithet as "a trifling sneeking [*sic*] puppy" ("Deposition of James Tate," in WFP 5:389). Slander was a serious issue throughout the colonial Americas. See Roger Thompson, "'Hold Watchfulness' and Communal Conformism"; Wyatt-Brown, *Southern Honor*.

14. "Deposition of James Tate" and "Deposition of Thomas Clayton," in WFP 5:389 and 5:387, respectively.

15. "Examination of and Testimony concerning the Corpse of a Drowned Man," WFP 3:265.

16. One of the difficulties of counting crimes is in determining what exactly to count. Derek Kerr counted seven incidents from 1799 to 1805, including the already-mentioned case of the murdered body washing up on the western shore. I have discounted that case (as well as another American found dead in the river) because there is no evidence that either crime occurred in Spanish West Florida (Kerr, *Petty Felony*, 128n93). See also, for example, a case in Natchez in which a group of men boarded a boat at night, killed three occupants, and dumped their bodies overboard, in NARA, record group 36, entry 1627, box 2, "Jonathan Davis to Messrs Meeker, Williamson & Patton," August 26, 1803. The body floated downstream to an unknown location, possibly Baton Rouge. I have omitted from my count all filibustering in the region, although these actions support my

conclusion that cross-border crime was extremely problematic for residents. However, filibustering is more a quasi-military action that despite the attendant thievery is not really comparable to a single person stealing a cow or a slave or murdering a schoolteacher. This brings the number of reported crimes occurring in Spanish West Florida to three between 1799 and 1805 (I cannot find crime reports for the period between 1783 and 1799) and sixteen from 1805 to 1810.

17. "Deposition of David B. Stuart," in "Proceedings concerning the accusation of robbery against Christopher Weaver, Richard Crozier and Elijah Toler, who were condemned after forty day imprisonment to be deported," in WFP 9:52.

18. Cutter, *Legal Culture*, chap. 2.

19. Note that in chapter 5 Passau engaged in a kind of self-expulsion by fleeing the territory when it seemed the court might render an unfavorable judgment.

20. "Pierre Goudeau's withdrawal of the proceedings with Andrew Gil," in WFP 16:113.

21. Landers, "Female Conflict," 560.

22. A monographical study of women's legal culture on the colonial Latin American borderlands is awaiting its historian, though scattered articles have touched on the ways in which women used the courts. See, for instance, McDonald's "Incest, Power, and Negotiation," for a study of the way that one woman used the courts to push against the boundaries of male power during this same period.

23. For more on Carlos Dehault De Lassus, see chap. 7.

24. Other documents in WFP refer to Gil as having once run a saloon. See WFP 10:172.

25. "Deposition of Joseph Sharp," in WFP 4:359; "Deposition of Joseph Gallup," in WFP 4:360.

26. Gorn, " 'Gouge And Bite,' "; Johnson, "Dangerous Words."

27. "Testimony of Alexander Bookter," in WFP 4:355.

28. Ibid., 4:356.

29. "Deposition of Jacob Rheams" and "Deposition of Hezemiah Williams," in WFP 4:354.

30. "Petition to Remove Alexander Bookter," in WFP 10:160.

31. "Deposition of John Glascock," in WFP 10:164. In fact, despite the appearance of his signature on the document, Glascock did not even know how to write.

32. "Testimony of William Bickham," in WFP 10:168.

33. "Deposition of William Bell," in WFP 10:165.

34. "William Bell against Captain Jones," in WFP 12:204–11.

35. Burkholder, "Honor and Honors," 29.

36. "Declaration of Andrew Cain," in "Jacob Byer vs. Alexander Bookter, concerning a Fight," in WFP 16:5; "Statement of Shepherd Brown," in WFP 16:22.

37. Wyatt-Brown, *Southern Honor*, 369.

38. U.S. Army recruiters visited Staunton, Winchester, and Fincastle, Virginia, in 1804. See, for example, NARA, record group 94, microfilm M-565, roll 2, Inspector's Office to Capt. Richard Sparks, February 24, 1804, and March 30, 1804; Inspector's Office to Capt. Edward D. Turner, February 25, 1804; Inspector's Office to Capt. Thomas Swain, February 29, 1804; Inspector's Office to Col. Henry Burbeck, April 18, 1804; Stagg, "Enlisted

Men"; Stagg, "Soldiers in Peace and War." Prior to the Louisiana Purchase, Spain had some of the same difficulties. See AGI, legajo 1555, no. 362, pp. 673 and 674, and no. 642, p. 586. For deserters prior to Spanish occupation, see Rea, "Military Deserters from British West Florida."

39. NARA, record group 59, microfilm T-260, roll 4, Capt. William Cooper to William C. C. Claiborne, April 14, 1804; M. Laussat to William C. C. Claiborne, April 14, 1804; John Watkins to Governor Claiborne, April 24, 1804; William C. C. Claiborne to James Madison, August 1, 1804. Lafitte's ships were eventually turned away, though they sold their cargo on the way back down the Mississippi.

40. "Robert Jones vs. Samuel Baker," October 14, 1807, in WFP 12:255.

41. NARA, record group 59, microfilm T-260, roll 9, Carlos de Grand-Pré to William C. C. Claiborne, August 3, 1808, and August 24, 1808; William C. C. Claiborne to Carlos de Grand-Pré, August 31, 1808, and November 13, 1808; William C. C. Claiborne to James Madison, November 14, 1808.

42. See, for example, the punishments meted out to John Greysey, William Walker, Thomas Sasthram, John Perkinson, Robert Ferguson, Peter Daniel, Dennis Willings, and Edward Towilliger, in NARA, record group 98, entry 137, "District Orders," August 2, 1807; record group 98, entry 13, "At a General Court Martial," August 19, 1807. These and other records from the period indicate that desertion to Spanish territory was a serious problem for the U.S. Army—enough so that the U.S. Army in the form of deserters and those seeking them maintained a near-constant presence in Spanish West Florida from 1804 onward.

43. John Herbert's name is spelled both "Herbert" and "Hubbert" in the records. I have used "Herbert" throughout to maintain consistent readability. "Summary proceeding and information on the wounding of the American John Hubbert," in WFP 11:172.

44. "Deposition of John Stephene," in WFP 11:174.

45. "Deposition of Joash Miller," in WFP 11:173.

46. "Deposition of John Stephene," and "Deposition of Hugh Coyle," in WFP 11:175.

47. "Deposition of Cupid, a slave," and "Deposition of Eliza, a slave," in WFP 13:132.

48. "Deposition of Sam," in WFP 11:138; Din, *Spaniards, Planters, and Slaves*, 26. On p. 158 Din notes that during the Pointe Coupee conspiracy of 1795, Spanish officials confiscated the guns of slaves in the Attakapas district, and that the "slaves could not recover their weapons *until the governor issued a new order*" (emphasis mine). The problem there was not that slaves owned guns, but that they had them during an uprising.

49. "Summary of the Case by Thomas Estevan," in WFP 13:144. On previous charges of Ellis's disloyalty, see WFP 13:206.

50. "Summary of the Case by Thomas Estevan," in WFP 13:145.

51. Despite requests by Grand-Pré, no extraditions appear in the West Florida papers, the Pintado papers, the Papeles de Cuba, the records of the Department of State, the records of the War Department, or the Territorial papers of the U.S. Congresses for this period and place. Among the more startling requests for extradition came one from Carlos de Grand-Pré. In June 1806, while George de Passau's murder trial was under way, Grand-Pré requested the extradition of a Pinckneyville, Mississippi, resident named

Keary. Keary's escaped slave had been arrested in Baton Rouge and then returned. At the jail and on the road back to Mississippi and in the presence of many witnesses, Keary had administered a beating so savage that the slave died. No record of a subsequent trial of anyone named Keary exists in records related to Baton Rouge, so Grand-Pré's request for extradition probably went unanswered. NARA, record group 59, entry 912, vol. 1, Cowles Meade to James Madison, June 27, 1806.

52. NARA, record group 45, microfilm m-149, Robert Smith to Commander David Porter, October 7, 1808.

53. Blount's name also appeared on the petition against Alexander Bookter.

54. "José Bernardo de Revia vs. George Mars," in WFP 13:234. Blount and his men probably crossed the lower border from West Florida into the northern part of Louisiana territory above New Orleans. Among other examples, see NARA, record group 59, entry 912, vol. 1, David Holmes to Robert Smith, May 30, 1810. In this incident two bounty hunters chased a U.S. Army deserter from southern Mississippi into West Florida, took him back to U.S. territory, and claimed a $150 reward.

55. Peter Lawrence was most likely the nephew of the Joseph Sharp from chap. 5. William Flanegan and several relatives' names also appear on the petition against Alexander Bookter. It is unclear from the records whether this was the same Joseph Sharp who had been assaulted in the Mink-Burris case, although my impression is that it was. If so, it adds dimension to the conflict and makes it all the more interesting.

56. "Deposition of Peter Lawrence, Jr.," in "Summary of the proceedings on the treacherous death of Joseph Sharp," in WFP 9:119–20. Flanegan's name is spelled different ways in the same document. I have again used the first iteration throughout for readability.

57. Ibid.

58. "Deposition of Thomas Crittenden," in WFP 9:128; "Report of Alcalde William Bell," in WFP 9:119.

59. This crime may or may not have had some kind of closure for the Sharp family. The Frankfort, Kentucky, *Palladium* reported that an armed Spanish party crossed the line in late 1805 and took a man named Flanegan and his wife into Spanish territory. The wife was released, but Spanish authorities took Flanegan on to Baton Rouge. See "Taken from a report out of Natchez," *Palladium* (Frankfort, Ky.), December 1, 1805, p. 2.

60. Patrick Marrin to Antonio Grass, November 17, 1803; Patrick Marrin to Vicente Pintado, December 11, 1803, both in PVP, reel 2, container 2. To some degree this was an accurate picture, but at the same time the reader gets the impression that the letter writer deliberately engaged in some tongue-in-cheek humor.

61. Patrick Legart to Vicente Pintado, June 20, 1803; Patrick Marrin to Vicente Pintado, November 17, 1803; Christopher Bolling to Vicente Pintado, November 27, 1803, all in PVP, reel 2, container 2.

62. Notice appeared in *Mississippi Herald and Natchez Gazette*, November 16, 1804, p. 2

63. "Petition of Catherine Rucker, Widow of John Turnbull," in WFP 8:404.

64. Vicente Pintado to Christopher Bolling, March 5, 1805, in PVP, reel 5, container 4; Vicente Pintado to Christopher Bolling, March 11, 1805, in PVP, reel 5, container 4.

65. Ira Kneeland to Vicente Pintado, March 27, 1805, May 1805, May 19, 1805, May 29, 1805, June 1805, July 2, 1805, August 25, 1805, in PVP, reel 5, container 4.

66. Ira Kneeland to Vicente Pintado, August 25, 1805, in PVP, reel 5, container 4.

67. Ira Kneeland to Vicente Pintado, July 1805, in PVP, reel 5, container 4.

68. Ira Kneeland to Nicholas Highland, August 15, 1807, in Center for American History, Natchez Trace Collection, 2E991.

69. Taken from database of land sales, WFP, vols. 1–18.

70. Alternately written as "Rhea and Cochran" and "Cochran and Rhea" in the records. Data taken from land database.

71. Land sales found in "Land Sale from Alexander Ross to John Mink," in WFP 4:256; "Land Sale from John Mink to John O'Connor," in WFP 4:259; "Land Sale from John O'Connor to William Cobb and Elijah Adams," in WFP 4:261. Unfortunately no data exist on the price of cattle in West Florida during this period. This was the same John Mink found in the Mink-Burris case.

72. "Sale of Land from Johnathan Longstreath to John Buck," in WFP 6:182; "Sale of Land from John Buck to John Murdock," in WFP 6:186.

73. Land prices taken from WFP, vols. 1–18. Total number of land sales equals 379. To obtain an average for each year, I sorted sales for each year by price, taking out the highest and the lowest prices in each category, and averaging the remainder. I combined the years 1787–91, 1792–95, 1796–99, and 1809–10 to obtain a large enough sample from which to draw conclusions. In each year several sales could not be included in the calculations because of missing information such as price or arpentage. I also did not include sales of plots within the towns of Baton Rouge or Saint Francisville, nor did I include sales of plantations that included farm implements, slaves, crops, and so on. Finally, I excluded land sales at estate auctions. The above-average spikes in Baton Rouge for 1802 and 1807 were due to the sale of several well-improved plantations in those years. Total N for land sales in table 5: 1787–91 = 19, 1792–95 = 43, 1796–99 = 19, 1800 = 16, 1801 = 19, 1802 = 24, 1803 = 45, 1804 = 34, 1805 = 15, 1806 = 25, 1807 = 16, 1808 = 20, 1809–10 = 30.

74. N = 1796–99 = 5 Feliciana, 14 all other; 1800 = 8 Feliciana, 8 all other; 1801 = 3 Feliciana, 16 all other; 1802 = 5 Feliciana, 19 all other; 1803 = 21 Feliciana, 24 all other; 1804 = 16 Feliciana, 18 all other; 1805 = 7 Feliciana, 8 all other; 1806 = 17 Feliciana, 8 all other; 1807 = 9 Feliciana, 7 all other; 1808 = 13 Feliciana, 7 all other; 1809–1810 = 13 Feliciana, 17 all other.

75. This seems to be a genuine rise in land prices rather than an anomaly.

76. Leslie Hall's *Land and Allegiance* and Holton's *Forced Founders* both show that the ability to purchase and retain land holdings outweighed political loyalty.

Chapter 7. Breaking the Bonds

1. Lynch's *Bourbon Spain*, Esdaile's *Spanish Army*, and Sutherland's *France* together present a full picture of the events of this period.

2. Lynch, *Bourbon Spain*, 403–4.

3. *El Misisipi* (New Orleans), October 12, 1808, pp. 1, 2.

4. Ibid., 3.

5. Lynch, *Spanish American Revolutions,* 34.

6. Kinsbruner, *Independence in Spanish America,* 37.

7. NARA, record group 59, microfilm M-40, roll 13, Robert Smith to Governor Holmes, July 12, 1810.

8. For a detailed examination of the Embargo Act, see Risjord, *Jefferson's America,* and McCoy, *Elusive Republic.*

9. Cox, *West Florida Controversy,* 218.

10. NARA, record group 45, microfilm M-149, Robert Smith to the Commanding Naval Officer, New Orleans, April 28, 1808.

11. Cox, *West Florida Controversy,* 325.

12. Michael Morris, "Dreams of Glory."

13. Elkins and McKitrick, *Age of Federalism,* 330–36, contains an excellent overview of Genet's American mission.

14. Landers, *Black Society in Spanish Florida,* 205–9.

15. Cox, *West Florida Controversy,* 313–14.

16. AGI, legajos 152–2, 156–2, 178, and 1565; Hall, *Africans in Colonial Louisiana,* 347–49.

17. AGI, legajo 572.

18. Cox, *West Florida Controversy,* 318.

19. This was proposed by Isaac Cox and picked up by subsequent historians. Ibid., 320.

20. Socolow, "Acceptable Partners," 210.

21. Lavrin and Couturier, "Dowries and Wills," 281, 282; Korth and Flusche, "Dowry and Inheritance."

22. Couturier, "Women and the Family," 295.

23. "Marriage Contract, Antonio Cavalier and Charlotte Sophie de Grand-Pré," in WFP 15:100; Seed, "American Law, Hispanic Traces."

24. Cummins, "Church Courts"; Schwartz, *Sovereignty and Society,* 339–41.

25. Ibid.

26. See Kinsbruner, *Independence in Spanish America,* chaps. 3 and 4 for a discussion of how this process culminated in various revolutions.

27. Cox, *West Florida Controversy,* 343, 333.

28. Very little in the way of critical work has been written about David Holmes. A somewhat hagiographical account of his administration can be found in McCain's "Administrations of David Holmes."

29. NARA, record group 59, entry 912, vol. 1., David Holmes to Robert Smith, June 20, 1810. Cox discusses this letter but interprets it in a different way. Where Holmes used the term "relaxed" to describe the government and went on to describe an "inefficient" and "unjust" local police force, Cox used this to describe the supposed anarchy in West Florida, claiming that little government control remained and that the police force could not maintain law and order.

30. NARA, record group 59, E912, vol. 1, David Holmes to the Secretary of State, July 11, 1810; David Holmes to the Secretary of State, July 31, 1810; David Holmes to Robert Smith, August 8, 1810; David Holmes to Robert Smith, September 12, 1810.

31. Ibid., David Holmes to Robert Smith, June 20, 1810.

32. Cox, *West Florida Controversy*, 331.

33. James Madison Papers at the Library of Congress, John Adair to James Madison, January 9, 1809. Accessed at http://hdl.loc.gov/loc.mss/mjm.10_0922_0924.

34. One of the best short explanations of the *cortés* and their role in Latin American independence movements remains Kinsbruner's *Spanish-American Independence Movement*. On p. 4 Kinsbruner notes that the Aragonese Spanish had established the idea of local parliaments based on a contractual relationship between king and subjects.

35. NARA, record group 59, E912, vol. 1, Holmes to Smith, June 20, 1810.

36. Cox, *West Florida Controversy*, 344.

37. *Natchez (Miss.) Weekly Chronicle*, June 18, 1810.

38. "Report, 1810," in WFP 18:79.

39. Cox, *West Florida Controversy*, 335.

40. Ibid., 365–66; "Journal of the Revolutionary Convention, St. John's Plains, Wednesday July 25th," reprinted in Padgett, *Official Records*, 4–5.

41. "Report of the Events on August 14, 1810, to be Relayed to the Superior Officers," in WFP 18:81–82.

42. Ibid.

43. NARA, record group 59, E912, vol. 1, John Johnson to Governor Holmes, August 14, 1810.

44. Ibid.

45. *Natchez (Miss.) Weekly Chronicle*, June 18, 1810.

46. "Report of the Events on August 14, 1810," in WFP 18:83.

47. Ibid, 18:84.

48. Ibid.

49. "Report, 1810," WFP 18:78.

50. Ibid., 18:79.

51. "Journal of the Revolutionary Convention, Saturday, August 25," in Padgett, *Official Records*, 28–29.

52. "Journal of the Revolutionary Convention, Monday August 27th," in Padgett, *Official Records*, 31–32.

53. Cox, *West Florida Controversy*, 387.

54. "Journal of the Constitutional Convention, St. Francisville, September 22d, 1810," in Padgett, *Official Records*, 35–36.

55. Ibid., 34–35.

56. Cox, *West Florida Controversy*, 393–94.

57. "Report, 1810," WFP 18:78.

58. Ibid.

59. This is Passau's first reappearance since the slave trial in 1806, after which he apparently fled to Missouri. No explanation exists for his apparent return to the territory, though hints exist that he was in West Florida in 1807 and 1808. He may have been among the French families expelled by De Lassus.

60. "Journal of the Constitutional Convention, Baton Rouge, Tuesday September 25, 1810," in Padgett, *Official Records*, 38.

61. Cox, *West Florida Controversy*, 399–400.

62. While Carlos de Grand-Pré spelled his name using a hyphen in "Grand-Pré," his children did not.

63. "One of the most respectable," *Louisiana Courier* (New Orleans), October 29, 1810, p. 3.

64. Ibid.

65. "Journal of the Constitutional Convention, Wednesday Septr. 26th," in Padgett, *Official Records*, 43.

66. Ibid. Note that the convention did not recognize Joseph Bonaparte as ruler of Spain.

67. Brading, *First America*; Rodríguez, *Independence of Spanish America*.

68. Padgett, *Official Records*, 43.

69. NARA, record group 59, E912, Volume 1, Governor Holmes to Secretary of State Smith, October 3, 1810.

70. Ibid.

71. Ibid., Governor Holmes to Secretary of State Smith, October 17, 1810.

Epilogue

1. NARA, record group 59, E912, vol. 1, Convention to Reuben Kemper, October 11, 1810.

2. NARA, record group 36, entry 1627, box 2, Governor Folch to Edmund P. Gaines, November 25, 1810; Judge Toumlin to the President, December 12, 1810, in Carter, *Territorial Papers of the United States*, 6:152–58; "West Florida and Its Attempts on Mobile, 1810–1811," *American Historical Review* 2, no. 4 (July 1897): 699–705.

3. NARA, record group 59, entry 38.

4. "Account of Combat between Tiger and Bayou Sara Bull," *St. Francisville Timepiece*, May 11, 1811, pp. 2–3. Emphasis in original.

5. Andersen, *Imagined Communities*, 9.

6. "Extract of a letter," *Charleston Gazette*, September 29, 1810, p. 3.

7. "West Florida Free," *Tennessee Gazette* (Nashville), October 9, 1810, p. 3.

8. "Revolutions," *Louisiana Gazette of St. Louis*, October 17, 1810, p. 3.

9. "At an hour last night," *Charleston Gazette*, October 20, 1810, p. 3.

10. "Florida Affairs," *Boston Repertory*, November 6, 1810, p. 1.

11. "More of the little mimick Revolution of Florida," *Boston Repertory*, December 7, 1810, p. 1.

12. Hobsbawm, *Nations and Nationalism since 1780*, 73. For a peculiarly Latin American perspective on this, see also Bolívar and Collier, "Nationality."

BIBLIOGRAPHY

Collections

Archives of the Spanish Government of West Florida: A Series of Eighteen Bound
Volumes of Written Documents Mostly in the Spanish Language. Deposited in the
Record Room of the Nineteenth Judicial District Court, Baton Rouge, La. [Works
Progress Administration] Survey of Federal Archives. Dr. P. M. Homer, National
Director; Stanley C. Arthur, Regional Director for Louisiana, Mississippi, Arkansas,
and Tennessee. Vols. 1 through 18.

Archivo General de Indias, Papeles Procedentes de la Isla de Cuba. Louisiana State
University Libraries, Special Collections, Baton Rouge.

Archivo Nacional de la República de Cuba, Havana, Cuba.

Asuntos Políticos. Legajo 8.

Reales Cédulas y Ordenes Negros, 1727–1861. Legajo 20.

Real Consulado y Junta de Fomentos. Legajo 73.

Realengos. Legajos 43, 70, 79.

British Library, London. Reprographic Section. Manuscripts, ADD. 59067, SCH. 52713.

Center for American History, University of Texas, Austin.

Natchez Trace Collection: Provincial and Territorial Documents.

Library of Congress, Washington, D.C.

The First American West: The Ohio River Valley, 1750–1820,
http://lcweb2.loc.gov/ammem/award99/icuhtml/fawhome.html.

James Madison Papers, series 1, reel 10, 11 December 1807–6 March 1809,
http://hdl.loc.gov/loc.mss/mjm.10_0922_0924.

Papers of Vicente Sebastián Pintado.

Thomas Jefferson Papers at the Library of Congress.

National Archives and Record Administration, Washington, D.C.

Record Group 36—Records of the U.S. Customs Service.

Entry 1627, Records of Customshouses in the Gulf States, New Orleans,
Letters Received 1804–1899, Aug. 1800–Dec. 1807, Boxes 1 & 2.

Record Group 45—Naval Records Collection of the Office of Naval Records
and Library.

Microfilm M 149, Letters Sent by the Secretary of the Navy to Officers, 1798–1868,
vol. 8, January 1, 1808–December 20, 1809, roll 8.

Record Group 46—Records of the U.S. Senate.

Microfilm M-1403, Unbound Records of the U.S. Senate, Eighth Congress:
Records of Legislative Proceedings, Sen 8A-F2, Reports and Communications
from the Secretary of the Treasury, roll 3.

Record Group 49—Records of the Bureau of Land Management.

Entry 333, vol. 1, "West of the Pearl River, Mississippi, Abstract of Certificates
A, B, C, D, & E, 1805–7."

Record Group 59—General Records of the Department of State.
    Entry 38, Lists of Special Agents, box 1.
    Entry 912, Records of the Department of State, Territorial Papers—Mississippi,
        1797–1810, vol. 1.
    Microfilm M-40, Domestic Letters of the Department of State, rolls 3, 12, 13.
    Microfilm M-78, Consular Instructions of the Department of State, 1801–34, vol. 1,
        October 12, 1801–February 26, 1817, roll 1.
    Microfilm T-225, Despatches from United States Consuls in New Orleans,
        1798–1807, vol. 1, March 17, 1798–February 6, 1807, roll 1.
    Microfilm T-260, State Department Territorial Papers, Orleans Series, 1764–1813,
        rolls 1–9.
Record Group 94—Records of the Adjutant General's Office, 1780s–1917.
    Microfilm M-565, Letters Sent by the Office of the Adjutant General (Main Series),
        1800–1890, vols. C–D, December 10, 1803–September 4, 1809, roll 2.
Record Group 98—Records of United States Army Commands.
    Entry 13, Records of Departments, Districts, Divisions, and Posts, 1784–1813,
        Orderly Books of the Adjutant of the Garrison of New Orleans, under the
        Command of Major William MacRea, Jan.–Feb. 1806; June 1807–March 1809,
        vol. 4 of 4.
    Entry 137, Records of Units, Infantry, 1789–1815, 2nd (1791–1815) Regiment,
        1802–1815, Orderly Books, Orderly Book of a Detachment or Company of Capt.
        Joseph Bowmar at Natchitoches, La., March–September, 1806, vol 1 of 1.
Record Group 107—Records of the Office of the Secretary of War.
    Entry 45, Subsistence Contracts, 1803–12, vol. 1.
    Microfilm M-222, Letters Received by the Secretary of War, Unregistered Series,
        1789–1860, roll 1.
    Microfilm M-370, Miscellaneous Letters Sent by the Secretary of War, 1800–1809,
        rolls 1 and 2.

Newspapers

Boston Repertory, 1810
Charleston (S.C.) Gazette, 1810
Hampshire Gazette (Northampton, N.H.), 1805
Louisiana Courier (New Orleans), 1810
Louisiana Gazette of St. Louis (New Orleans), 1810
El Misisipi (New Orleans), 1808
Mississippi Herald and Natchez Gazette, 1804–5
Natchez (Miss.) Weekly Chronicle, 1810
New Haven (Conn.) Visitor, 1803
New York American Citizen, 1804–5
Palladium (Frankfort, Ky.)
Pittsfield (Ohio) Sun, 1810

St. Francisville (La.) Timepiece, 1811
St. Francisville (La.) Democrat, 1933
Tennessee Gazette (Nashville), 1810
Virginia Argus (Richmond), 1804
Washington (D.C.) Federalist, 1804

Books, Articles, and Conference Papers

Abernethy, Thomas P. "Aaron Burr in Mississippi." *Journal of Southern History* 15 (February 1949): 19–21.

————. *The Burr Conspiracy*. New York: Oxford University Press, 1954.

Adelman, Jeremy, and Stephen Aron. "From Borderlands to Borders: Empires, Nation-States, and the Peoples in Between in North American History." *American Historical Review* 104 (June 1999): 814–41.

Andersen, Benedict. *Imagined Communities: Reflections on the Origins and Spread of Nationalism*. New York: Verso, 1991.

Armitage, David, and Michael Braddick, eds. *The British Atlantic World, 1500–1800*. New York: Palgrave-MacMillan, 2002.

Aron, Stephen. *How the West Was Lost: The Transformation of Kentucky from Daniel Boone to Henry Clay*. Baltimore: Johns Hopkins University Press, 1996.

Arthur, Stanley Clisby. *The Story of the West Florida Rebellion*. St. Francisville, La.: St. Francisville Democrat, 1935.

Axtell, James. *The Invasion Within: The Contest of Cultures in Colonial North America*. New York: Oxford University Press, 1985.

Bell, Caryn Cossé. *Revolution, Romanticism, and the Afro-Creole Protest Tradition in Louisiana, 1718–1868*. Baton Rouge: Louisiana State University Press, 1997.

Berlin, Ira. *Many Thousands Gone: The First Two Centuries of Slavery in North America*. Cambridge: Belknap Press of Harvard University Press, 1998.

Bice, David. *The Original Lone Star Republic: Scoundrels, Statesmen and Schemers of the 1810 West Florida Rebellion*. Clanton, Ala.: Heritage Publishing Consultants, 2004.

Bolívar, Simón, and Simon Collier. "Nationality, Nationalism, and Supranationalism in the Writings of Simon Bolivar." *Hispanic American Historical Review* 63 (February 1983): 37–64.

Bolton, Herbert Eugene. *The Spanish Borderlands: A Chronicle of Old Florida and the Southwest*. New York: U.S. Publishers Assn., 1921.

Boyd, Julian P., ed. *The Papers of Thomas Jefferson*. Vol. 9, *1 November 1785 to 22 June 1786*. Princeton, N.J.: Princeton University Press, 1954.

Brading, David A. *The First America: The Spanish Monarchy, Creole Patriots, and the Liberal State 1492–1867*. New York: Cambridge University Press, 1991.

Bradley, Jared W. "W. C. C. Claiborne and Spain: Foreign Affairs under Jefferson and Madison, 1801–1811." *Louisiana History* 12 (Fall 1971): 297–314.

Brevard, Caroline Mays. *A History of Florida from the Treaty of 1763 to Our Own Times*.

Vol. 1. Edited by James Alexander Robertson. Deland, Fla.: Florida State Historical Society, 1924.

Brooks, Philip C. "Spain's Farewell to Louisiana, 1803–1821." *Mississippi Valley Historical Review* 27 (June 1940): 29–42.

Burkholder, Mark. "Honor and Honors in Colonial Spanish America." In Johnson and Lipsett-Rivera, *Faces of Honor*, 18–44.

Bush, Barbara. *Slave Women in Caribbean Society, 1650–1838.* Bloomington: Indiana University Press, 1990.

Bush, Jonathan A. "The British Constitution and the Creation of American Slavery." In *Slavery and the Law*, edited by Paul Finkelman, 379–418. Madison, Wis.: Madison House, 1997.

Canny, Nicholas, and Anthony Pagden. *Colonial Identity in the Atlantic World, 1500–1800.* Princeton, N.J.: Princeton University Press, 1987.

Carter, Clarence E., ed. *Territorial Papers of the United States.* Vol. 5, *The Territory of Mississippi, 1798–1817.* Washington: U.S. Government Printing Office, 1837.

———, ed. *Territorial Papers of the United States.* Vol. 6, *The Territory of Mississippi, 1798–1817.* Washington: U.S. Government Printing Office, 1837.

Caughey, John Walton. *Bernardo de Gálvez in Louisiana, 1776–1783.* Gretna, La.: Pelican, 1972.

———. "Willing's Expedition down the Mississippi, 1778." *Louisiana Historical Quarterly* 15 (1932): 5–36.

Chaplin, Joyce. *An Anxious Pursuit: Agricultural Innovation and Modernity in the Lower South, 1730–1815.* Chapel Hill: University of North Carolina Press, 1993.

Clark, John G. "Economic Life before the Louisiana Purchase." In *The Spanish Presence in Louisiana, 1763–1803*, edited by Gilbert Din, 266–83. Lafayette: Center for Louisiana Studies, 1996.

Clark, Thomas. *A History of Kentucky.* Asheland, Ky.: J. Stuart Foundation, 1992.

Conrad, Glen, ed. *The French Experience in Louisiana History, 1763–1803.* Lafayette: Center for Louisiana Studies, 1996.

Cope, Douglas. *The Limits of Racial Domination: Plebeian Society in Colonial Mexico, 1660–1720.* Madison: University of Wisconsin Press, 1994.

Couturier, Edith. "Women and the Family in Eighteenth-Century Mexico: Law and Practice." *Journal of Family History* 10 (1985): 295.

Cox, Isaac Joslin. "Hispanic-American Phases of the 'Burr Conspiracy.'" *Hispanic American Historical Review* 12 (May 1932): 145–75.

———. *The West Florida Controversy, 1798–1813: A Study in American Diplomacy.* Baltimore: Johns Hopkins Press, 1918.

Crane, Verner. *The Southern Frontier, 1670–1713.* Ann Arbor: University of Michigan Press, 1929.

Cronon, William. *Changes in the Land: Indians, Colonists and the Ecology of New England.* New York: Hill and Wang, 1983.

Cummins, Light T. "Church Courts, Marriage Breakdown, and Separation in Spanish Louisiana, West Florida, and Texas." *Journal of Texas Catholic History and Culture* 4 (1993): 97–114.

————. "An Enduring Community: Anglo-American Settlers at Colonial Natchez and in the Felicianas, 1774–1810." *Journal of Mississippi History* 55 (1994): 133–54.

————. "Spanish Louisiana Land Policy: Antecedent to the Anglo-American Colonization of East Texas, 1769–1821." *East Texas Historical Journal* 33 (1995): 18–26.

Cusick, James. "Across the Border: Commodity Flow and Merchants in Spanish St. Augustine." *Florida Historical Quarterly* 69 (1991): 277–99.

————. *The Other War of 1812: The Patriot War and the American Invasion of Spanish East Florida.* Tallahassee: University Press of Florida, 2003.

Cutter, Charles. *The Legal Culture of Northern New Spain.* Albuquerque: University of New Mexico Press, 1995.

Davis, David Brion. *The Problem of Slavery in Western Culture.* Ithaca, N.Y.: Cornell University Press, 1966.

Dawdy, Shannon Lee. "Understanding Cultural Change through the Vernacular: Creolization in Louisiana." *Historical Archaeology* 34 (2000): 107–23.

Devereaux, Linda Ericson. "Philip Nolan and His 'Wild Horses.'" *Texana* 12 (1974): 88–100.

De Ville, Winston. *English Land Grants in West Florida: A Register for the States of Alabama, Mississippi, and Parts of Florida and Louisiana, 1766–1776.* Ville Platte, La.: Winston De Ville, 1986.

Din, Gilbert C. "The Canary Islander Settlements of Spanish Louisiana: An Overview." *Louisiana History* 27 (Fall 1986): 353–73.

————. "The Irish Mission to West Florida." *Louisiana History* 12 (Fall 1971): 315–34.

————. "Proposals and Plans for Colonization in Spanish Louisiana, 1787–1790." *Louisiana History* 11 (Summer 1970): 197–213.

————. "Spain's Immigration Policy in Louisiana and the American Penetration, 1792–1803." *Southwestern Historical Quarterly* 76 (January 1973): 255–76.

————. *Spaniards, Planters, and Slaves: The Spanish Regulation of Slavery in Louisiana, 1763–1803.* College Station: Texas A&M University Press, 1999.

Douglass, Elisha P. "The Adventurer Bowles." *William and Mary Quarterly*, 3rd ser., 6 (January 1949): 3–23.

Dowd, Gregory Evans. *A Spirited Resistance: The North American Indian Struggle for Unity, 1745–1815.* Baltimore: Johns Hopkins University Press, 1992.

Dysart, Jane E. "Another Road to Disappearance: Assimilation of Creek Indians in Pensacola, Florida, during the Nineteenth Century." *Florida Historical Quarterly* 61 (July 1982): 37–48.

Eccles, W. J. *The French in North America.* East Lansing: Michigan State University Press, 1998.

Edgerton, Douglas R. *Gabriel's Rebellion: The Virginia Slave Conspiracies of 1800 and 1802.* Chapel Hill: University of North Carolina Press, 1993.

Elkins, Stanley, and Eric McKitrick. *The Age of Federalism: The Early American Republic, 1788–1800.* New York: Oxford University Press, 1993.

Esdaile, Charles J. *The Spanish Army in the Peninsular War.* New York: Manchester University Press, 1988.

Fabel, Robin A. *Colonial Challenges: Britons, Native Americans, and Caribs, 1759–1775.* Gainesville: University Press of Florida, 2000.

———. *The Economy of British West Florida.* Tuscaloosa: University of Alabama Press, 1988.

Friend, Craig Thompson, ed. *The Buzzel about Kentuck: Settling the Promised Land.* Lexington: University Press of Kentucky, 1999.

———. " 'Work and Be Rich': Economy and Culture on the Bluegrass Farm." In Friend, *Buzzel about Kentuck,* 125–52.

Gaspar, David Barry, and David Patrick Geggus, eds. *A Turbulent Time: The French Revolution and the Greater Caribbean.* Bloomington: Indiana University Press, 1997.

Geggus, David. "The Haitian Revolution." In T*he Modern Caribbean,* edited by Franklin W. Knight and Colin Palmer, 21–50. Chapel Hill: University of North Carolina Press, 1989.

———. "Slavery, War and Revolution in the Greater Caribbean." In Gaspar and Geggus, *Turbulent Time,* 1–50.

Genovese, Eugene. *Roll, Jordan, Roll: The World the Slaves Made.* New York: Vintage, 1972.

Gorn, Elliott J. " 'Gouge and Bite, Pull Hair and Scratch': The Social Significance of Fighting in the Southern Backcountry." *American Historical Review* 90 (1985): 18–43.

Greene, Jack. *Pursuits of Happiness: The Social Development of Early Modern British Colonies and the Formation of American Culture.* Chapel Hill: University of North Carolina Press, 1988.

Gross, Ariele. "Pandora's Box: Slave Character on Trial in the Antebellum Deep South." In *Slavery and the Law,* edited by Paul Finkelman, 291–328. Madison, Wis.: Madison House, 1997.

Haarmann, Albert W. "The Spanish Conquest of British West Florida, 1779–1781." In *The Spanish Presence in Louisiana, 1763–1803,* edited by Gilbert Din, 203–18. Lafayette: Center for Louisiana Studies, 1996.

Hackett, Mary, ed. *Papers of James Madison: Secretary of State Series.* Vol. 6. Charlottesville: University of Virginia Press, 2002.

Hall, Gwendolyn Midlo. *Africans in Colonial Louisiana: The Development of Afro-Creole Culture in the Eighteenth Century.* Baton Rouge: Louisiana State University Press, 1992.

Hall, Leslie. *Land and Allegiance in Revolutionary Georgia.* Athens: University of Georgia Press, 2001.

Hamill, Hugh. *The Hidalgo Revolt: Prelude to Mexican Independence.* Gainesville: University of Florida Press, 1966.

Hanger, Kim. *Bounded Lives, Bounded Places: Free Black Society in Colonial New Orleans, 1769–1803.* Durham, N.C.: Duke University Press, 1997.

Harrington, J. Drew. "*Res* or *Persona*: Roman Civil Law's Influence on Southern Slave Law." *Labeo: Rassegna di Diritto Romano* 40 (1994): 236–45.

Hatfield, Joseph. *William Claiborne: Jeffersonian Centurion in the American Southwest.* Lafayette, La.: University of Southwestern Louisiana Press, 1976.

Haynes, Robert. "Territorial Mississippi, 1798–1817." *Journal of Mississippi History* 64, no. 4 (2002): 283–305.

Heyrman, Christine Leigh. *Commerce and Culture: The Maritime Communities of Colonial Massachusetts, 1690–1750.* New York: W. W. Norton, 1984.

Hickey, Donald. "America's Response to the Slave Revolt in Haiti, 1791–1806." *Journal of the Early Republic* 2 (Winter 1982): 361–80.

Hobsbawm, Eric J. *Nations and Nationalism since 1780: Programme, Myth, Reality.* New York: Cambridge University Press, 1990.

Hoffman, Paul E. *Florida's Frontiers.* Bloomington: Indiana University Press, 2002.

Holland-Braun, Kathryn E. "The Creek Indians, Blacks, and Slavery." *Journal of Southern History* 57 (November 1991): 601–36.

Holmes, Jack D. "*Dramatis Personae* in Spanish Louisiana." *Louisiana Studies* 6 (Summer 1967): 155–61.

———. *Gayoso: The Life of a Spanish Governor in the Mississippi Valley, 1789–1799.* Baton Rouge: Louisiana State University Press, 1965.

———. "The Provincial Governor-General Manuel Gayoso de Lemos." In *The Spanish Presence in Louisiana, 1763–1803,* edited by Gilbert Din, 94–112. Lafayette: Center for Louisiana Studies, 1996.

———. "Showdown on the Sabine: General James Wilkinson vs. Lieutenant-Colonel Simon De Herrera." *Louisiana Studies* 3 (1964): 46–76.

Holmes, Jack D., and J. Leitch Wright, trans. "Luis Bertucat and William Augustus Bowles: West Florida Adversaries in 1791." *Florida Historical Quarterly* 49 (July 1970): 49–62.

Holton, Woody. *Forced Founders: Indians, Debtors, Slaves, and the Making of the American Revolution in Virginia.* Chapel Hill: University of North Carolina Press, 1999.

Hyde, Samuel C., Jr. *Pistols and Politics: The Dilemma of Democracy in Louisiana's Florida Parishes, 1810–1899.* Baton Rouge: Louisiana State University Press, 1996.

Ingersoll, Thomas. *Mammon and Manon in Early New Orleans: The First Slave Society in the Deep South, 1718–1819.* Knoxville: University of Tennessee Press, 1999.

Isaac, Rhys. *The Transformation of Virginia, 1740–1790.* New York: W. W. Norton, 1982.

Johnson, Lyman. "Dangerous Words, Provocative Gestures, and Violent Acts." In Johnson and Lipsett-Rivera, *Faces of Honor,* 127–49.

Johnson, Lyman L., and Sonya Lipsett-Rivera, eds. *The Faces of Honor: Sex, Shame, and Violence in Colonial Latin America.* Albuquerque: University of New Mexico Press, 1998.

Jordan, Glen. "Philip Nolan: Trader or Filibuster?" *Texana* 12 (1973): 264–75.

Jordan, Winthrop. *White over Black: American Attitudes toward the Negro, 1550–1812.* Chapel Hill: University of North Carolina Press, 1968.

Joyner, Charles. *Down by the Riverside: A South Carolina Slave Community.* Urbana: University of Illinois Press, 1984.

Kastor, Peter. *The Louisiana Purchase: Emergence of an American Nation.* Washington, D.C.: CQ Press, 2002.

————. *The Nation's Crucible: The Louisiana Purchase and the Creation of America.* New Haven, Conn.: Yale University Press, 2004.

Kerr, Derek N. *Petty Felony, Slave Defiance, and Frontier Villany: Crime and Criminal Justice in Spanish Louisiana, 1770–1803.* New York: Garland, 1993.

Kesting, Robert. "A Common Bond: Masonic Intrigues in East Texas." *East Texas Historical Journal* 32 (1970): 20–31.

Kinnaird, Lawrence, and Lucia Kinnaird. "War Comes to San Marcos." *Florida Historical Quarterly* 62 (July 1983): 25–43.

Kinsbruner, Jay. *Independence in Spanish America: Civil Wars, Revolutions, and Underdevelopment.* Albuquerque: University of New Mexico Press, 1994.

————. *The Spanish-American Independence Movement.* New York: Krieger, 1973.

Kolchin, Peter. *American Slavery, 1619–1877.* New York: Hill and Wang, 1993.

Korth, Eugene H., and Della M. Flusche. "Dowry and Inheritance in Colonial Spanish America: Peninsular Law and Chilean Practice." *Americas* 58 (April 1987): 395–410.

Landers, Jane. "African American Women and Their Pursuit of Rights through Eighteenth-Century Spanish Texts." In *Haunted Bodies: Gender and Southern Texts,* edited by Susan Donaldson, 56–76. Charlottesville: University of Virginia Press, 1999.

————. *Black Society in Spanish Florida.* Urbana: University of Illinois Press, 1999.

————. "Female Conflict and Its Resolution in Eighteenth-Century St. Augustine." *Americas* 54 (April 1998): 557–74.

Landesman, Ned. "Nation, Migration, and the Province in the First British Empire: Scotland and the Americas, 1600–1800." *American Historical Review* 104 (April 1999): 463–75.

Lavrin, Asunción, and Edith Couturier. "Dowries and Wills: A View of Women's Socioeconomic Role in Colonial Guadalajara and Puebla, 1640–1790." *Hispanic American Historical Review* 59 (1979): 280–304.

Limerick, Patricia Nelson. *The Legacy of Conquest: The Unbroken Past of the American West.* New York: Norton, 1987.

Lofton, John. *Denmark Vesey's Revolt: The Slave Plot That Lit a Fuse to Fort Sumter.* Kent, Ohio: Kent State University Press, 1983.

Lynch, John. *Bourbon Spain, 1700–1808.* Cambridge, Mass: Basil Blackwell, 1989.

————. *The Spanish American Revolutions, 1808–1826.* New York: W. W. Norton, 1986.

Lyon, E. Wilson. "Document: The Closing of the Port of New Orleans." *American Historical Review* 37 (January 1931): 280–83.

Malone, Ann Patton. *Sweet Chariot: Slave Family and Household Structure in Nineteenth-Century Louisiana.* Chapel Hill: University of North Carolina Press, 1992.

Mattern, David B., ed. *The Papers of James Madison: Secretary of State Series.* Vol. 5. Charlottesville: University Press of Virginia, 2000.

Matthewson, Tim. "Jefferson and Haiti." *Journal of Southern History* 61 (May 1995): 209–48.

McAlister, Lyle N. "William Augustus Bowles and the State of Muskogee." *Florida Historical Quarterly* 40 (1962): 317–28.

McCain, William. "The Administrations of David Holmes, Governor of the Mississippi Territory, 1809–1817." *Journal of Mississippi History* 29 (1967): 328–47.

McCoy, Drew R. *The Elusive Republic: Political Economy in Jeffersonian America.* Chapel Hill: Published for the Institute of Early American History and Culture by the University of North Carolina Press, 1980.

McDonald, Dedra. "Incest, Power, and Negotiation in the Spanish Colonial Borderlands: A Tale of Two Families." *Colonial Latin American Historical Review* 6, no. 4 (1997): 525–57.

Miller, James J. *An Environmental History of Northeast Florida.* Gainesville: University Press of Florida, 1998.

Monette, John W. *History of the Discovery and Settlement of the Valley of the Mississippi, by the Three Great European Powers, Spain, France, and Great Britain, and the Subsequent Occupation, Settlement and Extension of Civil Government by the United States, until the Year 1846.* Vol. 2. New York: Harper and Brothers, 1846.

Morgan, Edmund. *American Slavery, American Freedom.* New York: W. W. Norton, 1975.

Morris, Christopher. *Becoming Southern: The Evolution of a Way of Life, Warren County and Vicksburg, Mississippi, 1770–1860.* New York: Oxford University Press, 1995.

———. "Impenetrable but Easy: The French Transformation of the Lower Mississippi Valley and the Founding of New Orleans." In *Transforming New Orleans and Its Environs,* edited by Craig C. Colton, 22–42. Pittsburgh: University of Pittsburgh Press, 2000.

Morris, Michael. "Dreams of Glory, Schemes of Empire: The Plan to Liberate Spanish Florida." *Georgia Historical Quarterly* 87 (2003): 1–21.

Morris, Thomas D. *Southern Slavery and the Law, 1619–1860.* Chapel Hill: University of North Carolina Press, 1996.

Moss, Kay. *Southern Folk Medicine, 1750–1820.* Columbia: University of South Carolina Press, 1999.

Murdoch, Richard. "Citizen Mangourit and the Projected Attack on East Florida in 1794." *Journal of Southern History* 14 (November 1948): 522–40.

Nasatir, Abraham P. "Anglo-Spanish Rivalry on the Upper Missouri." *Mississippi Valley Historical Review* 16 (March 1930): 507–28.

Nash, Gary. *Red, White, and Black.* Englewood Cliffs, N.J.: Prentice-Hall, 1992.

Oberg, Barbara, ed. *The Papers of Thomas Jefferson.* Vol. 31, *1 February 1799–31 May 1800.* Princeton, N.J.: Princeton University Press, 2004.

Owsley, Frank Lawrence, and Gene Smith. *Filibusters and Expansionists: Jeffersonian Manifest Destiny, 1800–1821.* Tuscaloosa: University of Alabama Press, 1997.

Padgett, James A. *Official Records of the West Florida Revolution and Republic.* Reprinted from the *Louisiana Historical Quarterly* 21 (July) 1938.

Paquette, Robert L. "Revolutionary Saint Domingue in the Making of Territorial Louisiana." In Gaspar and Geggus, *Turbulent Time,* 204–25.

Parker, Susan R. "The Cattle Trade in East Florida, 1784–1821." In *Colonial Plantations and Economy of Florida*, edited Jane Landers, 150–67. Gainseville: University Press of Florida, 2000.

Patrick, Rembert. *Florida Fiasco: Rampant Rebels on the Georgia-Florida Border, 1810–1815.* Athens: University of Georgia Press, 1954.

Philips, John C. "Flood Thy Neighbor: Colonial American Water-Powered Mills in West Florida." *Gulf Coast Historical Review* 14 (1998): 143–57.

Poyo, Geraldo, and Gilberto Hinojosa. "Spanish Texas and Borderlands Historiography in Transition: Implications for United States History." *Journal of American History* 75 (September 1988): 393–416.

Rankin, David C. "The Tannenbaum Thesis Reconsidered: Slavery and Race Relations in Antebellum Louisiana." *Southern Studies* 18, no. 1 (1979): 5–31.

Rea, Robert. "Military Deserters from British West Florida." *Louisiana History* 9, no. 2 (1968): 123–37.

———. "Planters and Plantations in British West Florida." *Alabama Review* 29 (July 1976): 220–35.

Richter, Daniel. *Facing East from Indian Country: A Native History of Early America.* Cambridge, Mass.: Harvard University Press, 2001.

Riddell, William Renwick. "Le Code Noir." *Journal of Negro History* 10, no. 3. (July 1925): 321–29.

Risjord, Norman K. *Jefferson's America, 1760–1815.* Madison, Wis.: Madison House, 1991.

Rodríguez, Jaime E. *The Independence of Spanish America.* New York: Cambridge University Press, 1998.

Rowland, Mrs. Dunbar, ed. *The Life, Letters, and Papers of William Dunbar of Elgin, Moray Shire, Scotland, and Natchez, Mississippi, Pioneer Scientist of the Southern United States.* Jackson: Press of the Mississippi Historical Society, 1930.

Rucker, Brian C. "Nixon's Raid: Precursor to Jackson's 1814 Invasion of Spanish West Florida." Paper presented to the Gulf Coast History and Humanities Conference, October 1997.

Schafer, Judith Kelleher. *Slavery, the Civil Law, and the Supreme Court of Louisiana.* Baton Rouge: Louisiana State University Press, 1994.

Schwartz, Stuart B. *Sovereignty and Society in Colonial Brazil: The High Court of Bahia and Its Judges, 1609–1751.* Berkeley: University of California Press, 1973.

Seed, Patricia. "American Law, Hispanic Traces: Some Contemporary Entanglements of Community Property." *William and Mary Quarterly*, 3rd ser., 52 (January 1995): 157–62.

Sidbury, James. *Ploughshares into Swords: Race, Rebellion, and Identity in Gabriel's Virginia, 1730–1810.* New York: Cambridge University Press, 1997.

Siebert, Wilbur. "Loyalists in West Florida and the Natchez District." *Mississippi Valley Historical Review* 2 (March 1916): 465–83.

Silver, Timothy. *A New Face on the Countryside: Indians, Colonists, and Slaves in South Atlantic Forests, 1500–1800.* New York: Cambridge University Press, 1990.

Smith, Gene. " 'Our Flag Was Displayed within Their Works': The Treaty of Ghent and the Conquest of Mobile." *Alabama Review* 52, no. 1 (1999): 3–20.

Smith, Joseph B. *The Plot to Steal Florida: James Madison's Phony War.* New York: Arbor House, 1983.

Smith, Mark M. *Mastered by the Clock: Time, Slavery, and Freedom in the American South.* Chapel Hill: University of North Carolina Press, 1997.

Smith, Theophus H. *Conjuring Culture: Biblical Formations of Black America.* New York: Oxford University Press, 1994.

Smith, Todd. "Indian Policy in Spanish Louisiana." In *The Spanish Presence in Louisiana, 1763–1803*, edited by Gilbert Din, 284–95. Lafayette: Center for Louisiana Studies, 1996.

Socolow, Susan M. "Acceptable Partners: Marriage Choice in Colonial Argentina, 1778–1810." In *Sexuality and Marriage in Colonial Latin America*, edited by Asunción Lavrin, 209–52. Lincoln: University of Nebraska Press.

Stagg, J. C. A. "Enlisted Men in the United States Army, 1812–1815: A Preliminary Survey." *William and Mary Quarterly*, 3rd ser., 43 (October 1986): 615–45.

———. "James Madison and the Coercion of Great Britain: Canada, the West Indies, and the War of 1812." *William and Mary Quarterly*, 3rd ser., 38 (January 1981): 3–34.

———. "Soldiers in Peace and War: Comparative Perspectives on the Recruitment of the United States Army, 1802–1815." *William and Mary Quarterly*, 3rd ser., 57 (January 2000): 79–120.

Starr, J. Barton. *Tories, Dons, and Rebels: The American Revolution in British West Florida.* Gainesville: University Press of Florida, 1976.

Sutherland, D. M. G. *France, 1789–1815: Revolution and Counterrevolution.* New York: Oxford University Press, 1986.

Tannenbaum, Frank. *Slave and Citizen: The Negro in the Americas.* New York: Random House, 1946.

Taylor, Joe Gray. *Louisiana: A Bicentennial History.* New York: W. W. Norton, 1976.

Taylor, Robert. "Prelude to Manifest Destiny: The United States and West Florida, 1810–1811." *Gulf Coast Historical Review* 7, no. 2 (1992): 45–62.

TePaske, John Jay. "Integral to Empire: The Vital Peripheries of Colonial Spanish America." In *Negotiated Empires: Centers and Peripheries in the Americas, 1500–1820*, edited by Christine Daniels and Michael V. Kennedy, 29–42. New York: Routledge, 2002.

"Thomas Rodney to T. Gammel, 2 October 1805." *Pennsylvania Magazine for History and Biography* 44 (1920): 187–88.

Thompson, Roger. "'Hold Watchfulness' and Communal Conformism: The Functions of Defamation in Early New England Communities." *New England Quarterly* 56, no. 4 (1983):504–22.

Turner, Frederick J. "The Origin of Genet's Projected Attack on Louisiana and the Floridas." *American Historical Review* 3 (July 1898): 650–71.

———. "The Policy of France toward the Mississippi Valley in the Period of Jefferson and Adams." *American Historical Review* 10 (January 1905): 249–79.

Usner, Daniel. *Indians, Settlers, and Slaves in a Frontier Exchange Economy: The Lower Mississippi Valley before 1783.* New Haven, Conn.: Yale University Press, 1992.

Vale, Thomas. *Fire, Native Peoples, and the Natural Landscape.* Washington, D.C.:
Island Press, 2002.

———. "The Pre-European Landscape of the United States: Pristine or Humanized."
In Vale, *Fire, Native Peoples, and the Natural Landscape,* 1–40.

Voeks, Robert A. *Sacred Leaves of Candomblé: African Magic, Medicine, and Religion in
Brazil.* Austin: University of Texas Press, 1997.

Waldrep, Christopher. "Opportunity on the Frontier South of the Green." In Friend,
Buzzel about Kentuck, 153–72.

Wall, Bennett H., ed. *Louisiana: A History.* Arlington Heights, Ill.: Forum Press, 1990.

Weber, David J. *The Spanish Frontier in North America.* New Haven, Conn.: Yale
University Press, 1992.

———. "The Spanish Legacy in North America and the Historical Imagination."
Western Historical Quarterly (February 1992): 4–24.

———. "Turner, the Boltonians, and the Borderlands." *American Historical Review* 91
(February 1986): 66–81.

Webre, Stephen. "The Problem of Indian Slavery in Spanish Louisiana, 1769–1803."
Louisiana History 25 (1984): 117–35.

"West Florida and Its Attempt on Mobile, 1810–1811." In "Documents," *American
Historical Review* 2 (July 1897): 699–705.

Whitaker, Arthur P. "Reed and Forde: Merchant Adventurers of Philadelphia: Their
Trade with Spanish New Orleans." In *The Spanish Presence in Louisiana, 1763–1803,*
edited by Gilbert Din, 246–65. Lafayette: Center for Louisiana Studies, 1996.

———. "Spanish Intrigue in the Old Southwest: An Episode, 1788–1789." *Mississippi
Valley Historical Review* 12 (September 1925): 155–76.

White, David H. "The Spaniards and William Augustus Bowles in Florida, 1799–1803."
Florida Historical Quarterly 54 (October 1975): 145–55.

———. *Vicente Folch, Governor in Spanish Florida, 1787–1811.* Washington, D.C.:
University Press of America, 1981.

White, Deborah Gray. *Ar'n't I a Woman?: Female Slaves in the Plantation South.* New
York: W. W. Norton, 1985.

White, Richard. *The Middle Ground: Indians, Empires, and Republics in the Great Lakes
Region, 1650–1815.* New York: Cambridge University Press, 1991.

Wilhelmy, Robert W. "Senator John Smith and the Aaron Burr Conspiracy." *Cincinnati
Historical Society Bulletin* 28 (1970): 38–60.

Wilson, Maurine T., and Jack Jackson. "Philip Nolan and Texas: Expeditions to the
Unknown Land, 1791–1801." *Southwestern Historical Quarterly* 93 (July 1989): 123–24.

Wood, Peter. *Black Majority: Negroes in Colonial South Carolina from 1670 through the
Stono Rebellion.* New York: W. W. Norton, 1974.

Works Progress Administration. *Spanish Land Grants in Florida.* Tallahassee, Fla.: State
Library Board, Tallahassee, Florida, 1941.

Wyatt-Brown, Bertram. *Southern Honor: Ethics and Behavior in the Old South.* New
York: Oxford, 1982.

INDEX

Anglo-Americans, 1; defined, 177n1; and dissatisfaction with Spanish government, 2

Atlantic world, 2, 7

Baton Rouge, 1, 2, 4, 6, 61, 90; and economy, 27–28, 31–32, 48–50; and trade, 53

Bayou Sara, 17, 88–89, 93, 170; as center of discontent, 88, 145, 159, 162, 163–64, 167

Bienville, Jean Baptiste, 29–30, 41, 44, 77–78

Black Legend, 2–4

Borderlands, surrounded, 2; as a problem, 5, 74–75, 129–30, 137–38

Bowles, William Augustus, 80–82, 94

Burr, Aaron, 69, 77, 91, 97–99, 158

Casa Calvo, Marquis de, 62, 63, 64–65, 70, 71, 72–73, 87, 93, 95–96

Catholicism, 11, 19, 41–42; influence of, on slavery, 36, 41–42

Census: 1726 (Louisiana), 12; 1785 (Baton Rouge), 17; 1795 (Bayou Sara), 28–29; 1803 (Baton Rouge), 54–55

Choctaws, 13–14, 71–72, 81, 134, 179n14

Claiborne, William C. C., 62–65 passim, 66–67, 72–73, 74, 170; and Kemper raids, 83, 86, 91, 92, 94–96; and Louisiana Purchase, 59–60; and national loyalty, 69–71

Clark, Daniel: and exploration, 27; and Kemper raids and rebellion, 83, 91, 94, 98; and land, 20, 65–66; and Louisiana Purchase, 58–59, 60; and national loyalty, 64, 67–68

Coartación (self-purchase), 37–38, 39

Code Noir, 36, 73

Creeks, 81

Crime, 203–4n16, 206n59; evasion of prosecution for, 139–42, 206n54; and filibustering, 77, 80, 93; meaning of, for West Florida, 129–36; murder, 14, 140–41, 205–6n51; and piracy, 99; and slavery; 44–45; theft, 18, 80

Cuba, 62, 81, 82, 154, 157, 163; and administration, 42; strategic value of, 15; trade with, 27, 32–33, 52–53, 56

Decoux, Marie, 21, 37, 45, 103

Derecho indiano, 36, 42

Derecho vulgar, 38

Deserters, U.S. Army, 128, 129, 131, 133, 134, 136–39, 205n42

Dunbar, William, 26, 67, 77–80, 83, 193n11; and exploration of frontier, 26–27, 61–62; farming practices of, 30–31; as slave owner, 27–28, 38–39

Economy: and indigo, 30–31; and slavery, 48–50; in United States, 43–44; of West Florida, 27–28, 29, 31–32, 55, 137, 151–53. *See also* Embargo; Land; Slavery; Trade

Embargo, 7; Act of 1807, 151–53

Feliciana district, 17, 59, 61, 76, 82, 86, 88, 90, 127; as center of discontent, 18, 128, 163–64

Filibustering, 7, 77, 78–80, 84–97, 99, 123. *See also* Burr, Aaron; Kemper brothers

Folch, Juan Vicente, 60, 70, 89–90, 91, 93, 143, 154, 161, 163

Fort San Carlos (Baton Rouge), 21, 23, 130, 161, 164–66